REPORT
OF THE TWENTIETH ANNUAL
ROUND TABLE MEETING
ON LINGUISTICS
AND LANGUAGE STUDIES

JAMES E. ALATIS
EDITOR

GEORGETOWN UNIVERSITY PRESS

Washington, D.C. 20007

Library of Congress Catalog Card Number 58-31607

Lithographed in U.S.A. by
EDWARDS BROTHERS, INC.
Ann Arbor, Michigan

CONTENTS

SECOND SESSION

THIRD SESSION

SECOND LUNCHEON ADDRESS

WASHINGTON LINGUISTICS CLUB 'EVE OF THE ROUND
TABLE MEETING'

Sociolinguistics and Urban Language Research
Moderator: Roger W. Shuy, Center for Applied Linguistics

INTRODUCTION

For the past twenty years Georgetown University's Annual Round Table Meeting on Linguistics and Language Studies has brought together scholars in linguistics and related disciplines to report on their latest research and to discuss current problems. The sixteen papers included in the present volume represent the proceedings of the 20th Annual Round Table Meeting, which was held at the School of Languages and Linguistics of Georgetown University on March 14 and 15, 1969.

The meeting consisted of three sessions and two luncheon addresses. Like the two previous Round Table Meetings, the 20th Annual Round Table Meeting had a central theme: 'Linguistics and the Teaching of Standard English to Speakers of Other Languages or Dialects'. The first session centered on 'Theoretical Linguistics and its Implications for Teaching SESOLD', the second session on 'Applied Linguistics and the Teaching of SESOLD: Materials, Methods, and Techniques', and the third session on 'Sociolinguistics: Sociocultural Factors in Teaching SESOLD'. A brief discussion period followed the reading of each paper. Respondents were asked to speak from microphones stationed throughout the meeting hall and to limit themselves to two minutes. The discussions which ensued were recorded, transcribed, and are included as a part of this volume.

On the evening before the Round Table the Washington Linguistics Club held its 'Eve of the Round Table Meeting' which this year centered on 'Sociolinguistics and Urban Language Research'. Since this topic was so pertinent to the theme of the 20th Round Table, and since there were so many references to the Thursday night papers in the Round Table discussions of Friday and Saturday, through the kindness of the officers of the Washington Linguistics Club the four papers read at their Thursday night meeting have been included in the present volume following the Round Table papers.

The general theme and, indeed, the topics for each of the sessions of this year's Round Table were selected and structured to assist a new

academic program which was established at Georgetown University last
year with the help of the United States Office of Education. The program is called the Experienced Teacher Fellowship Program (EXTFP)
for Teachers of Standard English to Speakers of Other Languages or
Dialects (SESOLD) and is supported from funds provided under the pro-
visions of the Higher Education Act of 1965, Title V, Part C. For this
program twenty-five fellows were selected from applicants from all
over the nation and were granted Government fellowships. Five tuition-
paying participants were also allowed to join the program. While the
majority of the 30 teachers came from the District of Columbia Public
Schools, some came from as far away as Hawaii, Texas, and California.

The program consisted of a highly integrated and coordinated series
of courses leading to a Master of Arts in Teaching (MAT). Among the
new courses which were developed to meet the needs of these predominantly urban teachers were 'Problems in Urban English' taught by Dr.
Roger Shuy of the Center for Applied Linguistics; 'The Language Laboratory: Theory and Practice' taught by Dr. Joseph Hutchinson, Academic Director of the Defense Language Institute; and 'Practice Teaching' guided by Supervisors of the D. C. Public School System, the Director of Language Arts of the D. C. Public School System, regular
members of the Georgetown University School of Languages and Linguistics faculty, and by Mrs. Charles W. Kreidler who was especially
employed for this function. Practice teaching took place in special
facilities of the School of Languages and Linguistics. Classrooms
were especially equipped for the program with the installation of closed
circuit television which allowed the practice teacher to be viewed,
video-taped, and evaluated. Elementary school children from the
Taylor School and older children from the Americanization School
came to the University for the month of February.

As part of an integrating colloquium, Dr. James E. Alatis, Associate Dean of the School of Languages and Linguistics and Director of
the Program, demonstrated to the participants various methods, approaches, and techniques of language teaching by teaching the Fellows
some of the basic elements of Modern Greek. Thus, teachers became
more sympathetic to students involved in language learning. Channel
4 in Washington produced a one-half hour color film showing the work
done in teacher training. The Northeast Language Conference financed
a film demonstrating how the closed circuit television was used in
teacher training.

It was thus our hope that this year's Round Table Meeting would
help round out the experience of these Fellows and assist them in their
attempt to integrate all the things they were learning, in such an intensive way, about theoretical linguistics, applied linguistics, and the
sociocultural aspects of learning a foreign language or dialect. We

felt that it was perhaps precisely through this specialized program for teachers and through this year's Round Table Meeting that Georgetown University could make at one and the same time a uniquely practical and truly academic contribution to the solution of some of the most pressing social problems of our day.

Thanks are due to the following graduate and undergraduate students of the School of Languages and Linguistics for their invaluable voluntary assistance at the 20th Round Table Meeting:

Student Committee Chairmen: Jurgen Heye, Bill Hoffman, Frances Reid, and Nic Stevens; Committee Members: Janet Ayers, Debbie Carr, Cynthia Cherry, Diana Crone, Jamela Feldman, Jane Hawkanson, Joy Newkerk, Wendy Powell, Sr. Frances Aid, Sr. Mary Rimblas, Sr. Sigrid Simlik, Pat Venditto, Kip Colegrove, Joe Matesi, Bill Wright, George Kelly, Jimmy Cato, Edward Cortner, Philip Dougherty, Douglass Gordon, Michael Herrington, and Carl Hundley.

Special thanks go to George Kelly, coordinator of the student effort, for the smooth operation of the conference. His assistance before and during the meeting is very much appreciated.

To Mrs. Margarita T. Hodge belongs the bulk of the credit for the success of the meeting. For her faithful cooperation, careful planning, and painstaking attention to the many details which go into a meeting such as this, I owe a heavy debt of gratitude.

I am most grateful to Mrs. Nevzer Stacey and Miss Carol LeClair for their great patience and skill in typing the manuscript for the present volume. Each in her own way was magnificent. In addition, Miss LeClair worked closely with Mr. Stewart in transcribing his paper from the original tape recordings and prepared the final photocopy of the entire volume.

Finally, for their invaluable attention to detail in the preparation of this manuscript, I should like to express my warmest thanks to my colleagues, Professors Neil J. Twombly, S.J. and Richard J. O'Brien, S.J. In addition I should also like to thank Rev. Stephen X. Winters, S.J. for his painstaking and patient proofreading of the final copy.

James E. Alatis
Editor

WELCOMING REMARKS

FRANK FADNER, S.J.

Regent, School of Languages and Linguistics
Georgetown University

Ladies and Gentlemen, Colleagues, Participants and Guests at Georgetown's yearly Round Table Meeting on Linguistics and Language Studies:

After a score of years I must confess that the old well begins to run dry as a source of original and witty remarks for him whose job it is to begin our unique annual show here at our School of Languages and Linguistics, which celebrates its twentieth anniversary this coming September.

But I assure you that the mat of welcome has never grown threadbare at the entrance to this place. And that goes for old faces and new ones alike.

As I first glanced through the proposed program yesterday I was afraid that we might be in for an aggravated rash of technical shorthand —what with the appearance of terms like SESOLD, TESL and ESL. The official portmanteau word is, of course, our Russian heritage. And the Russians had a greater excuse for recourse to such a device than we have, because of the polysyllabic nature of so many of their words. And so we had Sovnarkom, Komsomol, Cheka, and Ogpu. My latest discovery has been Gorsovet for City Hall.

I suppose it is a sign of vitality in a living language that our national bureaucracy should become the kitchen where alphabet soup and globaloney steam away so vigorously.

Here in the District, one goes to his 'shop', instead of his office where he may 'drag his feet' by way of postponing an operation indefinitely or he may 'phase it out' entirely, after too many 'slippages' or 'short falls'.

Or after 'contacting' a 'task force', the matter at hand becomes an 'ad hoc detail' which will have to be 'firmed up' before 'finalization'. And after a lifetime of this diet he does not simply 'die', but gets around it by 'passing on', or, even better, by merely 'passing away'.

And now, during the next two days we are going to seek to learn what precisely is the Standard English we're going to teach to Speakers of Other Languages and Dialects.

In this and in the solution of many of the historical and psychological problems which bedevil human communication and the science of Applied Linguistics, we your hosts at this University wish you all Godspeed and every success. Thank you.

WELCOMING REMARKS

ROBERT LADO

Dean, School of Languages and Linguistics
Georgetown University

From its founding in 1949—twenty years ago—the School of Languages and Linguistics, then the Institute of Languages and Linguistics,
has had as its purpose helping to identify and meet the Nation's needs in
languages and linguistics. In accomplishing this purpose, the Round
Table Meetings have provided in an outstanding way a national and international platform for scholars, teachers, government officials, and
professional and intellectual leaders to come together and discuss the
critical linguistic problems of the day.

The first Round Table Meeting, held in April 1950, dealt with the
wartime experience in language teaching and its applications to the
peacetime language needs of the nation. Throughout its history the
Round Table has had the fullest cooperation from outstanding leaders
in the various related fields of interest. Georgetown University is
justly proud to be a partner with them in organizing and supporting
these Round Tables. This 20th Round Table Meeting is a model in
keeping with the tradition started in 1950.

We have now discovered that our national language needs are not
only concerned with our neighbors in other countries and continents
but with our neighbors right here at home as well—our black neighbors
and our bilingual neighbors. And we are turning the light of objective
science and the knowledge and heart of teaching experience to this deep
and ill-defined problem. The results will, of necessity—in view of the
caliber of the participants—be highly productive and beneficial.

May I express the hope that we avoid the subtle error of our century,
that being so successful in perfecting instruments created to serve man-

kind we turn them into ends in themselves—and then use man to serve the instruments. Science is for man, not man for science. Man is for God and there is only one God.

On behalf of Georgetown University and the SLL, I welcome you to the proceedings.

THE LOGIC OF NONSTANDARD ENGLISH

WILLIAM LABOV

Columbia University

Abstract.   The traditional view of nonstandard English held by many public school teachers is that it is an illogical form of speech; that when children are taught the standard forms they are also being taught to think logically.   Linguists have endeavored for many years to show that differences in language are matters of social convention established by historical processes which shift continually the social prestige of dialect variants.

Recent programs for teaching the 'culturally disadvantaged', particularly those of Karl Bereiter and his associates, have revived the notion that nonstandard dialects are illogical, attributing poor educational performance to cognitive disabilities reflected in language.

The educational programs proposed are based upon sociological and linguistic misinterpretations of the data.   The linguistic behavior reported by Bereiter is merely the product of a defensive posture which children adopt in an alien and threatening situation.   Such behavior can be produced at will in any group of children and can be altered by changing the relevant sociolinguistic variables.

There are many important questions concerning the cognitive correlates of syntactic complexity which current research technique has not yet answered.   At present, there is no basis for attributing poor educational performance to the grammatical and phonological characteristics of any nonstandard dialect of English.

In the past decade, a great deal of federally-sponsored research has been devoted to the educational problems of children in ghetto schools. In order to account for the poor performance of children in these schools, educational psychologists have attempted to discover what kind of disadvantage or defect they are suffering from. The viewpoint which has been widely accepted, and used as the basis for large-scale intervention programs, is that the children show a cultural deficit as a result of an impoverished environment in their early years. Considerable attention has been given to language. In this area, the deficit theory appears as the concept of 'verbal deprivation': Negro children from the ghetto area receive little verbal stimulation, are said to hear very little well-formed language, and as a result are impoverished in their means of verbal expression: they cannot speak complete sentences, do not know the names of common objects, cannot form concepts or convey logical thoughts.

Unfortunately, these notions are based upon the work of educational psychologists who know very little about language and even less about Negro children. The concept of verbal deprivation has no basis in social reality: in fact, Negro children in the urban ghettos receive a great deal of verbal stimulation, hear more well-formed sentences than middle-class children, and participate fully in a highly verbal culture; they have the same basic vocabulary, possess the same capacity for conceptual learning, and use the same logic as anyone else who learns to speak and understand English.

The notion of 'verbal deprivation' is a part of the modern mythology of educational psychology, typical of the unfounded notions which tend to expand rapidly in our educational system. In past decades linguists have been as guilty as others in promoting such intellectual fashions at the expense of both teachers and children. But the myth of verbal deprivation is particularly dangerous, because it diverts attention from real defects of our educational system to imaginary defects of the child; and as we shall see, it leads its sponsors inevitably to the hypothesis of the genetic inferiority of Negro children which it was originally designed to avoid.

The most useful service which linguists can perform today is to clear away the illusion of 'verbal deprivation' and provide a more adequate notion of the relations between standard and nonstandard dialects. In the writings of many prominent educational psychologists, we find a very poor understanding of the nature of language. Children are treated as if they have no language of their own in the preschool programs put forward by Bereiter and Engelmann (1966). The linguistic behavior of ghetto children in test situations is the principal evidence for their genetic inferiority in the view of Arthur Jensen (1969). In this paper, I will examine critically both of these approaches to the language and intelligence of the populations labelled 'verbally' and 'culturally deprived'.[1] I will attempt to explain how the myth of verbal deprivation has arisen, bringing to bear the methodological findings of sociolinguistic work, and some substantive facts about language which are known to all linguists. I will be particularly concerned with the relation between concept formation on the one hand, and dialect differences on the other, since it is in this area that the most dangerous misunderstandings are to be found.

1. Verbality

The general setting in which the deficit theory has arisen consists of a number of facts which are known to all of us: that Negro children in the central urban ghettos do badly on all school subjects, including arithmetic and reading. In reading, they average more than two years behind the national norm. [2] Furthermore, this lag is cumulative, so that they do worse comparatively in the fifth grade than in the first grade. Reports in the literature show that this bad performance is correlated most closely with socioeconomic status. Segregated ethnic groups, however, seem to do worse than others: in particular, Indians, Mexican-Americans, and Negro children. Our own work in New York City confirms the fact that most Negro children read very poorly; however, our studies in the speech community show that the situation is even worse than has been reported. If one separates the isolated and peripheral individuals from the members of the central peer groups, the peer group members show even worse reading records, and to all intents and purposes are not learning to read at all during the time they spend in school. [3]

In speaking of children in the urban ghetto areas, the term 'lower-class' is frequently used as opposed to 'middle-class'. In the several sociolinguistic studies we have carried out, and in many parallel studies, it is useful to distinguish a 'lower-class' group from 'working-class'. Lower-class families are typically female-based or 'matrifocal', with no father present to provide steady economic support, whereas for the working-class there is typically an intact nuclear family with the father holding a semiskilled or unskilled job. The educational problems of ghetto areas run across this important class distinction; there is no evidence, for example, that the father's presence or absence is closely correlated with educational achievement. [4] The peer groups we have studied in South Central Harlem, representing the basic vernacular culture, include members from both family types. The attack against 'cultural deprivation' in the ghetto is overtly directed at family structures typical of lower-class families, but the educational failure we have been discussing is characteristic of both working-class and lower-class children.

In the balance of this paper, I will therefore refer to children from urban ghetto areas, rather than 'lower-class' children: the population we are concerned with are those who participate fully in the vernacular culture of the street and who have been alienated from the school system. [5] We are obviously dealing with the effects of the caste system of American society—essentially a 'color marking' system. Everyone recognizes this. The question is, by what mechanism does the color bar prevent children from learning to read? One answer is the notion of 'cultural deprivation' put forward by Martin Deutsch and others: the Negro children are said to lack the favorable factors in their home environment which enable middle-class children to do well in school. (Deutsch and assoc. 1967; Deutsch, Katz, and Jensen 1968). These factors involve the development of various cognitive skills through verbal interaction with adults, including the ability to reason abstractly, speak fluently, and focus upon long-range goals. In their publications, these psychologists also recognize broader social factors.[6] However, the deficit theory does not focus upon the interaction of the Negro child with white society so much as on his failure to interact with his mother at home. In the literature we find very little direct observation of verbal interaction in the Negro home; most typically, the investigators ask the child if he has dinner with his parents, and if he engages in dinnertable conversation with them. He is also asked whether his family takes him on trips to museums and other cultural activities. This slender thread of evidence is used to explain and interpret the large body of tests carried out in the laboratory and in the school.

The most extreme view which proceeds from this orientation—and one that is now being widely accepted—is that lower-class Negro children have no language at all. The notion is first drawn from Basil Bernstein's writings that 'much of lower-class language consists of a kind of incidental "emotional" accompaniment to action here and now'. (Jensen 1968:118). Bernstein's views are filtered through a strong bias against all forms of working-class behavior, so that middle-class language is seen as superior in every respect—as 'more abstract, and necessarily somewhat more flexible, detailed and subtle'. One can proceed through a range of such views until one comes to the practical program of Carl Bereiter, Siegfried Engelmann and their associates. (Bereiter et al 1966; Bereiter and Engelmann 1966). Bereiter's program for an academically oriented preschool is based upon their premise that Negro children must have a language with which they can learn, and their empirical finding that these children come to school without such a language. In his work with four-year-old Negro children from Urbana, Bereiter reports that their communication was by gestures, 'single words', and 'a series of badly-connected words or phrases', such as They mine and Me got juice. He reports that Negro children could not ask questions, that 'without exaggerating ... these four-year-olds could make no statements of any kind.' Furthermore, when these children were asked 'Where is the book?', they did not know enough to look at the table where the book was lying in order to answer. Thus Bereiter concludes that the children's speech forms are nothing more than a series of emotional cries, and he decides to treat them 'as if the children had no language at all'. He identifies their speech with his interpretation of Bernstein's restricted code: 'the language of culturally deprived children ... is not merely an underdeveloped version of standard English, but is a basically non-logical mode of expressive behavior' (Bereiter et al 1966: 113). The basic program of his preschool is to teach them a new language devised by Engelmann, which consists of a limited series of questions and answers such as Where is the squirrel? The squirrel is in the tree. The children will not be punished if they use their vernacular speech on the playground, but they will not be allowed to use it in the schoolroom. If they should answer the question Where is the squirrel? with the illogical vernacular form In the tree they will be reprehended by various means and made to say, The squirrel is in the tree.

Linguists and psycholinguists who have worked with Negro children are apt to dismiss this view of their language as utter nonsense. Yet there is no reason to reject Bereiter's observations as spurious: they were certainly not made up: on the contrary, they give us a very clear view of the behavior of student and teacher which can be duplicated in any classroom. In our own work outside of the adult-dominated environments of school and home, [7] we do not observe Negro children behaving like this, but on many occasions we have been asked to help analyze the results of research into verbal deprivation in such test situations.

Here, for example, is a complete interview with a Negro boy, one of hundreds carried out in a New York City school. The boy enters a room where there is a large, friendly white interviewer, who puts on the table in front of him a block or a fire engine, and says 'Tell me everything you can about this'. (The interviewer's further remarks are in parentheses.)

    [12 seconds of silence]
(What would you say it looks like?)
    [8 seconds of silence]
A space ship.
(Hmmmm.)
    [13 seconds of silence]
Like a je-et.
    [12 seconds of silence]
Like a plane.
    [20 seconds of silence]
(What color is it?)
Orange. [2 seconds]. An' whi-ite. [2 seconds]. An' green.
    [6 seconds of silence]
(An' what could you use it for?)
    [8 seconds of silence]
A je-et.

>   [6 seconds of silence]
> (If you had two of them, what would you do with them?)
>   [6 seconds of silence]
> Give one to some-body.
> (Hmmm. Who do you think would like to have it?)
>   [10 seconds of silence]
> Cla-rence.
> (Mm. Where do you think we could get another one of these?)
> At the store.
> (Oh ka-ay!)

We have here the same kind of defensive, monosyllabic behavior
which is reported in Bereiter's work. What is the situation that produces it? The child is in an asymmetrical situation where anything he
says can literally be held against him. He has learned a number of
devices to <u>avoid</u> saying anything in this situation, and he works very
hard to achieve this end. One may observe the intonation patterns of

$$\frac{^1a \quad \quad ^3\,{}'o'\,\, ^2\text{know}}{^2\text{a space } ^2\text{shi}^{\,\text{ip}^3}}$$

which Negro children often use when they are asked a question to which
the answer is obvious. The answer may be read as 'Will this satisfy
you?'

If one takes this interview as a measure of the verbal capacity of
the child, it must be as his capacity to defend himself in a hostile and
threatening situation. But unfortunately, thousands of such interviews
are used as evidence of the child's total verbal capacity, or more
simply his 'verbality'; it is argued that this lack of verbality <u>explains</u>
his poor performance in school. Operation Headstart and other intervention programs have largely been based upon the 'deficit theory'—
the notions that such interviews give us a measure of the child's verbal
capacity and that the verbal stimulation which he has been missing can
be supplied in a preschool environment.

The verbal behavior which is shown by the child in the test situation
quoted above is not the result of the ineptness of the interviewer. It is
rather the result of regular sociolinguistic factors operating upon adult
and child in this asymmetrical situation. In our work in urban ghetto
areas, we have often encountered such behavior. Ordinarily we worked
with boys 10-17 years old; and whenever we extended our approach
downward to 8- or 9-year olds, we began to see the need for different
techniques to explore the verbal capacity of the child. At one point we
began a series of interviews with younger brothers of the 'Thunderbirds'

in 1390 5th Avenue. Clarence Robins returned after an interview with 8-year-old Leon L., who showed the following minimal response to topics which arouse intense interest in other interviews with older boys.

CR: What if you saw somebody kickin' somebody else on the ground, or was using a stick, what would you do if you saw that?

Leon: Mmmm.

CR: If it was supposed to be a fair fight—

Leon: I don' know.

CR: You don' know? Would you do anything ... huh? I can't hear you.

Leon: No.

CR: Did you ever see somebody got beat up real bad?

Leon: ... Nope ? ? ?

CR: Well--uh--did you ever get into a fight with a guy?

Leon: Nope.

CR: That was bigger than you?

Leon: Nope.

CR: You never been in a fight?

Leon: Nope.

CR: Nobody ever pick on you?

Leon: Nope.

CR: Nobody ever hit you?

Leon: Nope.

CR: How come?

Leon: Ah 'on' know.

CR: Didn't you ever hit somebody?

Leon: Nope.

CR: [incredulous] You never hit nobody?

Leon: Mhm.

CR: Aww, ba -a-a-be, you ain't gonna tell me that.

It may be that Leon is here defending himself against accusations of wrong-doing, since Clarence knows that Leon has been in fights, that he has been taking pencils away from little boys, etc. But if we turn to a more neutral subject, we find the same pattern:

CR: You watch—you like to watch television? ... Hey, Leon ... you like to watch television? [Leon nods] What's your favorite program?

Leon: Uhhmmmm ... I look at cartoons.

CR: Well, what's your favorite one? What's your favorite program?

Leon: Superman ...

CR: Yeah? Did you see Superman--ah--yesterday, or day before yesterday: when's the last time you saw Superman?

Leon: Sa-aturday ...

CR: You rem--you saw it Saturday? What was the story all about? You remember the story?

Leon: M-m.

CR: You don't remember the story of what--that you saw of Superman?

Leon: Nope.

CR: You don't remember what happened, huh?

Leon: Hm-m.

CR: I see--ah--what other stories do you like to watch on T.V.?

Leon: Mmmm ? ? ? ? ... umm ... [glottalization]

CR: Hmm? [4 seconds]

Leon: Hh?

CR: What's th'other stories that you like to watch?

Leon: ^{2}Mi - ighty ^{2}Mouse^2 ...

CR: And what else?

Leon: Ummmm ... ahm ...

This nonverbal behavior occurs in a relatively favorable context for adult-child interaction; since the adult is a Negro man raised in Harlem, who knows this particular neighborhood and these boys very well. He is a skilled interviewer who has obtained a very high level of verbal response with techniques developed for a different age level, and he has an extraordinary advantage over most teachers or experimenters in these respects. But even his skills and personality are ineffective in breaking down the social constraints that prevail here.

When we reviewed the record of this interview with Leon, we decided to use it as a test of our own knowledge of the sociolinguistic factors which control speech. We made the following changes in the social situation: in the next interview with Leon, Clarence

(1) brought along a supply of potato chips, changing the 'interview' into something more in the nature of a party;

(2) brought along Leon's best friend, 8-year-old Gregory;

(3) reduced the height imbalance (when Clarence got down on the floor of Leon's room, he dropped from 6 ft. 2 in. to 3 ft. 6 in.);

(4) introduced taboo words and taboo topics, and proved to Leon's surprise that one can say anything into our microphone without any fear of retaliation.

The result of these changes is a striking difference in the volume and style of speech.

CR: Is there anybody who says your momma drink pee ?

Leon: [rapidly and breathlessly] Yee-ah!

Greg: Yup!

Leon: And your father eat doo-doo for breakfas'!

CR: Ohhh!! [laughs]

Leon: And they say your father--your father eat doo-doo for dinner!

Greg: When they sound on me, I say C. B. M.

CR: What that mean ?

Leon: Congo booger-snatch! [laughs]

Greg: Congo booger-snatcher! [laughs]

Greg: And sometimes I'll curse with B. B.

CR: What that ?

Greg: Black boy! [Leon—crunching on potato chips] Oh that's a M. B. B.

CR: M. B. B. What's that ?

Greg: 'Merican Black Boy !

CR: Ohh . . .

Greg: Anyway, 'Mericans is same like white people, right ?

Leon: And they talk about Allah.

CR: Oh yeah ?

Greg: Yeah.

CR: What they say about Allah ?

Leon: Allah--Allah is God.

Greg: Allah--

CR: And what else ?

Leon: I don' know the res'.

Greg: Allah i--Allah is God, Allah is the only God, Allah-

Leon: Allah is the son of God.

Greg: But can he make magic ?

Leon: Nope.

Greg: I know who can make magic.

CR: Who can ?

Leon: The God, the real one.

CR: Who can make magic ?

Greg: The son of po'-- [CR: Hm ?] I'm sayin' the po'k chop God! He only a po'k chop God![8] [Leon chuckles].

The 'nonverbal' Leon is now competing actively for the floor; Gregory and Leon talk to each other as much as they do to the interviewer.

One can make a more direct comparison of the two interviews by examining the section on fighting. Leon persists in denying that he fights, but he can no longer use monosyllabic answers, and Gregory cuts through his façade in a way that Clarence Robins alone was unable to do.

CR: Now, you said you had this fight, now, but I wanted you to tell me about the fight that you had.

Leon: I ain't had no fight.

{ Greg: Yes you did!   He said Barry,

  CR: You said you had one! you had a fight with Butchie,

{ Greg: An he say Garland ... an' Michael.

  CR: an' Barry ...

{ Leon: I di'n'; you said that, Gregory!

  Greg: You did.

{ Leon: You know you said that!

  Greg: You said Garland, remember that?

{ Greg: You said Garland!   Yes you did!

  CR: You said Garland, that's right.

Greg: He said Mich--an' I say Michael.

{ CR: Did you have a fight with Garland?

 Leon: Uh-uh.

CR: You had one, and he beat you up, too!

Greg: Yes he did!

Leon: No, I di--I never had a fight with Butch! ...

The same pattern can be seen on other local topics, where the interviewer brings neighborhood gossip to bear on Leon and Gregory acts as a witness.

CR: ... Hey Gregory! I heard that around here ... and I'm 'on' tell you who said it, too ...

Leon: Who?

{ CR: about you ...

{ Leon: Who?

 Greg: I'd say it!

CR: They said that--they say that the only person you play with is David Gilbert.

{ Leon: Yee-ah! yee-ah! yee-ah! ...

  Greg: That's who you play with!

{ Leon: I 'on' play with him no more!

  Greg: Yes you do!

Leon: I 'on' play with him no more!

Greg: But remember, about me and Robbie?

Leon: So that's not--

Greg: and you went to Petey and Gilbert's house, 'member? Ah haaah!!

Leon: So that's--so--but I would--I had came back out, an' I ain't go to his house no more ...

The observer must now draw a very different conclusion about the verbal capacity of Leon. The monosyllabic speaker who had nothing to say about anything and cannot remember what he did yesterday has disappeared. Instead, we have two boys who have so much to say they keep interrupting each other, who seem to have no difficulty in using the English language to express themselves. And we in turn obtain the volume of speech and the rich array of grammatical devices which we need for analyzing the structure of nonstandard Negro English (NNE): negative concord [I 'on' play with him no more], the pluperfect [had came back out], negative perfect [I ain't had], the negative preterite [I ain't go], and so on.

One can now transfer this demonstration of the sociolinguistic control of speech to other test situations—including I. Q. and reading tests in school. It should be immediately apparent that none of the standard tests will come anywhere near measuring Leon's verbal capacity. On these tests he will show up as very much the monosyllabic, inept, ignorant, bumbling child of our first interview. The teacher has far less ability than Clarence Robins to elicit speech from this child; Clarence knows the community, the things that Leon has been doing, and the things that Leon would like to talk about. But the power relationships in a one-to-one confrontation between adult and child are too asymmetrical. This does not mean that some Negro children will not talk a great deal when alone with an adult, or that an adult cannot get close to any child. It means that the social situation is the most powerful determinant of verbal behavior and that an adult must enter into the right social relation with a child if he wants to find out what a child can do: this is just what many teachers cannot do.

The view of the Negro speech community which we obtain from our work in the ghetto areas is precisely the opposite from that reported by Deutsch, Engelmann and Bereiter. We see a child bathed in verbal stimulation from morning to night. We see many speech events which depend upon the competitive exhibition of verbal skills: sounding, singing, toasts, rifting, louding—a whole range of activities in which the individual gains status through his use of language.[9] We see the younger child trying to acquire these skills from older children—hanging around on the outskirts of the older peer groups, and imitating this behavior to the best of his ability. We see no connection between verbal skill at the speech events characteristic of the street culture and success in the schoolroom.

2. Verbosity

There are undoubtedly many verbal skills which children from ghetto areas must learn in order to do well in the school situation, and some of these are indeed characteristic of middle-class verbal behavior. Precision in spelling, practice in handling abstract symbols, the ability

to state explicitly the meaning of words, and a richer knowledge of the
Latinate vocabulary, may all be useful acquisitions. But is it true that
all of the middle-class verbal habits are functional and desirable in the
school situation? Before we impose middle-class verbal style upon
children from other cultural groups, we should find out how much of
this is useful for the main work of analyzing and generalizing, and how
much is merely stylistic—or even dysfunctional. In high school and
college middle-class children spontaneously complicate their syntax to
the point that instructors despair of getting them to make their language
simpler and clearer. In every learned journal one can find examples of
jargon and empty elaboration—and complaints about it. Is the 'elaborated code' of Bernstein really so 'flexible, detailed and subtle' as some
psychologists believe? (Jensen 1968:119). Isn't it also turgid, redundant, and empty? Is it not simply an elaborated style, rather than a
superior code or system?[10]

Our work in the speech community makes it painfully obvious that in
many ways working-class speakers are more effective narrators, rea-
soners and debaters than many middle-class speakers who temporize,
qualify, and lose their argument in a mass of irrelevant detail. Many
academic writers try to rid themselves of that part of middle-class
style that is empty pretension, and keep that part that is needed for
precision. But the average middle-class speaker that we encounter
makes no such effort; he is enmeshed in verbiage, the victim of sociolinguistic factors beyond his control.

I will not attempt to support this argument here with systematic
quantitative evidence, although it is possible to develop measures
which show how far middle-class speakers can wander from the point.
I would like to contrast two speakers dealing with roughly the same
topic—matters of belief. The first is Larry H., a 15-year-old core
member of the Jets, being interviewed by John Lewis. Larry is one
of the loudest and roughest members of the Jets, one who gives the
least recognition to the conventional rules of politeness.[11] For most
readers of this paper, first contact with Larry would produce some
fairly negative reactions on both sides: it is probable that you would
not like him any more than his teachers do. Larry causes trouble in
and out of school; he was put back from the eleventh grade to the ninth,
and has been threatened with further action by the school authorities.

JL: What happens to you after you die? Do you know?
Larry: Yeah, I know.
JL: What?
Larry: After they put you in the ground, your body turns into--ah
         --bones, an' shit.
JL: What happens to your spirit?
Larry: Your spirit--soon as you die, your spirit leaves you.

JL: And where does the spirit go?

Larry: Well, it all depends ...

JL: On what?

Larry: You know, like some people say if you're good an' shit, your spirit goin' t'heaven ... 'n' if you bad, your spirit goin' to hell. Well, bullshit! Your spirit goin' to hell anyway, good or bad.

JL: Why?

Larry: Why? I'll tell you why. 'Cause, you see, doesn' nobody really know that it's a God, y'know, 'cause I mean I have seen black gods, pink gods, white gods, all color gods, and don't nobody know it's really a God. An' when they be sayin' if you good, you goin' t'heaven, tha's bullshit, 'cause you ain't goin' to no heaven, 'cause it ain't no heaven for you to go to.

Larry is a paradigmatic speaker of nonstandard Negro English (NNE) as opposed to standard English (SE). His grammar shows a high concentration of such characteristic NNE forms as negative inversion [don't nobody know ...], negative concord [you ain't goin' to no heaven ...], invariant be [when they be sayin' ...], dummy it for SE there [it ain't no heaven ...], optional copula deletion [if you're good ... if you bad ...], and full forms of auxiliaries [I have seen ...]. The only SE influence in this passage is the one case of doesn't instead of the invariant don't of NNE. Larry also provides a paradigmatic example of the rhetorical style of NNE: he can sum up a complex argument in a few words, and the full force of his opinions comes through without qualification or reservation. He is eminently quotable, and his interviews give us many concise statements of the NNE point of view. One can almost say that Larry speaks the NNE culture. [12]

It is the logical form of this passage which is of particular interest here. Larry presents a complex set of interdependent propositions which can be explicated by setting out the SE equivalents in linear order. The basic argument is to deny the twin propositions

(A) If you are good, (B) then your spirit will go to heaven.
(-A) If you are bad, (C) then your spirit will go to hell.

Larry denies (B), and asserts that if (A) or (-A), then (C). His argument may be outlined as follows:

(1) Everyone has a different idea of what God is like.
(2) Therefore nobody really knows that God exists.
(3) If there is a heaven, it was made by God.
(4) If God doesn't exist, he couldn't have made heaven.

(5) Therefore heaven does not exist.
(6) You can't go somewhere that doesn't exist.
(-B) Therefore you can't go to heaven.
(C) Therefore you are going to hell.

The argument is presented in the order: (C), because (2) because (1), therefore (2), therefore (-B) because (5) and (6). Part of the argument is implicit: the connection (2) therefore (-B) leaves unstated the connecting links (3) and (4), and in this interval Larry strengthens the propositions from the form (2) <u>Nobody knows if there is</u> ... to (5) <u>There is no</u> ... Otherwise, the case is presented explicitly as well as economically. The complex argument is summed up in Larry's last sentence, which shows formally the dependence of (-B) on (5) and (6):

An' when they be sayin' if you good, you goin' t'heaven,
[The proposition, if A, then B]
Tha's bullshit,
[is absurd]
'cause you ain't goin' to no heaven
[because -B]
'cause it ain't no heaven for you to go to.
[because (5) and (6)].

This hypothetical argument is not carried on at a high level of seriousness. It is a game played with ideas as counters, in which opponents use a wide variety of verbal devices to win. There is no personal commitment to any of these propositions, and no reluctance to strengthen one's argument by bending the rules of logic as in the (2-5) sequence. But if the opponent invokes the rules of logic, they hold. In John Lewis' interviews, he often makes this move, and the force of his argument is always acknowledged and countered within the rules of logic. In this case, he pointed out the fallacy that the argument (2-3-4-5-6) leads to (-C) as well as (-B), so it cannot be used to support Larry's assertion (C):

JL: Well, if there's no heaven, how could there be a hell?
Larry: I mean--ye-eah. Well, let me tell you, it ain't no hell,
         'cause this is hell right here, y'know!
JL: This is hell?
Larry: Yeah, this is hell right here!

Larry's answer is quick, ingenious and decisive. The application of the (3-4-5) argument to hell is denied, since hell is here, and therefore conclusion (C) stands. These are not ready-made or preconceived opinions, but new propositions devised to win the logical argument in the

game being played. The reader will note the speed and precision of
Larry's mental operations. He does not wander, or insert meaningless verbiage. The only repetition is (2), placed before and after (1)
in his original statement. It is often said that the nonstandard vernacular is not suited for dealing with abstract or hypothetical questions, but
in fact speakers from the NNE community take great delight in exercis-
ing their wit and logic on the most improbable and problematical matters. Despite the fact that Larry H. does not believe in God, and has
just denied all knowledge of him, John Lewis advances the following
hypothetical question:

JL: ... But, just say that there is a God, what color is he?
         White or black?
Larry: Well, if it is a God ... I wouldn' know what color, I
         couldn' say, --couldn' nobody say what color he is or
         really <u>would</u> be.
JL: But now, jus' suppose there was a God—
Larry: Unless'n they say ...
JL: No, I was jus' sayin' jus' suppose there is a God, would
         he be white or black?
Larry: ... He'd be white, man.
JL: Why?
Larry: Why? I'll tell you why. 'Cause the average whitey out
         here got everything, you dig? And the nigger ain't got
         shit, y'know? Y'understan'? So--um--for--in order
         for <u>that</u> to happen, you know it ain't no black God that's
         doin' that bullshit.

No one can hear Larry's answer to this question without being convinced
that they are in the presence of a skilled speaker with great 'verbal
presence of mind', who can use the English language expertly for many
purposes. Larry's answer to John Lewis is again a complex argument.
The formulation is not SE, but it is clear and effective even for those
not familiar with the vernacular. The nearest SE equivalent might be:
'So you know that God isn't black, because if he was, he wouldn't have
arranged things like that'.
     The reader will have noted that this analysis is being carried out in
standard English, and the inevitable challenge is: why not write in NNE,
then, or in your own nonstandard dialect? The fundamental reason is,
of course, one of firmly fixed social conventions. All communities
agree that SE is the 'proper' medium for formal writing and public communication. Furthermore, it seems likely that SE has an advantage
over NNE in explicit analysis of surface forms, which is what we are
doing here. We will return to this opposition between explicitness and
logical statement in sections 3 and 4. First, however, it will be helpful

to examine SE in its primary natural setting, as the medium for informal spoken communication of middle-class speakers.

Let us now turn to the second speaker, an upper-middle-class, college educated Negro man being interviewed by Clarence Robins in our
survey of adults in Central Harlem.

CR: Do you know of anything that someone can do, to have someone who has passed on visit him in a dream?

Chas. M.: Well, I even heard my parents say that there is such a thing as something in dreams some things like that, and sometimes dreams do come true. I have person-ally never had a dream come true. I've never dreamt that somebody was dying and they actually died, (Mhm) or that I was going to have ten dollars the next day and somehow I got ten dollars in my pocket. (Mhm). I don't particularly believe in that, I don't think it's true. I do feel, though, that there is such a thing as --ah--witchcraft. I do feel that in certain cultures there is such a thing as witchcraft, or some sort of science of witchcraft; I don't think that it's just a matter of believing hard enough that there is such a thing as witchcraft. I do believe that there is such a thing that a person can put himself in a state of mind (Mhm), or that--er--something could be given them to intoxicate them in a certain--to a certain frame of mind--that--that could actually be con-sidered witchcraft.

Charles M. is obviously a 'good speaker' who strikes the listener as
well-educated, intelligent and sincere. He is a likeable and attractive
person—the kind of person that middle-class listeners rate very high
on a scale of 'job suitability' and equally high as a potential friend. [13]
His language is more moderate and tempered than Larry's; he makes
every effort to qualify his opinions, and seems anxious to avoid any
misstatements or over-statements. From these qualities emerge the
primary characteristic of this passage—its verbosity. Words multiply,
some modifying and qualifying, others repeating or padding the main
argument. The first half of this extract is a response to the initial
question on dreams, basically:

(1) Some people say that dreams sometimes come true.
(2) I have never had a dream come true.
(3) Therefore I don't believe (1).

Some characteristic filler phrases appear here: such a thing as, some

THE LOGIC OF NONSTANDARD ENGLISH / 17

things like that, particularly. Two examples of dreams given after (2) are afterthoughts that might have been given after (1). Proposition (3) is stated twice for no obvious reason. Nevertheless, this much of Charles M.'s response is well-directed to the point of the question. He then volunteers a statement of his beliefs about witchcraft which shows the difficulty of middle-class speakers who (a) want to express a belief in something but (b) want to show themselves as judicious, rational and free from superstitions. The basic proposition can be stated simply in five words:

But I believe in witchcraft.

However, the idea is enlarged to exactly 100 words, and it is difficult to see what else is being said. In the following quotations, padding which can be removed without change in meaning is shown in brackets.

(1) 'I [do] feel, though, that there is [such a thing as] witchcraft.' Feel seems to be a euphemism for 'believe'.

(2) '[I do feel that] in certain cultures [there is such a thing as] witchcraft.]' This repetition seems designed only to introduce the word culture, which lets us know that the speaker knows about anthropology. Does certain cultures mean 'not in ours' or 'not in all'?

(3) '[or some sort of science of witchcraft.]' This addition seems to have no clear meaning at all. What is a 'science' of witchcraft as op-posed to just plain witchcraft?[14] The main function is to introduce the word 'science', though it seems to have no connection to what follows.

(4) 'I don't think that it's just [a matter of] believing hard enough that [there is such a thing as] witchcraft.' The speaker argues that witchcraft is not merely a belief; there is more to it.

(5) 'I [do] believe that [there is such a thing that] a person can put himself in a state of mind ... that [could actually be considered] witch-craft.' Is witchcraft as a state of mind different from the state of belief denied in (4)?

(6) 'or that something could be given them to intoxicate them [to a certain frame of mind] ...' The third learned word, intoxicate, is in-troduced by this addition. The vacuity of this passage becomes more evident if we remove repetitions, fashionable words and stylistic deco-rations:

But I believe in witchcraft.
I don't think witchcraft is just a belief.
A person can put himself or be put in a state of mind that is
    witchcraft.

Without the extra verbiage and the O.K. words like science, culture, and intoxicate, Charles M. appears as something less than a first-rate thinker. The initial impression of him as a good speaker is simply our long-conditioned reaction to middle-class verbosity: we know that people who use these stylistic devices are educated people, and we are inclined to credit them with saying something intelligent. Our reactions are accurate in one sense: Charles M. is more educated than Larry. But is he more rational, more logical, or more intelligent? Is he any better at thinking out a problem to its solution? Does he deal more easily with abstractions? There is no reason to think so. Charles M. succeeds in letting us know that he is educated, but in the end we do not know what he is trying to say, and neither does he.

In the previous section I have attempted to explain the origin of the myth that lower-class Negro children are nonverbal. The examples just given may help to account for the corresponding myth that middle-class language is in itself better suited for dealing with abstract, logically complex and hypothetical questions. These examples are intended to have a certain negative force. They are not controlled experiments: on the contrary, this and the preceding section are designed to convince the reader that the controlled experiments that have been offered in evidence are misleading. The only thing that is 'controlled' is the superficial form of the stimulus: all children are asked 'What do you think of capital punishment?' or 'Tell me everything you can about this.' But the speaker's interpretation of these requests, and the action he believes is appropriate in response is completely uncontrolled. One can view these test stimuli as requests for information, commands for action, as threats of punishment, or as meaningless sequences of words. They are probably intended as something altogether different: as requests for display;[15] but in any case the experimenter is normally unaware of the problem of interpretation. The methods of educational psychologists like Deutsch, Jensen and Bereiter follow the pattern designed for animal experiments where motivation is controlled by such simple methods as withholding food until a certain weight reduction is reached. With human subjects, it is absurd to believe that an identical 'stimulus' is obtained by asking everyone the 'same question'. Since the crucial intervening variables of interpretation and motivation are uncontrolled, most of the literature on verbal deprivation tells us nothing about the capacities of children. They are only the trappings of science: an approach which substitutes the formal procedures of the scientific method for the activity itself. With our present limited grasp of these problems, the best we can do to understand the verbal capacities of children is to study them within the cultural context in which they were developed.

It is not only the NNE vernacular which should be studied in this way, but also the language of middle-class children. The explicitness and precision which we hope to gain from copying middle-class forms are often the product of the test situation, and limited to it. For example, it was stated in the first part of this paper that working-class children hear more well-formed sentences than middle-class children. This statement may seem extraordinary in the light of the current belief of many linguists that most people do not speak in well-formed sentences, and that their actual speech production or 'performance' is ungrammatical. [16] But those who have worked with any body of natural speech know that this is not the case. Our own studies of the 'Grammaticality of Every-day Speech' show that the great majority of utterances in all contexts are complete sentences, and most of the rest can be reduced to grammatical form by a small set of 'editing rules'. [17] The proportions of grammatical sentences vary with class backgrounds and styles. The highest percentage of well-formed sentences are found in casual speech, and working-class speakers use more well-formed sentences than middle-class speakers. The widespread myth that most speech is ungrammatical is no doubt based upon tapes made at learned conferences, where we obtain the maximum number of irreducibly ungrammatical sequences.

It is true that technical and scientific books are written in a style which is markedly 'middle-class'. But unfortunately, we often fail to achieve the explicitness and precision which we look for in such writing; and the speech of many middle-class people departs maximally from this target. All too often, 'standard English' is represented by a style that is simultaneously over-particular and vague. The accumulating flow of words buries rather than strikes the target. It is this verbosity which is most easily taught and most easily learned, so that words take the place of thought, and nothing can be found behind them.

When Bernstein describes his 'elaborated code' in general terms, it emerges as a subtle and sophisticated mode of planning utterances, achieving structural variety, taking the other person's knowledge into account, and so on. But when it comes to describing the actual difference between middle-class and working-class speakers, we are presented with a proliferation of 'I think', of the passive, of modals and auxiliaries, of the first person pronoun, of uncommon words; these are the bench marks of hemming and hawing, backing and filling, that are used by Charles M., devices which often obscure whatever positive contribution education can make to our use of language. When we have discovered how much middle-class style is a matter of fashion and how much actually helps us express our ideas clearly, we will have done ourselves a great service; we will then be in a position to say what standard grammatical rules must be taught to nonstandard speakers in the early grades.

3. Grammaticality

Let us now examine Bereiter's own data on the verbal behavior of

the children he dealt with. The expressions They mine and Me got juice
are cited as examples of a language which lacks the means for expressing logical relations—in this case characterized as 'a series of badly
connected words'. (Bereiter 1966:113 ff.) In the case of They mine, it
is apparent that Bereiter confuses the notions of logic and explicitness.
We know that there are many languages of the world which do not have
a present copula, and which conjoin subject and predicate complement
without a verb. Russian, Hungarian, and Arabic may be foreign; but
they are not by that same token illogical. In the case of nonstandard
Negro English we are not dealing with even this superficial grammatical difference, but rather with a low-level rule which carries contraction one step farther to delete single consonants representing the verbs
is, have, or will. (Labov, Cohen, Robins & Lewis 1968:sect. 3.4) We
have yet to find any children who do not sometimes use the full forms
of is and will, even though they may frequently delete it. Our recent
studies with Negro children four to seven years old indicate that they
use the full form of the copula is more often than preadolescents 10 to
12 years old, or the adolescents 14 to 17 years old. [18]

Furthermore, the deletion of the is or are in nonstandard Negro
English is not the result of erratic or illogical behavior: it follows
the same regular rules as standard English contraction. Wherever
standard English can contract, Negro children use either the contracted
form or (more commonly) the deleted zero form. Thus They mine
corresponds to standard They're mine, not to the full form They are
mine. On the other hand, no such deletion is possible in positions
where standard English cannot contract: just as one cannot say That's
what they're in standard English, That's what they is equally impossible in the vernacular we are considering. The internal constraints
upon both of these rules show that we are dealing with a phonological
process like contraction, sensitive to such phonetic conditions as
whether or not the next word begins with a vowel or a consonant. The
appropriate use of the deletion rule, like the contraction rule, requires
a deep and intimate knowledge of English grammar and phonology.
Such knowledge is not available for conscious inspection by native
speakers: the rules we have recently worked out for standard contraction (Labov, Cohen, Robins & Lewis 1968:3.4) have never appeared
in any grammar, and are certainly not a part of the conscious knowledge of any standard English speakers. Nevertheless, the adult or
child who uses these rules must have formed at some level of psychological organization clear concepts of 'tense marker', 'verb phrase',
'rule ordering', 'sentence embedding', 'pronoun', and many other
grammatical categories which are essential parts of any logical system.

Bereiter's reaction to the sentence Me got juice is even more puz-
zling. If Bereiter believes that Me got juice is not a logical expression,
it can only be that he interprets the use of the objective pronoun me as

representing a difference in logical relationship to the verb: that the child is in fact saying that the juice got him rather than he got the juice! If on the other hand the child means 'I got juice', then this sentence form shows only that he has not learned the formal rules for the use of the subjective form I and oblique form me. We have in fact encountered many children who do not have these formal rules in order at the ages of four, five, six, or even eight. [19] It is extremely difficult to construct a minimal pair to show that the difference between he and him, or she and her, carries cognitive meaning. In almost every case, it is the context which tells us who is the agent and who is acted upon. We must then ask: what differences in cognitive, structural orientation are signalled by the fact that the child has not learned this formal rule? In the tests carried out by Jane Torrey it is evident that the children concerned do understand the difference in meaning between she and her when another person uses the forms; all that remains is that the children themselves do not use the two forms. Our knowledge of the cognitive correlates of grammatical differences is certainly in its infancy; for this is one of very many questions which we simply cannot answer. At the moment we do not know how to construct any kind of experiment which would lead to an answer; we do not even know what type of cognitive correlate we would be looking for.

Bereiter shows even more profound ignorance of the rules of discourse and of syntax when he rejects In the tree as an illogical, or badly-formed answer to Where is the squirrel? Such elliptical answers are of course used by everyone; they show the appropriate deletion of subject and main verb, leaving the locative which is questioned by wh + there. The reply In the tree demonstrates that the listener has been attentive to and apprehended the syntax of the speaker. [20] Whatever formal structure we wish to write for expressions such as Yes or Home or In the tree, it is obvious that they cannot be interpreted without knowing the structure of the question which preceded them, and that they presuppose an understanding of the syntax of the question. Thus if you ask me 'Where is the squirrel?' it is necessary for me to understand the processes of wh-attachment, wh-attraction to the front of the sentence, and flip-flop of auxiliary and subject to produce this sentence from an underlying form which would otherwise have produced The squirrel is there. If the child had answered The tree, or Squirrel the tree, or The in tree, we would then assume that he did not understand the syntax of the full form, The squirrel is in the tree. Given the data that Bereiter presents, we cannot conclude that the child has no grammar, but only that the investigator does not understand the rules of grammar. It does not necessarily do any harm to use the full form The squirrel is in the tree, if one wants to make fully explicit the rules of grammar which the child has internalized. Much of logical analysis consists of making explicit just that kind of internalized rule.

But it is hard to believe that any good can come from a program which begins with so many misconceptions about the input data. Bereiter and Engelmann believe that in teaching the child to say The squirrel is in the tree or This is a box and This is not a box they are teaching him an entirely new language, whereas in fact they are only teaching him to produce slightly different forms of the language he already has.

4. Logic

For many generations, American school teachers have devoted themselves to correcting a small number of nonstandard English rules to their standard equivalents, under the impression that they were teaching logic. This view has been reinforced and given theoretical justification by the claim that nonstandard Negro English lacks the means for the expression of logical thought.

Let us consider for a moment the possibility that Negro children do not operate with the same logic that middle-class adults display. This would inevitably mean that sentences of a certain grammatical form would have different truth values for the two types of speakers. One of the most obvious places to look for such a difference is in the handling of the negative; and here we encounter one of the nonstandard items which has been stigmatized as illogical by school teachers: the double negative, or as we term it, negative concord. A child who says He don't know nothing is often said to be making an illogical statement without knowing it. According to the teacher, the child wants to say He knows nothing but puts in an extra negative without realizing it, and so conveys the opposite meaning 'he does not know nothing' which reduces to 'he knows something'. I need not emphasize that this is an absurd interpretation: if a nonstandard speaker wishes to say that 'he does not know nothing', he does so by simply placing contrastive stress on both negatives as I have done here (He don't know nothing) indicating that they are derived from two underlying negatives in the deep structure. But note that the middle-class speaker does exactly the same thing when he wants to signal the existence of two underlying negatives: 'He doesn't know nothing'. In the standard form He doesn't know anything, the indefinite anything contains the same superficial reference to a preceding negative in the surface structure as the nonstandard nothing does. In the corresponding positive sentences, the indefinite something is used. The dialect difference, like most of the differences between the standard and nonstandard forms, is one of surface form, and has nothing to do with the underlying logic of the sentence.

The Anglo-Saxon authors of the Peterborough Chronicle were surely not illogical when they wrote For ne waeren nan martyrs swa pined alse he waeron, literally 'For never weren't no martyrs so tortured as these were'. The 'logical' forms of current standard English are simply the accepted conventions of our present-day formal style.

We can summarize the ways in which the two dialects differ in the following table:

	SE	NNE
Positive	He knows something.	He know something.
Negative	He doesn't know anything.	He don't know nothing.
Double negative	He doesn't know nothing.	He don't know nothing.

This array makes it plain that the only difference between the two dialects is in superficial form. When a single negative is found in the deep structure, SE converts something to the indefinite anything, NNE converts it to nothing. When speakers want to signal the presence of two negatives, they do it in the same way. No one would have any difficulty constructing the same table of truth values for both dialects.

English is a rare language in its insistence that the negative particle be incorporated in the first indefinite only. Russian, Spanish, French and Hungarian show the same negative concord as nonstandard English, and they are surely not illogical in this. What is termed 'logical' in standard English is of course the conventions which are habitual. The distribution of negative concord in English dialects can be summarized in this way:[21]

(1) In all dialects of English, the negative is attracted to a lone indefinite before the verb: Nobody knows anything, not * Anybody doesn't know anything.

(2) In some nonstandard white dialects, the negative also combines optionally with all other indefinites: Nobody knows nothing, He never took none of them.

(3) In other white nonstandard dialects, the negative may also appear in preverbal position in the same clause: Nobody doesn't know nothing.

(4) In nonstandard Negro English, negative concord is obligatory to all indefinites within the clause, and it may even be added to preverbal position in following clauses: Nobody didn't know he didn't meaning 'Nobody knew he did'.

Thus all dialects of English share a categorical rule which attracts the negative to an indefinite subject, and they merely differ in the extent to which the negative particle is also distributed to other indefinites in preverbal position. It would have been impossible for us to arrive at this analysis if we did not know that Negro speakers are using the same underlying logic as everyone else.

Negative concord is more firmly established in nonstandard Negro English than in other nonstandard dialects. The white nonstandard speaker shows variation in this rule, saying one time Nobody ever goes

<u>there</u> and the next <u>Nobody never goes there</u>; core speakers of the NNE vernacular consistently use the latter form. In the repetition tests which we conducted with adolescent Negro boys, [22] standard forms were regularly repeated back instantly with negative concord. Here, for example, are three trials by two 13-year-old members of the 'Thunderbirds':

Model: Nobody ever sat at any of those desks, anyhow.
Boot-1:   Nobody never sa--No [whitey] never sat at any o' tho' dess, anyhow.
   -2:   Nobody never sat at any o' tho' dess, anyhow.
   -3:   Nobody [es'] ever sat at no desses, anyhow.
David-1:   Nobody ever sat in-in-in-in- none o'--say it again?
   -2:   Nobody never sat in none o' tho' desses anyhow.
   -3:   Nobody--aww! Nobody never ex-- Dawg!

It can certainly be said that Boot and David fail the test; they have not repeated the sentence back 'correctly'—that is, word for word. But have they failed because they could not grasp the meaning of the sentence? The situation is in fact just the opposite: they failed because they perceived only the meaning and not the superficial form. Boot and David are typical of many speakers who do not perceive the surface details of the utterance so much as the underlying semantic structure, which they unhesitatingly translate into the vernacular form. Thus they have an asymmetrical system:

Perception:	Standard	Nonstandard
Production:	Nonstandard	

This tendency to process the semantic components directly can be seen even more dramatically in responses to sentences with embedded questions:

Model: I asked Alvin if he knows how to play basketball.
Boot: I ax Alvin do he know how to play basketball.
Money: I ax Alvin if--do he know how to play basketball.

Model: I asked Alvin whether he knows how to play basketball.
Larry F.-1:   I axt Alvin does he know how to play basketball.
       -2:   I axt Alvin does he know how to play basketball.

Here the difference between the words used in the model sentence and in the repetition is striking. Again, there is a failure to pass the test. But it is also true that these boys understand the standard sentence, and translate it with extraordinary speed into the NNE form—which is here the regular Southern colloquial form. This form retains the inverted order to signal the underlying meaning of the question, instead of the complementizer <u>if</u> or <u>whether</u> which standard English uses for this purpose. Thus Boot, Money, and Larry perceive the deep structure of the model sentence:

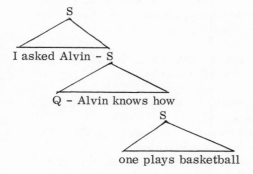

The complementizers <u>if</u> or <u>whether</u> are not required to express this underlying meaning; they are merely two of the formal options which one dialect selects to signal the embedded question. The colloquial Southern form utilizes a different device—preserving the order of the direct question. To say that this dialect lacks the means for logical expression is to confuse logic with surface detail.

To pass the repetition test, Boot and the others have to learn to listen to surface detail. They do not need a new logic; they need practice in paying attention to the explicit form of an utterance rather than its meaning. Careful attention to surface features is a temporary skill needed for language learning—and neglected thereafter by competent speakers. Nothing more than this is involved in the language training in the Bereiter and Engelmann program, or in most methods of 'teaching English'. There is of course nothing wrong with learning to be explicit—as we have seen, that is one of the main advantages of standard English at its best—but it is important that we recognize what is actually taking place, and what teachers are in fact trying to do.

I doubt if we can teach people to be logical, though we can teach them to recognize the logic that they use. Piaget has shown us that in middle-class children logic develops much more slowly than grammar, and that we cannot expect four-year-olds to have mastered the conservation of quantity, let alone syllogistic reasoning. Whatever problems working-class children may have in handling logical operations are not to be blamed on the structure of their language. There is nothing in the vernacular which will interfere with the development of logical thought, for the logic of standard English cannot be distinguished from the logic of any other dialect of English by any test that we can find.

5. What's wrong with being wrong?

If there is a failure of logic involved here, it is surely in the approach of the verbal deprivation theorists, rather than in the mental abilities of the children concerned. We can isolate six distinct steps in the reasoning which has led to programs such as those of Deutsch, Bereiter and Engelmann:

(1) The lower-class child's verbal response to a formal and threatening situation is used to demonstrate his lack of verbal capacity, or verbal deficit.

(2) This verbal deficit is declared to be a major cause of the lower-class child's poor performance in school.

(3) Since middle-class children do better in school, middle-class speech habits are seen to be necessary for learning.

(4) Class and ethnic differences in grammatical form are equated with differences in the capacity for logical analysis.

(5) Teaching the child to mimic certain formal speech patterns used by middle-class teachers is seen as teaching him to think logically.

(6) Children who learn these formal speech patterns are then said to be thinking logically and it is predicted that they will do much better in reading and arithmetic in the years to follow.

In sections 1-4 of this paper, I have tried to show that these propositions are wrong, concentrating on (1), (4), and (5). Proposition (3) is the primary logical fallacy which illicitly identifies a form of speech as the cause of middle-class achievement in school. Proposition (6) is the one which is most easily shown to be wrong in fact, as we will note below.

However, it is not too naive to ask, 'What is wrong with being wrong?' There is no competing educational theory which is being dismantled by this program; and there does not seem to be any great harm in having children repeat This is not a box for twenty minutes a day. We have already conceded that NNE children need help in analyzing language into its surface components, and in being more explicit. But there are serious and damaging consequences of the verbal deprivation theory which may be considered under two headings: (1) the theoretical bias, and (2) the consequences of failure.

(1) It is widely recognized that the teacher's attitude towards the child is an important factor in his success or failure. The work of Rosenthal on 'self-fulfilling prophecies' shows that the progress of children in the early grades can be dramatically affected by a single random labelling of certain children as 'intellectual bloomers'. (Rosenthal & Jacobson 1968) When the everyday language of Negro children is stigmatized as 'not a language at all' and 'not possessing the means

for logical thought', the effect of such a labelling is repeated many times during each day of the school year. Every time that a child uses a form of NNE without the copula or with negative concord, he will be labelling himself for the teacher's benefit as 'illogical', as a 'nonceptual thinker'. Bereiter and Engelmann, Deutsch and Jensen are giving teachers a ready-made, theoretical basis for the prejudice they already feel against the lower-class Negro child and his language. When they hear him say I don't want none or They mine, they will be hearing through the bias provided by the verbal deprivation theory: not an English dialect different from theirs, but the primitive mentality of the savage mind.

But what if the teacher succeeds in training the child to use the new language consistently? The verbal deprivation theory holds that this will lead to a whole chain of successes in school, and that the child will be drawn away from the vernacular culture into the middle-class world. Undoubtedly this will happen with a few isolated individuals, just as it happens in every school system today, for a few children. But we are concerned not with the few but the many, and for the majority of Negro children the distance between them and the school is bound to widen under this approach.

Proponents of the deficit theory have a strange view of social organization outside of the classroom: they see the attraction of the peer group as a 'substitute' for success and gratification normally provided by the school. For example, Whiteman and Deutsch introduce their account of the deprivation hypothesis with an eye-witness account of a child who accidentally dropped his school notebook into a puddle of water and walked away without picking it up.

A policeman who had been standing nearby walked over to the puddle and stared at the notebook with some degree of disbelief. (Whiteman and Deutsch 1968:86-7)

The child's alienation from school is explained as the result of his coming to school without the 'verbal, conceptual, attentional and learning skills requisite to school success.' The authors see the child as 'suffering from feelings of inferiority because he is failing; ... he withdraws or becomes hostile, finding gratification elsewhere, such as in his peer group.'

To view the peer group as a mere substitute for school shows an extraordinary lack of knowledge of adolescent culture. In our studies in South Central Harlem we have seen the reverse situation: the children who are rejected by the peer group are quite likely to succeed in school. In middle-class suburban areas, many children do fail in school because of their personal deficiencies; in ghetto areas, it is the healthy, vigorous popular child with normal intelligence who cannot read and fails all along the line. It is not necessary to document here the influence of the peer group upon the behavior of youth in our society; but we may note that somewhere between the time that children first learn to talk and puberty, their language is restructured to fit the rules used by their peer group. From a linguistic viewpoint, the peer group is certainly a more powerful influence than the family.[23] Less directly, the pressures of peer group activity are also felt within the school. Many children, particularly those who are not doing well in school, show a sudden sharp down turn in the fourth and fifth grades, and children in the ghetto schools are no exception. It is at the same age, at nine or ten years old, that the influence of the vernacular peer group becomes predominant.[24] Instead of dealing with isolated individuals, the school is then dealing with children who are integrated into groups of their own, with rewards and value systems which oppose those of the school. Those who know the sociolinguistic situation cannot doubt that reaction against the Bereiter-Engelmann approach in later years will be even more violent on the part of the students involved, and that the rejection of the school system will be even more categorical.

The essential fallacy of the verbal deprivation theory lies in tracing the educational failure of the child to his personal deficiencies. At present, these deficiencies are said to be caused by his home environment. It is traditional to explain a child's failure in school by his inadequacy; but when failure reaches such massive proportions, it seems to us necessary to look at the social and cultural obstacles to learning, and the inability of the school to adjust to the social situation. Operation Headstart is designed to repair the child, rather than the school; to the extent that it is based upon this inverted logic, it is bound to fail.

(2) The second area in which the verbal deprivation theory is doing serious harm to our educational system is in the consequences of this failure, and the reaction to it. If Operation Headstart fails, the interpretations which we receive will be from the same educational psychologists who designed this program. The fault will be found not in the data, the theory, nor in the methods used, but rather in the children who have failed to respond to the opportunities offered to them. When Negro children fail to show the significant advance which the deprivation theory predicts, it will be further proof of the profound gulf which separates their mental processes from those of civilized, middle-class mankind.

A sense of the 'failure' of Operation Headstart is already in the air. Some prominent figures in the program are reacting to this situation by saying that intervention did not take place early enough. Bettye M. Caldwell notes that:

... the research literature of the last decade dealing with social-class differences has made abundantly clear that all

> parents are not qualified to provide even the basic essentials of
> physical and psychological care to their children. (Caldwell
> 1967:16)

The deficit theory now begins to focus on the 'long-standing patterns of
parental deficit' which fill the literature. 'There is, perhaps unfortunately,' writes Caldwell, 'no literacy test for motherhood.' Failing
such eugenic measures, she has proposed 'educationally oriented day
care for culturally deprived children between six months and three
years of age.' The children are returned home each evening to 'maintain primary emotional relationships with their own families', but during the day they are removed to 'hopefully prevent the deceleration in
rate of development which seems to occur in many deprived children
around the age of two to three years.' (Caldwell 1967:17)
  There are others who feel that even the best of the intervention
programs, such as those of Bereiter and Engelmann, will not help the
Negro child no matter when they are applied—that we are faced once
again with the 'inevitable hypothesis' of the genetic inferiority of the
Negro people. Many readers of this paper are undoubtedly familiar
with the paper of Arthur Jensen in the <u>Harvard Educational Review</u>
(1969) which received early and widespread publicity. Jensen begins
with the following quotation from the United States Commission on
Civil Rights as evidence of the failure of compensatory education.

> The fact remains, however, that none of the programs appear
> to have raised significantly the achievement of participating
> pupils, as a group, within the period evaluated by the Commis-
> sion. (p. 138)

Jensen believes that the verbal deprivation theorists with whom he had
been associated—Deutsch, Whiteman, Katz, Bereiter—have been
given every opportunity to prove their case—and have failed. This
opinion is part of the argument which leads him to the overall conclusion that 'the preponderance of the evidence is ... less consistent with
a strictly environmental hypothesis than with the genetic hypothesis';
that racism, or the belief in the genetic inferiority of Negroes, is a
correct view in the light of the present evidence.
  Jensen argues that the middle-class white population is differentiated
from the working-class white and Negro population in the ability for
'cognitive or conceptual learning', which Jensen calls Level II intelligence as against mere 'associative learning' or Level I intelligence:

> certain neural structures must also be available for Level II
> abilities to develop, and these are conceived of as being differ-
> ent from the neural structures underlying Level I. The genetic

factors involved in each of these types of ability are presumed
to have become differentially distributed in the population as a
function of social class, since Level II has been most important for scholastic performance under the traditional methods
of instruction.

Thus Jensen found that one group of middle-class children were helped
by their concept-forming ability to recall twenty familiar objects that
could be classified into four categories: animals, furniture, clothing,
or foods. Lower-class Negro children did just as well as middle-class
children with a miscellaneous set, but showed no improvement with
objects that could be so categorized.
    The research of the educational psychologists cited here is presented
in formal and objective style, and is widely received as impartial scientific evidence. Jensen's paper has already been reported by Joseph
Alsop and William F. Buckley Jr. as 'massive, apparently authorita-
tive ... ' (N.Y. Post 3/20/69) It is not my intention to examine these
materials in detail; but it is important to realize that we are dealing
with special pleading by those who have a strong personal commitment.
Jensen is concerned with class differences in cognitive style and verbal
learning. His earlier papers incorporated the cultural deprivation theory which he now rejects as a basic explanation.[25] He classifies the
Negro children who fail in school as 'slow-learners' and 'mentally-
retarded', and urged that we find out how much their retardation is due
to environmental factors and how much is due to 'more basic biological
factors.' (Jensen 1968:167) His conviction that the problem must be
located in the child leads him to accept and reprint some truly extraordinary data. To support the genetic hypothesis he cites the following
table of Heber for the racial distribution of mental retardation.

Estimated prevalence of children with IQs below 75.

SES	White	Negro
1	0.5	3.1
2	0.8	14.5
3	2.1	22.8
4	3.1	37.8
5	7.8	42.9

This report, that almost half of lower-class Negro children are mentally retarded, could be accepted only by someone who has no knowledge
of the children or the community. If he had wished to, Jensen could
easily have checked this against the records of any school in any urban
ghetto area. Taking IQ tests at their face value, there is no correspondence between these figures and the communities we know. For
example, among 75 boys we worked with in Central Harlem who would

fall into Heber's SES 4 or 5, there were only three with IQs below 75: one spoke very little English, one could barely see, and the third was emotionally disturbed. When the second was retested, he scored 91, and the third retested at 87. [26] There are of course hundreds of realistic reports available to Jensen: he simply selected one which would strengthen his case for the genetic inferiority of Negro children, and deliberately deleted the information that this was a study of an area selected in advance because of its high incidence of mental retardation. [27]

In so doing, Jensen was following a standing tradition among the psychologists who developed the deficit hypothesis. The core of Martin Deutsch's environmental explanation of low school performance is the Deprivation Index—a numerical scale based on six dichotomized variables. One variable is 'The educational aspirational level of the parent for the child'. Most people would agree that a parent who did not care if a child finished high school would be a disadvantageous factor in the child's educational career. In dichotomizing this variable Deutsch was faced with the embarrassing fact that the educational aspiration of Negro parents is in fact very high—higher than for the white population, as he shows in other papers. [28] In order to make the Deprivation Index work, he therefore set the cutting point for the deprived group as 'college or less'. (Whiteman and Deutsch 1968:100) Thus if a Negro child's father says that he wants his son to go all the way through college, the child will fall into the 'deprived' class on this variable. In order to receive the two points given to the 'less deprived' on the index, it would be necessary for the child's parent to insist on graduate school or medical school! This decision is never discussed by the author: it simply stands as a fait accompli in the tables. This is the type of data manipulation carried on by those who are strongly committed to a particular hypothesis; the selection and presentation of the data are heavily determined by the desire of the writers to make things come out right.

No one can doubt that the inadequacy of Operation Headstart and of the verbal deprivation hypothesis has now become a crucial issue in our society. [29] The controversy which is beginning over Jensen's article will undoubtedly take as given that programs such as Bereiter and Engelmann's have tested and measured the verbal capacity of the ghetto child. The cultural sociolinguistic obstacles to this intervention program are not considered; and the argument proceeds upon the data provided by the large, friendly interviewers that we have seen at work in the extracts given above.

6. The linguistic view

Linguists are in an excellent position to demonstrate the fallacies of the verbal deprivation theory. All linguists agree that nonstandard dialects are highly structured systems; they do not see these dialects as accumulations of errors caused by the failure of their speakers to master standard English. When linguists hear Negro children saying He crazy or Her my friend they do not hear a 'primitive language'. Nor do they believe that the speech of working-class people is merely a form of emotional expression, incapable of expressing logical thought.

All linguists who work with nonstandard Negro English recognize that it is a separate system, closely related to standard English, but set apart from the surrounding white dialects by a number of persistent and systematic differences. Differences in analysis by various linguists in recent years are the inevitable products of differing theoretical approaches and perspectives as we explore these dialect patterns by different routes—differences which are rapidly diminishing as we exchange our findings. For example, Stewart differs with me on how deeply the invariant be of She be always messin' around is integrated into the semantics of the copula system with am, is, are, etc. The position and meaning of have ... -ed in NNE is very unclear, and there are a variety of positions on this point. But the grammatical features involved are not the fundamental predicators of the logical system. They are optional ways of contrasting, foregrounding, emphasizing, or deleting elements of the underlying sentence. There are a few semantic features of NNE grammar which may be unique to this system. But the semantic features we are talking about here are items such as 'habitual', 'general', 'intensive'. These linguistic markers are essentially points of view—different ways of looking at the same events, and they do not determine the truth values of propositions upon which all speakers of English agree.

The great majority of the differences between NNE and SE do not even represent such subtle semantic features as these, but rather extensions and restrictions of certain formal rules, and different choices of redundant elements. For example, SE uses two signals to express the progressive: be and -ing, while NNE often drops the former. SE signals the third person in the present by the subject noun phrase and by a third singular -s; NNE does not have this second redundant feature. On the other hand, NNE uses redundant negative elements in negative concord, uses possessives like mines, uses or either where SE uses a simple or, and so on.

When linguists say that NNE is a 'system', we mean that it differs from other dialects in regular and rule-governed ways, so that it has equivalent ways of expressing the same logical content. When we say that it is a 'separate' sub-system, we mean that there are compensating sets of rules which combine in different ways to preserve the distinctions found in other dialects. Thus as noted above NNE does not use the if or whether complementizer in embedded questions, but the meaning is preserved by the formal device of reversing the order of subject and auxiliary.

Linguists therefore speak with a single voice in condemning Bereiter's view that the vernacular can be disregarded. I have exchanged views on this matter with all of the participants in the Round Table, and their response shows complete agreement in rejecting the verbal deprivation theory and its misapprehension of the nature of language. The other papers in this series will testify to the strength of the linguistic view in this area. It was William Stewart who first pointed out that Negro English should be studied as a coherent system; and in this all of us follow his lead. Dialectologists like Raven McDavid, Albert Marckwardt, and Roger Shuy have been working for years against the notion that vernacular dialects are inferior and illogical means of communication; and their views are well represented here. As the overwhelming testimony of this conference shows, linguists agree that teachers must know as much as possible about nonstandard Negro English as a communicative system.

The exact nature and relative importance of the structural differences between NNE and SE are not in question here. It is agreed that the teacher must approach the teaching of the standard through a knowledge of the child's own system. The methods used in 'teaching English as a foreign language' are invoked, not to declare that NNE is a foreign language, but to underline the importance of studying the native dialect as a coherent system for communication. This is, in fact, the method that should be applied in any English class.

Linguists are also in an excellent position to assess Jensen's claim that the middle-class white population is superior to the working-class and Negro populations in the distribution of 'Level II' or 'conceptual' intelligence. The notion that large numbers of children have no capacity for conceptual thinking would inevitably mean that they speak a primitive language, for even the simplest linguistic rules we discussed above involve conceptual operations more complex than those used in the experiment cited by Jensen. Let us consider what is involved in the use of the general English rule that incorporates the negative with the first indefinite. To learn and use this rule, one must first identify the class of indefinites involved: any, one, ever, which are formally quite diverse. How is this done? These indefinites share a number of common properties which can be expressed as the concepts 'indefinite', 'hypothetical', and 'nonpartitive'. One might argue that these indefinites are learned as a simple list by 'association' learning. But this is only one of the many syntactic rules involving indefinites—rules known to every speaker of English, which could not be learned except by an understanding of their common, abstract properties. For example, everyone 'knows' unconsciously that anyone cannot be used with preterite verbs or progressives. One does not say, Anyone went to the party or Anyone is going to the party. The rule which operates here is sensitive to the property [+hypothetical] of the indefinites. Whenever the proposition is not inconsistent with this feature, anyone can be used. Everyone 'knows' therefore that one can say Anyone who was anyone went to the party, or If anyone went to the party ... or Before anyone went to the party ... There is another property of anyone which is grasped unconsciously by all native speakers of English: it is [+distributive]. Thus if we need one more man for a game of bridge or basketball, and there is a crowd outside, we ask, Do any of you want to play? not Do some of you want to play? In both cases, we are considering a plurality, but with any we consider them one at a time, or distributively.

What are we then to make of Jensen's contention that Level I thinkers cannot make use of the concept 'animal' to group together a miscellaneous set of toy animals? It is one thing to say that someone is not in the habit of using a certain skill. But to say that his failure to use it is genetically determined implies dramatic consequences for other forms of behavior, which are not found in experience; the knowledge of what people must do in order to learn language makes Jensen's theories seem more and more distant from the realities of human behavior. Like Bereiter and Engelmann, Jensen is handicapped by his ignorance of the most basic facts about human language and the people who speak it.

There is no reason to believe that any nonstandard vernacular is in itself an obstacle to learning. The chief problem is ignorance of language on the part of all concerned. Our job as linguists is to remedy this ignorance: Bereiter and Engelmann want to reinforce it and justify it. Teachers are now being told to ignore the language of Negro children as unworthy of attention and useless for learning. They are being taught to hear every natural utterance of the child as evidence of his mental inferiority. As linguists we are unanimous in condemning this view as bad observation, bad theory, and bad practice.

That educational psychology should be strongly influenced by a theory so false to the facts of language is unfortunate; but that children should be the victims of this ignorance is intolerable. It may seem that the fallacies of the verbal deprivation theory are so obvious that they are hardly worth exposing; I have tried to show that it is an important job for us to undertake. If linguists can contribute some of their available knowledge and energy towards this end, we will have done a great deal to justify the support that society has given to basic research in our field.

NOTES

[1] I am indebted to Rosalind Weiner, of the Early Childhood Education group of Operation Headstart in New York City, and to Joan Baratz, of the Educational Development Corp., Washington D.C., for

pointing out to me the scope and seriousness of the educational issues involved here, and the ways in which the cultural deprivation theory has affected federal intervention programs in recent years.

[2]A report of average reading comprehension scores in New York City was published in the New York Times on December 3, 1968. The schools attended by most of the peer group members we have studied showed the following scores:

School	Grade	Reading score	National norm
J. H. S. 13	7	5. 6	7. 7
	9	7. 6	9. 7
J. H. S. 120	7	5. 6	7. 7
	9	7. 0	9. 7
I. S. 88	6	5. 3	6. 7
	8	7. 2	8. 7

The average is then more than two full years behind grade in the ninth grade.

[3]See W. Labov and C. Robins, 'A Note on the Relation of Reading Failure to Peer-Group Status in Urban Ghettos'. (1968).

[4]There are a number of studies reported recently which show no relation between school achievement and presence of a father in the nuclear family. Preliminary findings to this effect are cited from a study by Bernard Mackler of CUE in Thos. S. Langer and Stanley T. Michaels, Life Stress and Mental Health (New York : Free Press), Chapter 8. Jensen 1969 cites James Coleman's study Equality of educational opportunity, p. 506, and others to illustrate the same point.

[5]The concept of 'nonstandard Negro English', and the vernacular culture in which it is embedded, is presented in detail in Labov, Cohen, Robins and Lewis 1968, sections 1.2.3 and 4.1. See Volume II, section 4.3, for the linguistic traits which distinguish speakers who participate fully in the NNE culture from marginal and isolated individuals.

[6]For example, in Deutsch, Katz and Jensen 1968 there is a section on 'Social and Psychological Perspectives' which includes a chapter by Proshansky and Newton on 'The Nature and Meaning of Negro Self-Identity' and one by Rosenthal and Jacobson on 'Self-Fulfilling Prophecies in the Classroom'.

[7]The research cited here was carried out in South Central Harlem and other ghetto areas in 1965-1968 to describe structural and functional differences between nonstandard Negro English and standard English of the classroom. It was supported by the Office of Education as Cooperative Research Projects 3091 and 3288. Detailed reports are given in Labov, Cohen and Robins 1965, Labov 1965, and Labov, Cohen, Robins and Lewis 1968.

[8]The reference to the pork chop God condenses several concepts of

black nationalism current in the Harlem community. A <u>pork chop</u> is a
Negro who has not lost traditional subservient ideology of the South, who
has no knowledge of himself in Muslim terms, and the <u>pork chop God</u>
would be the traditional God of Southern Baptists. He and his followers
may be pork chops, but he still holds the power in Leon and Gregory's
world.

[9]For detailed accounts of these speech.events, see Labov, Cohen,
Robins and Lewis 1968, section 4.2.

[10]The term <u>code</u> is central in Bernstein's description of the differences between working-class and middle-class styles of speech. (1966)
The restrictions and elaborations of speech observed are labelled as
'codes' to indicate the principles governing selection from the range of
possible English sentences. No rules or detailed description of the
operation of such codes are provided as yet, so that this central concept remains to be specified.

[11]A direct view of Larry's verbal style in a hostile encounter is
given in Labov, Cohen, Robins and Lewis 1968, Vol. II, pp. 39-43.
Gray's Oral Reading Test was being given to a group of Jets on the
steps of a brownstone house in Harlem, and the landlord tried unsuc-
cessfully to make the Jets move. Larry's verbal style in this encounter matches the reports he gives of himself in a number of narratives
cited in section 4.8.

[12]See Labov, Cohen, Robins and Lewis 1968, Volume II, p. 38,
71-73, 291-292.

[13]See Labov, Cohen, Robins and Lewis 1968, section 4.6, for a
description of subjective reaction tests which utilize these evaluative
dimensions.

[14]Several middle-class readers of this passage have suggested that
<u>science</u> here refers to some form of control as opposed to belief; the
'science of witchcraft' would then be a kind of engineering of mental
states; other interpretations can of course be provided. The fact remains that no such subtleties of interpretation are needed to understand Larry's remarks.

[15]The concept of a 'request for verbal display' is here drawn from
Alan Blum's treatment of the therapeutic interview in <u>The Sociology of
Mental Illness</u>, mimeographed, (to appear in <u>For Thomas Szaz</u>).

[16]In a number of presentations, Chomsky has asserted that the great
majority of the sentences which a child hears are ungrammatical ('95
percent'). In Chomsky 1965:58, this notion is presented as one of the
arguments in his general statement of the 'nativist' position: 'A consideration of the character of the grammar that is acquired, <u>the degenerate quality and narrowly limited extent of the available data,</u> [my
emphasis] the striking uniformity of the resulting grammars, and their
independence of intelligence, motivation, and emotional state, over

THE LOGIC OF NONSTANDARD ENGLISH / 37

wide ranges of variation, leave little hope that much of the structure of the language can be learned ...'

[17]The editing rules are presented in W. Labov, 'On the the Grammaticality of Every-day Speech,' paper given at the annual meeting of the Linguistic Society of America, New York City, December 1966.

[18]From work on the grammars and comprehension of Negro children four to eight years old being carried out by Professor Jane Torrey of Connecticut College in extension of the research cited above in Labov, Cohen, Robins and Lewis 1968.

[19]From the research of Jane Torrey cited in footnote 18.

[20]The attention to the speaker's syntax required of the listener is analyzed in detail by Harvey Sacks in his unpublished 1968 lectures.

[21]For the detailed analysis of negative concord in NNE, see Labov, Cohen, Robins and Lewis 1968, section 3.6, and W. Labov, 'Negative Attraction and Negative Concord in Four English Dialects', paper given at the 1968 annual meeting of the Linguistic Society of America, New York, December 1968.

[22]More complete data on these Memory Tests is given in Labov, Cohen, Robins and Lewis 1968, section 3.9.

[23]See for example, Herbert Gans on 'The Peer Group Society', The Urban Villagers (N.Y.: Free Press, 1962).

[24]For the relationship between age and membership in peer groups, see Peter Wilmott, Adolescent Boys of East London, (London: Routledge and Kegan Paul, 1966).

[25]In Deutsch, Katz and Jensen 1968, Jensen expounds the verbal deprivation theory in considerable detail. For example: 'During this "labeling" period ... some very important social-class differences may exert their effects on verbal learning. Lower-class parents engage in relatively little of this naming or "labeling" play with their children... That words are discrete labels for things seems to be better known by the middle-class child entering first grade than by the lower-class child. Much of this knowledge is gained in the parent-child interaction, as when the parent looks at a picture book with the child...' (p. 119).

[26]Heber's studies of 88 Negro mothers in Milwaukee are cited frequently throughout Jensen 1969. The estimates in this table are not given in relation to a particular Milwaukee sample, but for the general population. Heber's study was specifically designed to cover an area of Milwaukee which was known to contain a large concentration of retarded children, Negro and white, and he has stated that his findings were 'grossly misinterpreted' by Jensen. (Milwaukee Sentinel, June 11, 1969)

[27]The IQ scores given here are from group rather than individual tests and must therefore not be weighted heavily: the scores are from the Pintner-Cunningham test, usually given in the first grade in New York City schools in the 1950s.

[28]Table 15-1 in Deutsch and associates 1967: 312, section C, shows that some degree of college training was desired by 96, 97 and 100 percent of Negro parents in Class Levels I, II and III respectively. The corresponding figures for whites were 79, 95, and 97 percent.

[29]The negative report of the Westinghouse Learning Corporation and Ohio University on Operation Headstart was published in the New York Times (on April 13, 1969). This evidence for the failure of the program is widely publicized, and it seems likely that the report's discouraging 'conclusions will be used by conservative Congressmen as a weapon against any kind of expenditure for disadvantaged' children, especially Negroes. The two hypotheses mentioned to account for this failure are that the impact of Headstart is lost through poor teaching later on, and more recently, that poor children have been so badly damaged in infancy by their lower-class environment that Headstart cannot make much difference. The third 'inevitable' hypothesis of Jensen is not reported here.

REFERENCES

Bereiter, Carl et al. 1966. An Academically Oriented Pre-School for Culturally Deprived Children. In Fred M. Hechinger (ed.) Pre-School Education Today. (New York, Doubleday) 105-137.

_____ and Siegfried Engelmann. 1966. Teaching Disadvantaged Children in the Preschool. Englewood Cliffs, N.J., Prentice-Hall.

Caldwell, Bettye M. 1967. What is the Optimal Learning Environment for the Young Child? American Journal of Orthopsychiatry, Vol. XXXVII, No. 1, 8-21.

Chomsky, Noam. 1965. Aspects of the Theory of Syntax. Cambridge, Mass., M.I.T. Press.

Deutsch, Martin and Associates. 1967. The Disadvantaged Child. New York, Basic Books.

_____, Irwin Katz and Arthur R. Jensen (eds.). 1968. Social Class, Race, and Psychological Development. New York, Holt.

Jensen, Arthur. 1968. Social Class and Verbal Learning. In Deutsch, Katz, and Jensen 1968.

_____. 1969. How Much Can We Boost IQ and Scholastic Achievement? Harvard Educational Review, Vol. 39, No. 1.

Labov, William. 1967. Some Sources of Reading Problems for Negro Speakers of Non-Standard English. In A. Frazier (ed.), New Directions in Elementary English (Champaign, Ill., National Council of Teachers of English) 140-167. Reprinted in Joan C. Baratz and Roger W. Shuy. 1969. Teaching Black Children to Read. (Washington, D.C., Center for Applied Linguistics) 29-67.

_____, Paul Cohen and Clarence Robins. 1965. A Preliminary Study of the Structure of English Used by Negro and Puerto Rican Speakers in New York City. Final Report, Cooperative Research Project

No. 3091, Office of Education, Washington, D. C.
_____, Paul Cohen, Clarence Robins and John Lewis. 1968. A Study
of the Non-Standard English of Negro and Puerto Rican Speakers in
New York City. Final Report, Cooperative Research Project
No. 3288, Office of Education, Washington, D. C. Vol. I and
Vol. II.
_____, and Clarence Robins. 1969. A Note on the Relation of Reading
Failure to Peer-Group Status in Urban Ghettos. The Teachers Col-
lege Record, Volume 70, Number 5.
Rosenthal, Robert and Lenore Jacobson. 1968. Self-Fulfilling Proph-
ecies in the Classroom: Teachers' Expectations as Unintended De-
terminants of Pupils' Intellectual Competence. In Deutsch, Katz
and Jensen 1968.
Whiteman, Martin and Martin Deutsch. Social Disadvantage as Related
to Intellective and Language Development. In Deutsch, Katz and
Jensen 1968.

DISCUSSION

Raven I. McDavid, Jr., The University of Chicago: Bill, I'm very
much interested to say—although there's a small number of myths—
let us speak optimistically. I think in the Chicago area, just judging
from what is going on in the teacher-training institutions, the Bereiter
myth has no particular standing.

My second point is that I am a little bit worried about the way people
toss the term middle class around. I don't know what you mean by
middle class. In the community I grew up in, we would have assumed
that multiple negatives were middle class forms; they were not upper
class forms. Middle class speech was something the educated looked
down on. Maybe it is undemocratic to use the term upper class.

The third is—although I'm sure, in view of various other things,
the social consequences of this attitude are perhaps worse when the
people in the schools ignore the cultural background of Negro students
in the cities—it is my experience, demonstrated empirically and even
dramatically, that in any school the student who comes in with an ab-
errant set of interests and background from that which the community,
the neighborhood, has been working on, is likely to get a rough time.
To be specific, my oldest savage, many years ago in Cleveland in the
Murray School, which was basically Italian in its constituency—well,
he was the only faculty child and one of two Nordics in the kindergarten class; after six weeks we had a report from the principal saying
that she thought that he was mentally retarded. I think stupidity, sad-
ism, and other such vices in the classroom are not the peculiar property of any group of teachers in dealing with any group of students. I

think there is just too damn much ignorance among the classroom teachers on all levels.

Labov: I think these three points are all well taken, Raven. You hearten me very much about the Chicago situation, but the verbal deficit theory shouldn't be underestimated. Two educational psychologists have alerted me to how dominant this view really is: Joan Baratz here at the Center for Applied Linguistics, and Rosalind Wiener of the Early Childhood Education Division at Operation Headstart in New York City. The notion of verbal deprivation is deeply embedded in the views of Deutsch, Whiteman, and Jensen in the writings that form a large part of the justification for Operation Headstart. In Bedford-Stuyvesant the Bereiter method has been adopted; the Appalachian project has adopted it; in fact, it is so widespread that one of the leading journals in child development refused to print an article on the grounds that it did not incorporate the deficit theory within its framework. If you look at the book by Bereiter and Engelmann, Teaching Disadvantaged Children in the Pre-school, you will see that they provide a complete method for these pre-schools. The approach is well worked out; it has a lot of ingenious ideas, and you can easily see what a powerful impact this has upon people who are looking for something concrete to do.

Your point about the class situation is well taken. I'm using the term middle class in the same way that it is used in most sociological surveys in urban areas. Roger Shuy follows the same practice in his Detroit study. You are perfectly right in saying that this middle class/ working class opposition doesn't cover the social divisions in many regions of the country. But in the big cities, the 'middle class' is the group that shows the greatest achievement in school, clearly opposed in its educational success to the ghetto areas. The teachers themselves have no doubt that they represent the 'middle class'.

On your third point, that this is not a new situation, I think you are absolutely right. I have observed that you've been trying to hammer home the value of regional dialects for years; you haven't succeeded, as you point out, because it is a big education system that isn't easily moved. By and large, the American educational system has staggered on with all of its deficiencies—because people are pretty resilient, I guess. But, now we have an enormous number of children in the ghetto areas who are not learning to read; so that it is a question of the majority of children in these areas who are now considered deviant and deficient. If the school system is going to cope with this, I think it has to bend in a way it's never bent before.

David D. DeCamp, The University of Texas at Austin: Bill, I would like to add one incident to help document this case of yours against Carl Bereiter. Several years ago at an NCTE National Meeting, Bereiter talked on this subject to a panel; perhaps some of you in this room were there and heard this. He was talking at that time about black children in the rural south, and he said, 'There is no point in teaching these kids language, or arithmetic or anything else. They are so deprived that they can't count.' He said that it isn't just a matter of not being able to count to high numbers. These kids don't know the numbers from 1 to 10. They can't even count to 2, and as his example for this he gave one sentence, something like 'Them three boy play with them bicycle.' He said, 'Notice, them three boy ... boy, you see, they can't even count to 2.' Fortunately, Beryl Bailey, who was on the same panel, very, very neatly demolished him. The only difficulty was that he was the only one in the room there, apparently, who didn't seem to realize he was demolished. I, by general nature, abhor violence, but I mean he is the kind of guy that you have got to stomp on.

Shaligram Shukla, Georgetown University: Your conclusion was that there was no basis for attributing poor educational performance to the grammatical and phonological characteristics of a very nonstandard dialect of English. I have little doubt about this; because if one speaks a nonstandard variety of English, and if language is a system of rules, then certainly he has to perform some more rules than a speaker or a child that grows up in a society where the standard variety of English is spoken. In other words, if this nonstandard-speaking child is faced with learning a language which is standard, then he has to perform some more transformations in order to be able to express or to use that language, as compared to the child who comes up from the community where the standard language is spoken. Therefore, it does have some bearing, I think, on the learning of the child who comes from a nonstandard speech community, at least on the learning of the language.

Labov: I think that your point is well taken. I hope you didn't think I was implying that the child should not be taught standard English. There is nobody on this panel or in this room, I am sure, who would advise that a child speaking a nonstandard dialect should not be given every opportunity to learn the standard dialect. We all realize he needs this in order to have access to the scientific literature and to become a full member of the community. We have to distinguish between this long-range goal of education and our analysis of why the first steps in the educational system are failing. The question we're raising is: What is the 'cognitive disadvantage' that accrues to speakers of a nonstandard dialect? Now let us consider just for a moment some other nonstandard dialects in various parts of the world—Parisian argot in France, nonstandard Hindi or Marathi, in India. As a rule, these language forms represent somewhat more advanced stages

in the evolution of the language as far as internal syntactic and phonological developments are concerned. They have usually added rules to
the original grammars. There are also pidgins used as contact languages, in which it may be difficult to express certain complex ideas;
when these languages become creoles and develop into fully-fledged,
still nonstandard, vernaculars, they develop their own new syntactic
devices. We have to know more about this process. It is also true
that many colloquial speakers lack the ability to follow the convoluted
syntax of literary language. It remains to be proven that the complex
syntax which proliferates in high school in the writing of middle-class
children is at all functional. Before we begin to instruct working-class
children in the details of 'middle-class', or, let us say, elaborated,
highly educated syntax, we have to be very clear in our minds about
how much of this is functional and contributes to the precision of
thought. Much of it may be purely stylistic—a status symbol which
may impress people, but does not advance the processes of analysis
and generalization that we want to teach.

Kreidler: Is there another comment?

Robert J. DiPietro, Georgetown University: I'd be the last one to
defend Bereiter. I've been a victim of Bereiters myself in learning
foreign languages. In a sense, however, isn't he right when he says
that the student can't tell the difference between these forms? What
he really means is that they can't tell the difference between these
forms in standard English. Don't we learn much in linguistics throughout the centuries even from the Bereiters? For example, we've
learned from the Appendix probi that people said speclum when they
should have said speculum. Such documents give us a good deal of information about the history of languages and about varieties of languages. I'm sure, in future centuries, that the Bereiters of today will
be looked upon as sources of information about what contemporary language was really like. Although what you are saying is something that
has been said by people for a long time, i.e. it is important to know the
native language of the student in teaching him a foreign language or a
standard variety of his own language, I wonder about its practical application in the classroom.

Labov: Well, there are a number of linguists who are exploring the
notion—William Stewart in particular. It may be practical to introduce
the child to reading with texts that contain a certain amount of vernacular structure—partly for cultural reasons, partly for structural reasons. The surprising thing is that the nonstandard speaker has incorporated a great deal more of standard English syntax than one would
imagine. In our repetition tests, for example, we give 14-year old

boys sentences such as this to repeat: <u>I asked Alvin if he knew how to play basketball</u>. This contains the conditional <u>if</u>; Joan Baratz has pointed out that this <u>if</u> has been picked up by Bereiter as terribly important for logic. If you don't have the <u>if</u>, you're said not to understand conditions. And the sentence comes back instantly with no <u>if</u>: <u>I axed Alvin, did he know how to play basketball</u>. This tells us two things: first of all, the listener did not pass the test; secondly, he understood perfectly well the underlying logic of the sentence. To signal 'question', he used the southern colloquial form, retaining the flip-flop order in the embedded question instead of the complementizer <u>if</u>. A speaker who operates in this way has an asymmetrical system whereby he perceives both the standard and the nonstandard forms, but produces only by the nonstandard route.

Though what you say is true in many cases—there are pretty complicated things that go right past kids—it's surprising how much is fairly well integrated into their passive system of perception.

A THEORY OF DIALECT

RAVEN I. MC DAVID, JR.

University of Chicago

Abstract. This paper discusses some of the features that seem to
set off dialects, and some of the forces that cause them. It deals with
differences between regional and social dialects, and gives some attention to the ways by which a regional dialect becomes a social one.
Thinking in terms of the misuse of the term, it recommends discarding
the term 'dialect' altogether in dealing with varieties of American
English, and proposes that we confine ourselves to a discussion of
regional and social variations, accepting a pluralism of standards and
styles just the same.

1. To those who know me, it must seem incredible that I begin my
remarks with a reference to Noam Chomsky, most of whose work—
however eloquent for other purposes—I find for mine (in his own words)
trivial and uninteresting. But the learned Fathers here have assured me
that, just as the Devil may quote Scripture (a matter over which they
have no jurisdiction), it is lawful, on occasion, for a serious Christian
to quote the Devil, provided it is done with serious intent, to the end that
the true faith may be propagated. So it comes to pass that a peace-loving
and independent taxonomist finds that he must refer to a belligerent
transformationalist shaman heavily subsidized by the military establishment.
   In his 1964 appearance in Oklahoma City, in which he sought to dis-
credit language laboratories, contrastive grammar, pattern practices
and the entire established methodology of oral-aural second language
teaching (Udell 1964), Chomsky also took the dialectologists to task.

As he put it, their fault was that they recorded what people actually
said, not what people intended to say.

When asked how one should go about recording what people intended
to say, Chomsky could not provide an answer. Yet, indeed, as happens
many times with theoretical scientists, an incidental suggestion may be
validated later and elsewhere by an experimentalist. As I interpret it,
much of Bill Labov's fine work on the speech of New York City is concerned with this very problem, the discrepancy between what one actually says and what one thinks he has said—or at least what he thinks he
ought to have said. In Roger Shuy's study of Detroit speech there also
seems to be at least an implicit concern with the discrepancy between
what is locally said and the values the schools place upon it.

Indeed, much of the cross-purposeful talking that some of us have
indulged in of late about dialect differences might have been avoided had
it been possible to keep in mind the fact that our very designata may
vary considerably in their affective value according to the purpose for
which we use them. To a taxonomist like myself, in my scientific rôle
I have to insist on strictly comparable data; while granting that certain
linguistic forms may be more common in social group A than in social
group B, in the same community, I find it difficult to accept the notion
of inherent differences if I encounter the same forms in both groups.
Furthermore, I would expect that any assertion of such inherent differences be supported by objectively recorded evidence, which outsiders
may test independently, gathered from both groups under conditions as
nearly identical as possible. The corollary, of course, is that one
should be ready, nay eager, to revise one's conclusions when the evidence appears. For example, when I began my fieldwork for the Linguistic Atlas in 1941, it was inconceivable to me that any Low-Country
South Carolinian, or any South Carolinian with any degree of culture,
should have the barbarous constricted post-vocalic /-r/ in barn and
beard that my school contemporaries associated with the Middle West.
Yet field experience demonstrated that this kind of /-r/ is found throughout the state in a very complicated pattern of distribution, and in the
speech of a number of Carolinians of impeccable cultural credentials,
and I was happy to revise my opinions and put the new conclusions in
print for the benefit of other scholars (McDavid, 1948).

2. But an accurate taxonomic description, no matter how thoroughly
and elegantly done, is only part of the story. Haugen 1966 points out a
part of the difficulty: that the word dialect itself has a shifting range of
emotive associations, and its acceptability varies unpredictably from
person to person. In fact, he would reject the term as applicable to
cultivated usage:

Martinet is therefore beside the mark when he writes that in
America 'the term denotes every local form of English but

without any suggestion that a more acceptable form of the language exists distinct from the dialects' (1964:116). It is quite
different with the word 'accent': an American may inoffen-
sively be described as having a 'New England accent' or a
'Southern accent', and of course all Americans speak of the
English as having an 'English accent' [in my experience 'Oxford accent' is more common]. 'Dialect' is here as elsewhere a term that suggests informal or lower-class or rural
speech. (924)[1]

My own experience is somewhat different. Most Southerners of my acquaintance accept 'dialect' with equanimity if not with pride. But if it
is a term that arouses resentment in others of like sophistication, it is
probably wise to drop it for all references to regional comparisons of
educated speech, and substitute 'accent' as Haugen suggests[2] or some
other term. At the same time, since there are scholars and even
school texts that freely refer to dialects without social perjoration, it
would be a mistake to retain the term 'dialect' in the sense of nonstandard varieties of American English. Awaiting the coining of short, familiar and acceptable terms, I propose for the moment that we speak
of regional and social varieties, with the understanding not only that
each regional variety subsumes many social varieties, but that population movements may transfer large numbers of speakers of certain social levels from one region to another, and thereby complicate the social dialect picture of the host region, or at least of certain communities in it. Nor is it without precedent that where a group of immigrants settles in communities where the full range of social mobility
is denied them, as in certain executive bedroom suburbs, new composite social varieties will develop out of regional mixture.[3]
      Yet even if we did not have to worry about terms, we find it difficult
to understand when a variety of a language leaves off and a new language
begins. Those who have worked with the Ojibwa of the upper Great
Lakes know that almost mutual intelligibility is not sufficient to establish the unity of a speech community so far as the speakers themselves
are concerned. On more than one occasion an Ojibwa informant has
spoken disparagingly of another Indian, to the effect that he is only an
Ottawa /otáawa/; while others, with a similar variety of the language,
even in minuscule details, have been eager to identify themselves as
Ottawas and to reject the association with the Ojibwas.
      Even among languages with a long written tradition it is often the
chances of political and cultural history rather than any structural dis-
creteness that determines whether we have a separate tongue. Bloomfield (1933) points out that the Dutch-German speech community is a
continuum, stretching from the English Channel to the Oder and the
Bohemian mountains (and once much further); but nationalism in the

Netherlands and later in Belgium has established beside standard German two prestigious local varieties in the northwest as official languages under the names of Dutch and Flemish.   In the Soviet Union there seems to be no sharper boundary between Great and Little Russian than that in northern Pennsylvania between the Northern and Midland varieties of American English.   In the United States, however, where most of the non-Jewish immigrants from Imperial Russia came from the Ukraine, Ukrainian is identified as a separate language (Fishman 1966) and its specific encouragement is one of the instruments used to strengthen the ethnic identity of parishes and neighborhoods. It is speculative whimsy to suggest that a different issue of the Late Unpleasantness of the 1860s might have resulted in signs in Washington store-windows 'Confederate Spoken Here', but the various plaints issuing from the power bloc in the Northeastern States over the past half dozen years suggest that for them Texan might be a foreign language.

As Sapir and Sturtevant and others have repeatedly pointed out, a language is the medium by which a social group cooperate and interact and transmit their culture; and a large part of the taxonomic record on which we establish the identity of a language or of its subvarieties is the way the speech community feels about it.

3.   It is, however, useful to sort out the regional and social variation from other ways in which usage differs within a speech community.   Then we may show how these other modes of variation are interrelated with regional and social differences.   For much of this I am indebted to Joos (1962a, 1962b) and to Allen (1964); for the general picture to Card, McDavid and McDavid (1964).[4]   Responsibility for the interpretation, however, is my own.

One of the most obvious scales is that of maturity (cf. Labov 1965), by which not only do we expect someone to speak his age (as well as dress and act it) but to acquire a fuller mastery of the ranges of variety that a language permits.   On the first we have the evidence of children's development.   A child who has stubbornly clung to a deviant analogical preterite like brang may suddenly give it up; the once modish slang of adolescents, however derived, may be looked on with contempt.   But more important is the range of versatility that seems to emerge at some period between twelve and eighteen.   Negatively, of course, the failure to increase the range of versatility in this period may be a symptom of impending academic difficulties; and the overstrained efforts of parents to keep with it by following the vogue language of the moment are sure to be unsuccessful, if not as grotesque as the appearance at Miami Beach of bikinis and miniskirts on zaftig figures for which they were never designed.

Another scale, and that a significant one, is that of responsibility. For each occasion there is a more or less definable range between the extremes of sloppiness on one side and prissiness on the other.   What-

ever the merits of the case argued by our overprivileged hippie establishment, it is undeniable that their disregard for working-class standards of cleanliness makes it difficult for them to get an objective
hearing (if that is what they wish) on their concrete proposals. At the
other end of the spectrum, Firth has reported informally (and my own
experience in the South supports it) that a too meticulous observation,
in informal situations, of the canons of grammatical precision is likely
to breed distrust.

Another scale is that of vogue. Slang, of course, comes to mind,
as notoriously volatile and transient, though gams 'legs' and the verb
to bamboozle have been in English for more than two centuries and are
still slang. There is similar vogue in the jargon and counter-words
that are used, very often, as little more than sentence-fillers. About
1950 there was a certain efflorescence of new adverbs in -wise: cur-
riculum-wise, sermon-wise, discipline-wise, and the like. About
1958 it became fashionable to use on-going for continuing, and about
the same time hopefully became a sentence-connective of all work, with
a vague connotation of optimism. At the moment, inter alia, we are
surfeited with dialogue, confrontation, and relevance. Some of these
terms have had their origins in the usage of such subsaline professions
as advertising and colleges of education, but they soon became endemic
among the laity.

Of a slightly different nature is the associational scale. As any kind
of work becomes more scientific and technical, it develops its specialized terminology that becomes almost unintelligible to those not of the
true bond. This is demonstrated, most impressively, by the various
competing schools in our profession, so that stratificationalists find it
difficult to comprehend transformationalists, and tagmemicists cannot
follow either. And it is a rare physicist that can follow a technical discussion among literary critics.

But in addition to the technical language of the discipline, its prac-
titioners rapidly develop their informal shop talk about the day to day
work. Model railroad fans speak of pikes 'track layouts' and reefers
'refrigerator cars'; Anglo-Catholic clergy casually mention spikes
'brethren who imitate Roman ceremonial without an understanding of
the spirit of Catholicism'; amateur (and perhaps even professional)
strategists rate the striking power of nations in terms of nukes 'nuclear
warheads'. From this kind of shop talk it is but a short step to the ar-
gots by which the parasitic subcultures of the criminal professions
identify themselves: the big store of the high-grade confidence racket,
an impressive layout which is used to help the mark go for the send—
the operation of getting from his bank or other source adequate funds
to invest in the business opportunity the con-man has let him learn
about; in picking pockets, the stall who maneuvers Mr. Bates, the victim, into a position where the tool can best extract the okus, or leather,

from the left prat (hip pocket). And the cult of the addict as hero has made even us squares cognizant of the argot of drug use, and of the ways in which this argot passes from the subculture through the talk of musicians into the lingo of the fans and often into general use. What all of these subvarieties of the language have in common is that their use sets off the group member from the outsider—whether the group is composed of Trappist monks (who have their informal sign-language argot they will not divulge to their bishop), Chicago critics, or safe-crackers. For the narcotic addict, indeed, David Maurer has pointed out on a number of occasions that though it is possible to become addicted without mastering the argot, he has not yet found it mastered by a person who was not addicted.[5]

The attitudinal scale may involve either what the speaker thinks about someone or something, or how the reader or listener understands something spoken or written. Like news coverage on television, most of these usages are adverse—derogatory on the part of the speaker, offensive to the listener. For the first, I need only cite designations I learned in my childhood for various poor white groups: ridge-runners, lintheads, piney-woods rooters, swamp-rats, clay-eaters, shrimp-dippers, poor buckra, poor white trash, crackers, and hoosiers.[6] On the other side, Civil War was usually taken with umbrage at home, and the friendly British use of Yank as a generic for any U.S. soldier has provoked some epic pub-wreckings by irate Alabamians. Nor would I advocate promiscuous use of Canuck in the working-class areas of Toronto. And in Louisiana either Creole or Cajun may cause difficulty if one is unaware of his auditor's group identification in Franco-American society.

Nor are even occupational titles free from these overtones. Mencken (1963: 321-2) points out the degeneration of professor in the mouths of the laity; but even where there have not been the misapplications by extension, the term is likely to connote an absent-minded boob. English teacher is even worse, with its epicene associations; at the beginning of my field work I learned that it was a sure barrier to folk confidence; and since linguist and dialectologist are too difficult to explain, I took upon myself the more testiculate title of historian. It is alleged that one can reduce a Russian diplomat to tears of rage by calling him gospod'in, which roughly means Sir; and it is well-attested that in the politest of American communities, the use of Sir with certain concomitants of intonation and paralanguage can make it the most insulting word in one's vocabulary.

There is also a difference according to the medium of communication, of speech versus writing. Many of the humbler sort of words never get written down except sometimes in local-color fiction: such children's terms as rinktums or larrows, or fice as the designation of a small, usually worthless, nervously noisy dog of uncertain ancestry.

At the other end of the scale, the more complicated names of organic compounds are seldom spoken, even by chemists. Likewise there are differences in syntax, between spoken and written usage; and one of the problems of learning to write is that of substituting certain syntactic devices for providing the emphasis that in speech is carried by stress and intonation. But of course there are gradations between the two extremes; a skillfully written essay may create the illusion of speech, which one could never expect of a formal parliamentary resolution. [7]

It is hardly necessary to elaborate on Martin Joos's The Five Clocks (1962), with its discussion of the way the tone of discourse varies according to the size of the audience and the familiarity between the audience and the speaker. What is interesting is that the two extremes—the intimate style that arises between those who know each other well and the frozen style characteristic of great literature—have high allusiveness, the ability to convey breadth and depth of meaning in a few syllables. This scale, of course, is closely involved in the scale of responsibility, but they may operate independently.

The historical dimension is the first of three where, by and large, the speaker has no choice. One may accept or reject slang, participate of his own volition in a profession, hobby, or racket with its own in-group language, heed or ignore the expectations of the audience or the demands of the situation; however, he cannot choose the century of his birth, no matter how nostalgic he is for the medieval grace of iron clothing or the togas of the Roman Senate. It takes only a little familiarity with earlier literature to realize that by our standards Shakespeare would speak with a pronounced brogue, Chaucer could be understood with difficulty if at all, and King Alfred would sound like a wild Icelander. Less dramatic is the practical evaluation of a word or syntactic structure as dated, contemporaneous, or neologistic. The editors of dictionaries are pretty well agreed on the principles for designating entries as obsolete or archaic, though they recognize their fallibility and the need for revision of judgment. [8] A much harder problem is posed by those linguistic forms that are still current, still widely distributed, but more or less restricted to the older and least educated speakers. As yet, no dictionary has provided a way for indicating such forms, let alone a generally acceptable label. [9] And still harder is the problem of recognizing innovations; for by the time the lexicographers get to classifying and defining such forms, they are usually well established in the language. [10] Few words in English can be dated as precisely as sputnik, from the Russian success in October 1957, or such medical coinages as anaesthesia, appendicitis, and geriatrics.

Even more important—with the historical discussion and the two remaining ones—is the fact that these almost always involve differences in the linguistic system as well as in details. Systematic variation is not unknown in the other dimensions, but not inevitable: with history, territory, and social class it is very likely.

Territorial variation in language has been recognized for several millenia, and the techniques of investigating such variations have been gradually refined by a century of research. Even such practices as the drawing and weighting of isoglosses in determining the boundaries of speech-areas and regions have gone beyond mere intuition (Kurath 1970), and the characteristics of focal, relic, and transition areas are generally agreed on. The findings for American English of the first half of this century have been summarized in such works as Kurath (1949), Kurath and McDavid (1961), Atwood (1953, 1962), and dozens of perceptive shorter studies. Not all regions have been surveyed by these methods, but the amount of uninvestigated territory is steadily shrinking, and by the bicentennial of Independence this first stage will be virtually complete.

As such surveys are completed and the data is analyzed, one becomes aware that the territorial extent of linguistic forms is extremely variable, and that in some instances not only national but even linguistic boundaries are transgressed. At one end of the spectrum is such a term as tippety-bounce 'seesaw', apparently restricted to Block Island; at the other are many of the new scientific and technical terms, especially those of nuclear physics, that have been taken bodily into a wide range of languages. It is a commonplace that British and American railroad terminology differ sharply, but that that of aviation is almost identical. Within the Germanic languages, only English seems to retain glove; elsewhere it has been replaced by the phrase 'hand-shoe'.

By and large, one has no choice about the geographical variety of language he first learns, any more than he has about the temporal variety. And though it is not impossible to acquire a new variety, it is not easy. Sometimes a long change of residence effects a change: my sister informed me, after the first decade of my exile from the Confederacy, that I was now talking like a Yankee; and some speakers have undergone even more dramatic changes by osmosis. And the adoption of a new regional variety of speech for professional purposes is characteristic of many radio announcers, actors, hog-callers, clergymen and other public performers. In the South, among Episcopal clergymen, especially those who take their seminary training at Virginia Theological Seminary, a facsimile of eastern Virginia pronunciation is adopted for liturgy and pulpit, presumably on the assumption that it is the only kind of English the Almighty can understand. But in all such instances it is wise to proceed cautiously, for overt attempts to alter one's native variety of speech often result in alienation from one's own community and ridicule by those with whom one wishes to associate. Again, it is important to recognize that territorial varieties of a language may show important systematic differences.

The final dimension, that of social differences, is probably the one which is of most immediate concern in the schools. Until relatively recently, it was not seriously studied, and the prevailing pedagogical attitude was that there was a binary opposition between 'good' and 'bad' usage (Joos 1962b). The first attempt at systematic investigation of such social differences was Kurath (1939-1943), as an outgrowth of the peculiar American language situation, where the standard appeared in a variety of phonetic shapes, and where the relationship between the standard and the most extreme uneducated speech varied from community to community, with intermediate types sometimes closer to one extreme, sometimes to the other. Consequently, three basic types of informants were included—educated, extremely unsophisticated, and intermediate—in a proportion of about 1:5:5 (since educated speech varies less than the other types, from community to community). This procedure offered, at least, reliable social bench marks, so far as the natives of a community were concerned, and some indications of the directions of change.

None of those who have directed any of the American regional atlases have any illusion that their work is definitive for all time. [11] It has always been recognized that other kinds of investigations were necessary for a variety of purposes: to give more detailed pictures of the social differences in the language practices within communities of various types (Kurath 1968), to assay the degree to which recent immigration (both from other regions and from other nations) has affected the traditional speech patterns, to study intensively the aspects of communication that are only partially handled (if at all) in the general-purpose questionnaires for a traditional linguistic atlas—syntax, suprasegmentals, and paralanguage[12]—to develop more effective teaching programs, and simply to see what changes the passage of time has wrought. For these reasons, and others, a large number of interesting studies have been undertaken in the past decade, with a variety of techniques. Thanks to such investigations as those of Pederson in Chicago (1964), Labov in New York City (1966), Shuy in Detroit (1967, 1968), Dillard and Stewart in the District of Columbia (see Loman 1967), and Dunlap in Atlanta (1969), we are on our way to broader and deeper knowledge of the kinds of variations that exist in the language practices of a wide range of social groups in a number of American communities. And perhaps we will be able to make some useful generalizations about the trends in the social status of various linguistic forms in American English. For the moment, it is unfortunate that much of the data on which our conclusions are based resides in the files of various projects. But perhaps this is inevitable in a time when the investigator is called on to apply his research before he can adequately organize and publish his evidence.

Again, as with temporal and territorial varieties of language, no one

can choose the social variety he starts with. He may acquire a new
variety with a change in status—education, certain kinds of jobs, mov-
ing to a different kind of neighborhood, or in various other ways. As
with a change in territorial variety, a change in social variety may
come from osmosis and observation, or from deliberate intent. It is
fraught with its own kind of perils, too: the politician who achieves
only a superficial command of the folk speech of his constituents may
lose their votes, and school programs to 'raise the level' of children's
usage too often concentrate on trivia and ignore substantive matters—
even when they do not alienate the children from the schools.

In times past, it was possible to let the process of acculturation of
a family to new social varieties take a couple of generations. The
British entrepreneur of the early Nineteenth Century would never expect to speak like the established orders; but he could get his son into
the kind of good school that would assure his way of speaking. Today,
however, with a more open society than ever before, with rapidly rising incomes and even more rapidly rising expectations, and with technology creating new jobs which demand assorted academic skills, there
is a demand for accelerating the process. How this demand will be
met, and to what degree, is the business of those who direct the
schools; it is our business to provide the schools with the best information we can get, remembering that what may be valid for one community is not necessarily valid for another.

What we can be sure of is that whatever we call the standard language (McDavid 1970) will not remain unchanged in the process. For
the standard language, when push comes to shove, is but the language
used by those who make the important decisions in the speech community, and as the body of decision makers continues to change, so will the
prestigious forms of the language. There is one bit of evidence available from the South. In my childhood, in the Up-Country, educated
speakers had a monophthong [a·] in final position and before voiced
consonants, except /g/ and nasals followed by voiceless consonants;
we had a diphthong before voiceless consonants, /g/, and /n/ followed
by voiceless consonants, giving rye, ride, find, but tiger, pint, rice.
The leveled monophthong we considered uneducated. Now, however,
with the expansion of economic and educational opportunities, the body
of the educated is drawn increasingly from those whose families have
the monophthong in all positions; and this feature has to be considered
a part of Southern educated speech. Such changes are not without precedent. The Yorkshiremen who came to London with the wool trade are
at least partly responsible for establishing in standard English the
plural third person pronouns they, their, them, the feminine she, and
the indicative plural are (in place of the older be). It is interesting to
speculate on the influence that Mississippians and West Virginians may
ultimately have on the educated speech of Chicago and Cleveland.

4. Finally, let us see how these dimensions interact with each other. Because there is neither time nor space to deal with all situations, let alone competence to handle them in depth, I shall take one situation, that of the South as I have known it, and of the Southerners with whom I have interacted.

Despite my sister's comments, I suspect my basic speech-pattern is that of Up-Country South Carolina. I would no more think of deliberately trying to change than I would of denying the legitimacy of my descent. I have perhaps fewer regional prejudices than I had as a child; if I recognize that educated Middle Westerners have some of the pronunciations that characterize the uneducated Southerner, I am not so naïve as to equate the two populations: after all, my wife is from Minneapolis, and my children have all been brought up in the Great Lakes region. I have overcome most of my early prejudices against New York speech, and even a good deal of that against Bostonians. [13] I have observed that in field interviews or in classroom discussion I am likely to shift unconsciously in the direction of the phonemic norms of my audience; on the other hand, in a lecture situation before my fellow professionals I stick pretty closely to my basic speech-type, as one should in the presence of one's peers.

My upbringing was middle class, in the days before that became a pejorative for the self-styled 200-proof liberal, and that situation was given point by the fact that we lived halfway—half a block in each direction—between the wealthiest neighborhood in town and one of the poorest. I do not recall having heard a nonstandard speech form in my home, except quotatively or in jest; yet through various associations I was aware that other varieties of English were spoken in our community. Our attitude seemed to be that these were natural variations, that with changes of circumstance there would come changes in the way of speaking; meanwhile, we would accept each speaker on his merits as a person rather than on the shape of his inflections. As our contacts broadened, through playgrounds, camps, and jobs, we learned to shift linguistic gears according to the status of those we were speaking to— just as we had noticed our elders doing. Even I, far less privileged in this respect than most of my contemporaries, discovered—through the observations of a friend in the C.I.O. —that I was apparently able to talk to farmers and cotton-mill workers without betraying my academic background.

With the other dimensions there were approximately the same relationships one would encounter in other regions. Responsibility ranked high; it was beyond decorum to talk down to one's audience or over their heads. Slang and technical language were all right in their limited place;[14] if we used derogatory terms in the presence of their human referents we knew we would have to back up our utterances with our fists. We were well aware of the differences between speech and writing; we accepted English spelling as a poor reflection of the language, and something to be learned as a special skill—and indeed, as I recall, we were pretty good at the skill. To this day I say <u>six</u>, one <u>sixth</u> of the money and five-<u>sixths</u> of the class as homonyms /sɪks/, but I have never had the slightest problem in spelling them—nor do the simplifications of final consonant clusters seem to bother those I grew up with. Perhaps—lapsing into chomskemics—we have a different set of rules in our computer programs.[15] And of course—with a slight exception, which I shall mention later—we spoke English of the Twentieth Century.

Our scale of maturity, too, was pretty conventional, with the exception of the subspecies, female, often designated as the professional Southern belle. During the mating season, which varied with individuals, she would often assume, in the presence of males, the linguistic practices associated with girls in their late teens. But for the most part even this type of speaker observed the rules of speaking as chronological age required.

Where there seems to be the greatest difference is in the width of the intervals on the Joosish style-scale. It is interesting to note that, just as Southern speech seems to have a wider difference between strongest and weakest stresses,[16] between highest and lowest pitches, so it seems to have greater differences between formal and consultative and casual styles. There may also be a greater tendency of the Southerner to shift into his casual style as he comes to accept someone as an equal, or at least worth talking to. This is possibly the legacy of an aristocratic tradition, where everyone was assured of his social status and consequently was able to relax freely;[17] it is possibly another evidence of the cultural lag in the South—the retention of something of the Seventeenth Century relaxation in the informal speech of ladies and gentlemen, so well attested in the Restoration drama and so deplored by the would-be 'ascertainers' of the language. Whatever its origins, its manifestations are clear, in various social clues. In Charleston, particularly, the obscene <u>ain't</u> drops into the conversation, signalling that ladies and gentlemen recognizing each other's status can afford to relax. In most communities the copula-auxiliary will disappear, or at least its frequency will be reduced. Weak-stressed vowels will be further shortened,[18] and various consonants and clusters will weaken. At the other end of the scale we can recall the high formality of Lyndon Johnson's addresses to the nation, to say nothing of the bourbon-soaked tremolos of such veteran campaigners as the late Alben Barkley.

What this all comes down to is that we have to continue our research and leave our conclusions open ended, even while we try to adapt to practical situations the knowledge we have so far attained. It is im-

possible to exaggerate the complexity of human communication, especially of language, that most peculiar and typical attribute of the very
amusing animal that we call man.

NOTES

[1] The pejorative use of 'dialect' is apparent in some of the well-
meant programs for educating the culturally disadvantaged. Leaving
out of account the fact that, for many of the proponents of these programs, 'dialect' is restricted to one race, such phrases as 'dialect
remediation' and 'dialect eradication' and the opposition between 'standard English' and 'local dialect' are too common, and reflect a lack of
appreciation of the dignity of every naturally acquired variety of language as an intimate part of the speaker's cultural experience. They
probably reflect a certain kind of local lower-middle-class ethnocen-
trism as that which in Detroit schools assigns to classes in 'corrective
speech' pupils originating south of the Ohio and the Missouri.

[2] That, as Haugen points out, the term 'dialect' is a loan from
French, and that France has not only educationally but legally downgraded language varieties—so that we do not even know the number of
speakers of Breton—is relevant; as I have pointed out (McDavid 1966),
the Romance tradition has been hostile to the objective study of usage;
the lynching of Germanic studies in World War I left Romance authori-
tarianism inadequately balanced by Germanic realism in American universities; and the products of the Romance educational tradition were
among the most violent critics of the alleged 'permissiveness' of the
Merriam Webster's Third New International Dictionary (1961).

[3] My colleague Sol Tax has suggested it would be worthwhile to study
the linguistic acculturation of faculty children in the University of Chicago area, especially in the Laboratory Schools; so far, however, we
have not found a student ready to undertake the project. Perhaps even
more interesting would be the study of the language development of the
children of Army and Navy and Air Force officers, since they combine
high geographical mobility and a strong sense of identification with
their professional subculture.

[4] These scales were developed in their final form as a part of the
task of evaluating the usage levels for the Random House Dictionary.
Implicit, of course, is the possibility that in addition to words and
meanings, syntax and inflections, most scales involve potential variation in pronunciation (system of phonemes, phonic quality of phonemes,
incidence of phonemes), stress, intonation, juncture, paralanguage,
kinesics, haptics, and proxemics; the latter, of course, are not relevant for the medium-scale (writing vs. speech), and for the historical
dimension they can be recovered only in fragmentary detail, as in the
elegant nasality of Chaucer's prioress.

[5]The boundaries between slang and argot are often difficult to delimit; originally, they connoted much the same thing, and today, as Maurer points out, much of the most vivid slang is fed into the dominant culture from the alert wordsmiths in the various rackets. Even if one considers slang as something more or less public and argot the private possession of a closely knit group, the lines are not always clear. Certainly, the greater vividness of the language in the service academies and other military colleges, as opposed to the rather pallid utterances that pass for college slang in civilian institutions, is due to the intimacy of barracks life and the continued emphasis on esprit de corps (see McDavid 1939).

[6]Most of the popular nicknames for states and their inhabitants were originally disparaging, though they are now accepted as a matter of course since time has blunted the recollection of their origins (see McDavid 1967).

[7]A number of writers (of whom I am one) are in the habit of preparing a paper for oral presentation and then translating it into a style suitable for printing. For such, nothing can be more distressing than an editor's insistence that a version be ready for publication before the oral version is actually delivered.

[8]One of the definitions in the Merriam Third most severely excoriated as example of letting down the standards of usage was disinterested in the sense of 'apathetic'. This sense was the earliest in the language and is attested from the Seventeenth Century in such writers as John Donne, but the editors of the Oxford English Dictionary adjudged it probably obsolete, since there was no evidence after the 1790s. However, by the time the Oxford Supplement was issued in 1933, the editors had found enough evidence from the 1920s to justify removing the label (whether the meaning had been revived or had simply continued unnoticed is irrelevant here). Strangely, none of the hostile critics of the Third who objected to its unlabeled inclusion of this meaning had noticed that its predecessor, the New International, second edition (1934), which they considered a more elegant model than the Third, had also included the offensive meaning, unlabeled.

[9]For this category we proposed the label old-fashioned. Most of the commercial dictionaries use the label dial. ('dialectal'), which is also used for various linguistic forms of very limited distribution.

[10]Here another reference to the Merriam Third is in order. Much was made, by its detractors, of the inclusion of finalize, with an illustrative citation from Dwight D. Eisenhower; when, two months after the appearance of the Third, John F. Kennedy used the same word in a press conference, he provoked a violent barrage of editorial diatribe, launched by The New York Times. It was scientifically interesting, though unconvincing to the embattled belletristes, that the word had

been in the language since World War I, and was supported by a variety of citations, including some from the stately <u>Times</u> itself.

[11]Of course, it is a common failing of the public, both the <u>Gelehrte</u> and the laity, to attribute omniscience where the participating scholars made no such assertion. Orton's <u>Linguistic Survey of England</u> was delayed in its execution because many British scholars felt that all the relevant information had been recorded in the Nineteenth Century investigations of A. J. Ellis and Joseph Wright. And a Georgia official whom I approached about possible informants, asked in all seriousness, 'Isn't all of that in <u>Gone with the Wind</u>?'

[12]For many of these features, it is difficult to frame questions that will give unequivocal responses in the traditional interviewing situation; moreover, suprasegmentals and paralanguage are apt to be distorted in direct eliciting. And of course in the period before lightweight tape recorders were available, there were practical limits to the length of syntactic constructions that could be accurately transcribed by even the best field investigators.

[13]In the South the Bostonians were particularly suspect, as having provoked, through their propaganda mills, the Late Unpleasantness. Much of Southern coolness to Massachusetts political figures is probably due to this cultural memory.

There is, of course, a well-documented record of Northern prejudices against Southern speech-forms; amusingly enough, this is particularly strong among the constituents of the late Joseph McCarthy. For documentation see McDavid (1969) and Appleby (1970).

[14]To make a personal statement, I am inclined to imitate, usually unconsciously, the style of H. L. Mencken, than whom there are many worse rhetorical models.

[15]It is interesting that not only do educated Southerners simplify such putative clusters, but that they feel it inconceivable that any native speaker of English should try to pronounce them.

Perhaps some of the educational difficulties by poor Southerners moving north are due to two causes: (1) they have not mastered Southern formal, but only consultative and casual, and (2) the limited experience of Northern teachers has not prepared them for casual style so sharply different from the formal.

[16]Without meaning irreverence toward St. Martin the Clockmaker, I should point out that in the summer of 1957 James H. Sledd and I agreed that in our pronunciation of <u>nonsense</u> the proper trageremic superfix was ´ + ˆ , which Joos interpreted as ´ | ˆ .

[17]It is interesting that poor Southerners of all racial and ethnic groups refer to those who are unable to relax as 'strivers and strainers'.

[18]To Southerners, one of the irritating features of Middle Western pronunciation is the use of such full vowels as /o/ and /e/ in the final syllables of <u>borrow</u> and <u>Tuesday</u> rather than the reduced /ə/ and /i/.

REFERENCES

Allen, Harold B. 1964. Readings in Applied English Linguistics.
2d ed. New York, Appleton-Century-Crofts.
Appleby, Jane. 1970, Northern Prejudice against Southern Speech.
Athens, Georgia: University of Georgia Press.
Atwood, E. Bagby. 1953. A Survey of Verb Forms in the Eastern
United States. Ann Arbor, Mich.: University of Michigan Press.
_____. 1962. The Regional Vocabulary of Texas. Austin, Texas:
University of Texas Press.
Bloomfield, Leonard. 1933. Language. New York, Henry Holt and
Company.
Card, William, Raven I. McDavid, Jr., and Virginia McDavid. 1964.
A Proposed System of Labels for the Random House Dictionary.
Chicago, privately circulated.
Fishman, Joshua. 1966. Language Loyalties in the United States.
The Hague, Mouton.
Haugen, Einar. 1966. Dialect, Language, Nation. American Anthro-
pologist. 68.922-35.
Joos, Martin. 1962a. The Five Clocks. International Journal of
American Linguistics. Indiana U. Research Center in Anthropolo-
gy, Folklore and Linguistics, Publication 22.
_____. 1962b. Homeostasis in English Usage. College Composition
and Communication. 8 (Oct. 1962) 18-22.
Kurath, Hans. 1949. A Word Geography of the Eastern United States.
Ann Arbor, Michigan: University of Michigan Press.
_____. 1968. New Directions in Dialectology. Publication of the
American Dialect Society. 49.
_____. 1970. Area Linguistics. Bloomington, Indiana: Indiana
University Press.
_____ et al. 1939-43. Linguistic Atlas of New England. 3 vol., 26
parts. Providence, Rhode Island: American Council of Learned
Societies.
_____ and Raven I. McDavid, Jr. 1961. The Pronunciation of English
in the Atlantic States. Ann Arbor, Michigan: University of Michi-
gan Press.
Labov, William. 1965. Stages in the Acquisition of Standard English.
In Social Dialects and Language Learning, ed. Roger W. Shuy,
77-103. Champaign, Illinois: National Council of Teachers of
English.
_____. 1966. The Social Stratification of English in New York City.
Washington, D.C.: Center for Applied Linguistics.
Loman, Bengt A. 1967. Conversations in a Negro-American Dialect.
Washington, D.C.: Center for Applied Linguistics.

McDavid, Raven I. Jr. 1939. A Citadel Glossary. American Speech. 14.23-32.

_____. 1948. Postvocalic /-r/ in South Carolina: A Social Analysis. American Speech. 23.194-203.

_____. 1966. The Merriam Third: Self-Inflicted Wounds? Paper read before the Present-Day English section (English 13) of the Modern Language Association.

_____. 1967. Word Magic? or, 'Would You Want Your Daughter to Marry a Hoosier?' Indiana English Journal. vol. 2, no. 1, 1-7.

_____. 1969. The Teacher of Minorities. Nebraska English Journal.

_____. 1970. The Sociology of Language. In Yearbook of the National Society for the Study of Education, ed. Albert H. Marckwardt.

Martinet, André. 1964. Elements of General Linguistics. Chicago: University of Chicago Press.

Mencken, Henry Louis. 1963. The American Language: the Fourth Edition and the Two Supplements, abridged, with annotations and new material, by Raven I. McDavid, Jr., with the assistance of David W. Maurer. New York: Alfred A. Knopf.

Shuy, Roger, and Walter A. Wolfram. 1969. Field Techniques in an Urban Language Study. Washington, D.C.: Center for Applied Linguistics.

Shuy, Roger, Walter A. Wolfram and William K. Riley. 1967. Linguistic Correlates of Social Stratification in Detroit Speech. Final Report, Cooperative Research Project, 6-1397, U.S. Office of Education.

[Udell, Gerald]. 1964. Report of a Conversation. Chicago: privately circulated.

DISCUSSION

William Labov, Columbia University: What you said about the change in the standard in various regional areas is extremely interesting. In some parts of Europe we seem to see the solidification of regional dialects. Do you think that this influence of Southern speech—the Deep South influencing the Midwest—would actually lead to regional differences in the standard? Have you detected this, for example, in network broadcasts or in the general speech heard in universities?

McDavid: One of the things which I have spoken of otherwise is what seems to be a well ingrained attitude on the part of, let us use the cliché, the 'establishment', a hostility towards Southern speech forms. Jane Appleby at Georgia is making a study of this. Well, suppose these originally-arrived West Virginians and Mississippians become the majority of the power structure in Cleveland. Certain things will happen. As a matter of fact, I have already noticed one thing happening in Cleveland; I didn't mention it partly because I am not a native Clevelander, thank God, and partly because of space. The inland Northern dialect area characteristically contrasts such words as cot and caught, collar and caller, etc., as it has an /a/ vs. /ɔ/ distinction, and whether you Tragerize it or otherwise—whatever other phonemic church you may go to—the particular point is the fact that it is a working contrast. In the five years I was at what we affectionately called 'Western Reverse', I noticed that about a third of the natives of Cuyahoga County had lost this cot-caught contrast. I didn't know from these words whether the Pirates and Steelers were able to out-prestige the Indians and Browns; but for whatever reason the Pittsburgh feature had spread to Cleveland. It also extends for some distance—I'm not sure at the moment how far—down into West Virginia.

Labov: Can I ask you one more question that I have no answer to? When we turn on the radio in the South and listen to Atlanta or Charleston stations, we hear what seems to be a very close approximation to Northern broadcast speech. Do you think there is going to be a real disjunction in the South between the prestige speech of natural people and broadcast radio?

McDavid: There is already. I mean there is a tendency of a great many Southerners to make fun of the fact that such a barbarous foreign way of speaking comes out of the radio. Because we've also made fun of some of the excessive rotundity of our professional political spokesmen and certain kind of evangelists and the like. But I think we say that they're acting and it doesn't mean a damn thing. I think that this may be also part of this particular social attitude of, 'Okay, if they want to do it that way, but we don't intend to.' Of course, now that the White House is occupied by a speaker of network English—I can describe him in no better terms, whose chief fault (in the eyes of my two-hundred-proof Northern colleagues) is his breach of Washington tradition by treating Southerners as human beings, that attitude, too, may change.

RECEPTIVE COMPETENCE, PRODUCTIVE COMPETENCE, AND PERFORMANCE

RUDOLPH C. TROIKE

The University of Texas at Austin

Abstract. Recent experimental work in teaching standard English to speakers of nonstandard dialects of English has shown that such speakers often have a good receptive command of the standard dialect, and readily re-encode stimuli presented in the standard dialect into their own nonstandard forms. This fact shows that some modification is needed in the concept of 'understanding' as 'analysis by synthesis', and suggests that a distinction is necessary between <u>receptive competence</u> and <u>productive competence</u>. Whereas the latter may be inferred to a large extent from free performance, the former is not so directly attested, and special eliciting techniques are required in order to get at it. Materials and methods for second-dialect teaching need to give greater recognition to receptive competence, and its relevance for developing productive competence in speakers. This recognition may have importance for second-language teaching, as well as for native-language teaching programs in the schools.

In their now-classic paper, 'Speech Recognition: A Model and a Program for Research,' Halle and Stevens (1964) proposed the idea that a hearer of a language, given that he knows the language, recognizes the phonological (and, by extension, the lexical and grammatical) elements in an utterance by a process they call 'analysis by synthesis'. The hearer, on receiving a linguistic input, undertakes to match this against strings produced by his own internal linguistic synthesizer. When a sufficiently close match occurs, 'understanding' is said to take place. In this view, the role of hearer in a linguistic transaction is shifted from that of a passive to an active participant, since the processing of the linguistic input engages the language faculties of the hearer in a definitely active way.

The notion that we understand sentences by matching input against an internally-constructed output is a very fruitful one, and has much to recommend it, for it serves to account for a whole range of everyday phenomena which are so often taken for granted that they rarely receive recognition. I have in mind, for example, the fact that we often subconsciously project the form and even the specific content of a sentence ahead of a speaker's own oral delivery of it. This frequently shows up when someone to whom we are listening 'gets stuck' and cannot think of the word he wants to use. Depending on how impolite or compassionate we are, we may supply the word for him; or we may let him wallow in his misery while we await confirmation of our prediction. Not infrequently we are able to predict the whole content of a sentence after only the first part of it has been fed into our linguistic analyzer. I well remember one acquaintance who used to make himself obnoxious by completing other people's sentences for them whenever they got hung up on a word. What made it so annoying, of course, was that he was usually right.

The same sort of thing happens while we are reading, and when we are occasionally led astray by ambiguous signals, we back-track and reproject until we get a structure which permits coherent mapping into the material on the page. Usually this occurs so rapidly and so unconsciously that we are not even aware that it has taken place. But occasionally we do notice it, as in a sentence I recently encountered:

Coleman had matched groups of speakers
read, once, passages containing many passives ...

I was conscious of trying no less than twice to force <u>read</u> and <u>once</u> into a structure that had been projected on the basis of taking <u>had matched</u> as the VP and <u>groups</u> as the object, before I undertook to retrace my steps to the point of ambiguity and project a new structural analysis.

Analysis-by-synthesis, then, helps us to explain these commonplace phenomena, as well as our ability to correct, either silently or aloud, another speaker's slips in pronunciation or mistakes in word-choice. Understanding therefore results, not from a post hoc analysis of things heard or read, nor even singing along with Mitch, but rather largely from the satisfaction of predictions made propter hoc on the basis of linguistic and extra-linguistic clues and information.

Analysis-by-synthesis also helps to explain a common problem of perception in inter-dialectal and inter-language situations. As is well known, many speakers in the northern and western U.S. and parts of Canada make no distinction in the vowels of <u>cot</u> and <u>caught</u>, while many

speakers in the southern U.S. do not differentiate the vowels of <u>pin</u> and
<u>pen</u>. Furthermore, many North Midland speakers typically pronounce
<u>horse</u> and <u>hoarse</u> alike. It is a frequent experience that speakers whose
phonological grammars contain no surface distinction between /a/ and
/ɔ/ are unable to 'hear' any difference between these vowels when they
are presented in such pairs of words as <u>stock</u> and <u>stalk</u>. Conversely,
as one for whom both <u>pin</u> = <u>pen</u> and <u>horse</u> = <u>hoarse</u>, I find the distinctions difficult to hear in the speech of others, and unless I pay special
attention to the matter, I am usually unaware of the distinctions at all.
These facts are easily accounted for in terms of the Halle-Stevens
model, since if the linguistic synthesizer in the brain does not contain
specifications for making particular distinctions, they will not be noted
in the process of analysis. The same would be true for the difficulty
of Spanish speakers in hearing the [iy] vs. [I] distinction in English, or
of English speakers in distinguishing the high central vowel of Turkish.
At the same time, potential confusion of my [pIn] to a northern speaker
is predictable from the model, since this would match his production of
<u>pin</u> only, never <u>pen</u>.

These observations would seem to refute, at least on the phonological level, the claim recently advanced by Charles-James N. Bailey
(1968) that a speaker's competence at any given time includes all of the
styles and dialects of a language with which he is familiar. In another
paper (Troike 1969) I have proposed a generative diaphonemic system
for describing the dialects of English. In such a system, $|I|$ and $|\varepsilon|$
would be set up as underlying diaphonemes for all dialects, but Southern dialects would contain a rule

$$|\varepsilon| \;\rightarrow\; [I] \,/ \underline{\quad\quad}\, [+\text{nasal}]$$

Likewise $|o|$ and $|ɔ|$ would undergo merger before $|r|$ in North Mid-
land dialects. I have been asked by Noam Chomsky (personal communication) what psychological reality these underlying diaphonemes might
have. I think I would have to answer that the diaphoneme as I have conceived it is strictly a descriptive device, with no particular claim to
psychological reality (and therefore 'understanding'). For as a speaker,
myself, of a creole dialect which contains both of the merger rules
mentioned above, I long ago learned to adopt other strategies for identifying the reference of [pIn] and [hors], since I could not rely on phonological cues. Conversely, as a speaker of a relic [r]-preserving
dialect, I am repeatedly shocked by the references of a New England
school-teacher friend of mine to [makIŋ] her students' papers, which I
invariably decode first as <u>mocking</u> before doing a double-take and recognizing as <u>marking</u>.

So far the analysis-by-synthesis model has been shown to account
satisfactorily for a number of observed linguistic phenomena, but there

remain some problems which suggest that amplifications in the model
and associated concepts may be necessary. At the time the model was
conceived, the object of linguistic description was the competence
(knowledge) of an ideal mono-dialectal, mono-stylistic speaker/hearer
who only knew a particular variety of academic Philadelphia speech.
He was permitted only a little latitude in his speech-ways, as between
such innocuous alternatives as John phoned up the girl and John phoned
the girl up, or John expected the doctor to examine Harry and John expected Harry to be examined by the doctor. However, recent concentration of studies on sociolinguistic and dialectal variation in English
has shown that this idealized construct needs considerable amplification
and modification in order to account for a whole new and significant
range of data. (It is not so much that the data are new as that our
awareness of them is.)

In particular, I wish to cite some of the evidence which I and some
of my co-workers in Texas have gathered which has a bearing on this
question. Slobin (1967) has noted the utility of oral-repetition testing in
the study of child language development; several years ago we independently came upon this same technique, and have used it as a rapid diagnostic instrument for dialect study with children of ages five to seven.

Of particular interest is the response of many Negro children and
white Appalachian children to the task of repeating a sentence they hear
on tape while watching a coordinated colored cartoon filmstrip. Some
examples follow (N indicates Negro, A indicates Appalachian white):[1]

Model	Response
Mother helps Gloria.	Mother help Gloria. (N)
Gloria has a toothbrush.	Gloria have a toothbrush. (N)
She cleans her teeth with her brush.	Her clean her teeth with her brush. (N)
David has a brush for his hair.	David have a brush for he hair. (N)
She has soap on her head.	She has soap(t) on hers head. (A)
David and Gloria are clean.	David and Gloria is clean. (A)
They are on their knees.	They are on theirs knees. (A)
The socks are on Gloria's feet.	The socks is on Gloria's feet. (A)
The children go to bed.	The children goes to bed. (A)

These examples show very clearly, I think, that the child has not
merely attempted to repeat the stimulus, but has decoded it first and
then re-encoded it in the form he might have used in framing the sentence as an original utterance.[2] The rapidity with which this is accomplished suggests that the performance is closely akin to that often attributed to the coordinate bilingual speaker (and might therefore be
considered a type of instantaneous translation).

It is clear also, that the stimulus form and the output form differ sufficiently, albeit primarily in low-level lexical realization rules and agreement rules, that somewhat different grammars (rules of competence) must be assumed to underlie them. It is this sense, then, in which I have used the terms 'receptive competence' and 'productive competence' in the title of this paper. Since a (generative) grammar is a competence model (Chomsky 1965), and real differences in grammatical specification (including T-markers) must underlie the input and output forms given here, it follows that a difference between the receptive and productive competence of these children must be hypothesized. Thus they are bidialectal, with an asymmetry in their bidialectal performance, since they can presumably both understand and produce the forms of one, 'nonstandard', dialect, while understanding, but not producing, the forms of a second, 'standard', dialect.

A somewhat parallel situation has been found in a study of Spanish-speaking first-graders. Carefully-structured interviews, designed to reveal both receptive and productive competence in the area of verb structure, showed, for example, that most of the children could respond appropriately to stimuli containing the inflected future (infinitive + -é, etc.), but in their own utterances consistently employed the periphrastic future (ir a + infinitive). From their performance in these interviews, we must infer that the difference is not a fortuitous matter of sampling error, but reflects real differences in their receptive and productive competence. (We are currently conducting studies to determine whether these variations are developmental or dialectal in character.)

The productive competence of a speaker may range over a wide repertoire of styles and dialects, which may involve differences of lexicon, grammar, or pronunciation. In general, however, linguists have not been willing to credit children with much breadth of competence in any of these respects. While this may be true for many children, we have found that even six-year-olds are sensitive to stylistic differences. Two examples will suffice. In one instance, in which a middle-class white first-grader was interviewed, the interviewer asked her to make up a story about a picture she was shown in a magazine. At this point, the girl drew herself up, and beginning 'Once upon a time, ... ' launched into a discourse which was very formally delivered and which was notable for containing no contractions. At the end of the story, she audibly relaxed, and from there on freely used contractions for the remainder of the interview.

A second-grade Negro girl in a small East Texas town also showed stylistic shifts in phonology in going from a simple conversation to a 'storified' account of an event. Although she was not consistent in maintaining the shift, she at least showed clear sensitivity to it. The whole subject of the range of styles and dialects in the repertoire of

children is only just beginning to receive attention, and a great deal
yet remains to be learned.

A common complaint from white teachers is that they cannot understand their Negro pupils; from this report I think we may infer that the
teachers simply lack the receptive competence which they tacitly expect
of their pupils in reverse. Since most students are able to understand
their teachers, it should be clear that the dialectal range of their receptive, if not their productive, competence, often exceeds that of their
teachers. But the clear realization that the speaker who says ain't,
don't, and it is a book / some books on the table, can understand the
speaker who says isn't, doesn't, and there is/are a book/some books
on the table, and that this situation must involve a distinction in the two
types of competence (with partially different sets of grammatical, lexical, and phonological rules), could not easily emerge until the compe-
tence/performance distinction itself was recognized.

The study of linguistic performance is only in its infancy, and before
an adequate model of language use is possible, much more must be understood about linguistic competence. It is for this reason that the
study of linguistic competence continues to remain central to the discipline of linguistics. But for linguistic study to progress, both within
its own parameters as well as in relation to the larger areas of anthropology, psychology, and philosophy, the somewhat antiseptic ideal
speaker/hearer of the past must give way to sociolinguistic man, whose
linguistic performance can best be understood in terms not only of his
multi-dialectal and multi-stylistic competence, but in terms of his sociolinguistic competence as well. In this way, linguistic theory as
presently conceived can take its proper place within the broader context
of a true science of language, and sociolinguistic theory can realize its
potential contribution to the even wider field of the science of man.

NOTES

[1]I am grateful to Mr. Gib Devine, of Austin, Texas, for permission
to use and quote this material, which is taken from the Gloria and David materials (Devine 1958). Mr. Devine first drew my attention to
this phenomenon when some of the tapes in this series, which had been
prepared for TESOL purposes, began to be used with speakers of nonstandard English dialects.

[2]For a parallel situation in reading, see the 1724 quotation from
Defoe reported in Troike (1968).

REFERENCES

Bailey, Charles-James N. 1968. Integrating diachronic and synchronic linguistic theory. Manuscript.

Chomsky, Noam. 1965. Aspects of the theory of syntax. Cambridge, Massachusetts: The M. I. T. Press.

Devine, Gib. 1958. Gloria and David series. No. 6. Austin, Texas: Devine and Associates.

Halle, Morris and Kenneth N. Stevens. 1964. Speech recognition: a model and a program for research. In Jerry A. Fodor and Jerrold J. Katz, eds., The structure of language: readings in the philosophy of language. Englewood Cliffs, New Jersey: Prentice-Hall, Inc. Pp. 604-612.

Slobin, Dan I., ed. 1967. A Field manual for the cross-cultural study of the acquisition of communicative competence. 2nd draft. Berkeley, California: University of California.

Troike, Rudolph C. 1968. Social dialects and language learning: implications for TESOL. TESOL Q 2, 3, 176-80.

_____. 1969. Overall pattern and generative phonology. In Harold B. Allen, ed., Readings in American dialectology. New York: Appleton-Century-Croft.

DISCUSSION

Robert J. DiPietro, Georgetown University: I was very interested in your concept of the diaphoneme. I noticed in some varieties of Caribbean English you get sentences to parallel the one you have here, Her clean her teeth with her brush. I've heard, She clean she teeth when she brush, and I was wondering if you have thought of the possibility of paralleling your diaphoneme with diamorpheme or dialexeme.

Troike: I guess the simplest answer is that I have not tried pushing it beyond that point of the concept of the diaphoneme. This, of course, would certainly be a conceivable point. It would make sense in some terms, at any rate, for trying to understand the translation process that goes on. That is to say, that the speaker is able to recognize that she or her in the other dialect would have the same reference as the other form of his own dialect, and would simply re-encode that in terms of whatever semantic features were involved.

J. C. Thompson, CIA Language School: I think that it is worth noting in the first example here of when our predictions mislead us in reading that the problem is one of stress pattern. When your predictions mislead you in reading and it is not a matter of vocabulary, the problem will nearly always be that you have read with a stress or intonation that wasn't what the writer intended. In this case when you read Coleman has matched ..., you miss the fact that the writer did not intend minimum stress on has. With minimum stress on has, you read has matched as an inflected form of the verb to match, which is not what the writer intended. It is a feature of good editing to spot these misleading structures and correct them, as for instance, <u>Coleman takes matched groups of readers and has them read ...</u> and so on, which is quite unambiguous.

William A. Stewart, Education Study Center: I was very pleased by Troike's hint that there are similarities between intelligibility in bilingualism and bidialectalism, in that there are many families in which the parents speak one language or dialect and the children another, and yet they can speak back and forth. This is a fairly common phenomenon, so I think that Troike is right in pointing out that the use of different languages or dialects by different speakers need not indicate total unintelligibility. I would merely question his blanket statement that because we get accurate translations of this type that we have <u>full</u> intelligibility and accurate and successful translation in all cases. There are certain situations where I would say that is not so. That one gets near-complete intelligibility for speakers who speak different dialects but who have had long-term contact with each other in many situations, is partially true. I think a lot of this has gone on in the South between radical forms of nonstandard Negro dialect and white speech, such as between Gullah and Charlestonian standard English, where I have heard one speaker use Gullah and the other standard English, and the two seem to understand each other most of the time. Yet, when the listener is faced with a less familiar dialect, he may not really understand all that has been said, and the failure of intelligibility may in fact be greatest if the two dialects are superficially so similar that he thinks that he has understood, when in fact he has not.

Troike: I certainly agree, first of all, with the last comments here. I want to go back very briefly to the reference to the reading passage before commenting on the other matter. In the process of reading, we make predictions, we analyze and predict these structures ahead; and as we read we assign stresses and pitches and so forth, in terms of the structures we internally generate as we go through our reading. So, obviously the writer had intended that we should assign these stresses in a particular way as a result of a particular analysis; but the stresses get assigned as a result of the analysis, not the other way around.

In respect to the second point, I had intended originally, if there had been more time, to bring and play a tape showing exactly one of the things that Mr. Stewart was talking about, and that was intelligibility between some children in school—a Negro girl speaking her particular dialect and a white girl speaking her dialect—and showing that they were mutually intelligible between themselves. I didn't really intend to make a completely blanket statement on the other matter. By and large, it does seem that the Negro children do understand their white teachers. They have had a lot of exposure to the teachers' dialect over television and things of this sort now, when in the past this was not always the case; whereas the white teachers have not had the exposure to the other dialect and so they have not developed that bilateral receptive competence. With regard to the children, Bill Labov commented just earlier on the use of whether, pointing out that this would be a word that had simply not come into their experience to the point where they would be able to decode it. So you are quite right that a blanket statement would not be in order there.

John Behling, New York University: As I heard the tapes, there appeared to me to be a distinct difference in the intonation pattern, particularly in the fluidity or the smoothness with which the little girl repeated them. I wonder, therefore, if the later phrasing, which more closely corresponded to that of interrogator, represented to some considerable extent an improved ability in mimicry, rather than necessarily an improved competence or performance. We see this a great deal with children learning foreign languages under the ALM system, when they can become very fine parrots but don't really know what they are saying. I wonder if your experiments either did, or anticipate, any testing to detect how much of this is due to an improved ability in mimicry, rather than improved ability in competence and performance?

Troike: As I indicated, we were using the test primarily as a dialectal diagnostic, and we just simply happened to have this one example to show the before-and-after effects of actual instructional procedures. But I think, if you remember, in listening you will have noted that there was actually rather little change in the overall phonology of the production there. The change was primarily in terms of the production of the grammatical signals, e.g. the final s, the change of her to she, and this sort of thing, so that the rest of the phonology was not very much affected by that.

William Labov, Columbia University: I wish you would comment on the Appalachian examples. I think they show that the sort of correction that the school environment brings about, I would assume from what little I know about this dialect, is an unsystematic behavior, that the hers head and the theirs knees represent a different phenomenon from dropping the -s in helps. Even without instruction you can get some kind of a hyper-correction in this formal setting.

The other question I want to ask you concerns the more abstract kind of differences in repetition tests with older children that I mentioned before: I asked Alvin did he know? for I asked Alvin if he knew. James Gibson at Cornell felt that this was strong evidence against the motor theory of perception. I think you are right in connecting your data to the asymmetry of production and perception which means a fundamental change in our theoretical approach. What do you think the implications are here for a motor theory of perception?

Troike: To respond first of all to the matter of the Appalachian forms, I wanted to comment that these children were all preschool. These were all in five to six range, so they would presumably not have been affected by any kind of instruction except that which might have been done through their own older siblings or friends, or whatever, who were actually in school. So this presumably does represent native forms of the local dialect, and since Mr. Stewart has been out in that area and done some work, he might have some observations on that.

The second point: I wish we could have had on this tape one particular sentence that I think was extremely instructive. The children by and large, as we have seen, are able to respond rather quickly; in fact, almost before the sentence actually finishes they start coming out with their re-encoding of it. But there is one sentence in the text which contains the word both: Gloria and David both have their shoes on. This one difference in structure, with both in the sentence, apparently completely throws them. For some reason they are blocked on being able to decode that and to get it re-encoded, so that reproduction simply falls to pieces. I think this gives very strong support to the notion of their receptively being unable to decode this, i.e. having the internalized grammar to do so, and where they don't have the particular rules they are not able to deal with it.

Tsung Chin, Georgetown University: I think your point about the dichotomy between the receptive competence and productive competence is a very good point. We all know, and probably all agree, that children, speaking of children's language acquisition, do understand a lot more than they can speak. However, I question the approach, or rather I do not understand very well about the approach, to rely on intelligibility or understanding between speaker A and speaker B. If speaker A understands what speaker B says, does this mean necessarily that speaker A has acquired the so-called receptive competence of speaker B's linguistic system? Especially the examples you gave: for example, if speaker A understands speaker B's sentence He has a book, yet speaker A himself says He have a book, does this necessarily indicate that speaker A has acquired the competence, or simply that there are lexical items which help speaker A understand?

Troike: I think that is a very good question, certainly one that deserves a deeper analysis and some rather critical testing. Unquestionably we do rely on all sorts of other clues for the actual analysis which goes on in our heads, and we know extremely little about this. People have hypothesized various things about it, and I think the psycholinguists are just now beginning to get on the trail of trying to figure out some of these cues that people may use. The thing which I was emphasizing here was taking competence itself as a purely abstract notion of the knowledge which is involved and the kinds of rules one has to set up to describe the grammar of the dialect, in the input and the output, and arguing that one is obliged to set up different sets of rules to describe the structure of the input in this system and the structure of the output. So competence here is a rather abstract notion; it does not refer directly to the performance of the person in the process of understanding or in the process of producing. It is rather an abstract model set up to describe the structures of the two systems that are involved in the input and the output.

TRANSFORMATIONAL THEORY AND ENGLISH AS A SECOND LANGUAGE/DIALECT

CHARLES T. SCOTT

University of Wisconsin

Abstract. Chomsky's numerous criticisms of formerly well-accepted beliefs about the nature of language learning (e. g. in his review of Skinner's Verbal Behavior) have led to a diversity of views regarding the potential application of transformational theory to the teaching of English as a second language/dialect. It seems clear, moreover, that his criticisms have shaken the faith of many teachers in the efficiency of the audio-lingual approach to second language/dialect teaching. While Chomsky's views have been directed towards problems in the general theory of human language acquisition rather than to principles involved in the teaching and learning of second languages/dialects, it has not, I think, been a mistake on the part of ESL specialists to attempt to relate his views to the latter situation. This paper explores a number of notions developed in transformational theory which appear to have direct bearing on a theory of language acquisition; these notions are discussed with a view to their relevance in the second language/dialect situation. Tentative conclusions concerning the pedagogical effects of these notions are drawn, with appropriate distinctions made between effects on the teaching of English as a second language and the teaching of English as a second dialect.

Chomsky's numerous criticisms of formerly well-accepted beliefs about the nature of language learning (starting principally with his review of Skinner's Verbal Behavior, and now more recently as a recurrent theme in his lectures under the general title Language and Mind) have led to a diversity of views regarding the potential application of transformational theory to the teaching of English as a second language, and even as a second dialect. Quite appropriately, of course, Chomsky has in effect disclaimed any direct significance of transformational theory for the teaching of languages (1966a: 43), but it is perfectly understandable, given the pre-eminence of transformational-generative theory in contemporary linguistics, that teachers and ESL specialists will, and should, look to the theory for insights that may nourish their own pedagogical discipline. Thus, although Chomsky and his fellow theorists may choose to suspend judgment on the relevance of their theory to the teaching of languages, teachers of English as a second language need not take this as an invitation to ignore any possible applications of the theory to the theoretical basis of their own discipline. Fortunately, this kind of response has not been the case.

Fortunately, also, two kinds of active response to transformational theory on the part of language teachers can be dismissed briefly, because they are trivial and uninformed. One was the initial response of some teachers to the theory when it was first announced, and is, therefore, nearly ten years behind us. This was a negative response, most frequently expressed as a flippant dismissal of the early form of transformational rules as merely a notational novelty for dealing with certain types of conversion drills, e.g. statements and yes/no question structures. The response was often stated in the form of a declaration: 'We've been using transformations for years.' The second response is both positive and recent; I have heard it expressed in somewhat the following way by a teacher of Swahili: 'I'm happy to see that analysis is once again acceptable in language teaching.' The response is positive to transformational theory because it reacts favorably, but unknowledgeably, to those concerns of the theory which have to do with notions like 'intuition', 'competence', 'rule-governance', 'syntactic labeling', etc. Curiously, this positive response comes mainly from language teachers whose orientation is towards traditional grammar—a distinct minority these days, but one whose attitude has generally been more hostile to transformational theory than that of the structuralists, probably because of what Ferguson referred to several years ago as the 'trend toward mathematicization' in linguistics. This positive response, however, is recent, reflecting perhaps a kind of appreciation for Chomsky's current interest in demonstrating the historical connections between transformational theory, traditional grammar, and the rationalists' approach to a philosophy of science. Whatever the motivations for the response, it springs from the same ignorance of transformational theory as the first response does, though it is potentially more pedagogically dangerous than the first. I will return to the issue raised by this response.

The entire question as to whether there are practical applications for language teaching to be derived directly from any linguistic theory seems dubious at best. But that is a question which is related to the more fundamental consideration of the theoretical nature of second language teaching, i.e. how, and whether, one construes second language teaching in terms of a theory. Wardhaugh (1969 : 4) has argued that previous attempts to formalize a theory of second language teaching, e.g. Lado's Language Teaching, may in fact be no more than rationalizations to justify actual practices in the teaching of second languages. He is undoubtedly correct in this interpretation, but the only substitute that he offers is a kind of personal and public commitment to whatever system of belief about second language teaching that may, in the future, replace our present belief in the oral approach. I would myself prefer a more positive effort to construct a theory of second language teaching and learning that would be responsive to the same kind of fundamental principle that Chomsky has urged with reference to human language itself: 'If we hope to understand human language and the psychological capacities on which it rests, we must first ask what it is, not how or for what purposes it is used' (1968: 62). Nevertheless, these are questions which are quite beyond the intention of this paper. I wish only to establish the point that in what follows I do not want the discussion to be interpreted in the context of 'applications', but rather of potential problems or insights.

If this decade has indeed been the winter of our discontent in our national political and social life, it is no less true that is has been a decade of dissatisfaction with established positions in linguistics and second language teaching. In the latter case, however, the process of change has been much more strikingly successful in linguistics than it has in the language teaching field. It is clear that the transformationalism of the sixties has emerged as a flourishing replacement for the structuralism of the fifties, whereas we still seem to be groping for a convincing and appropriate replacement for the oral approach in second language teaching. I suggest that we seem to be searching for a replacement for the oral approach, mainly because our sense of symmetry and parallelism as one of the proprieties of the linguistics-language teaching axis virtually dictates an expectation of a replacement. After all, on the linguistics-psychology axis, Chomsky has in fact compelled a parallel type of replacement process involving behaviorism and an updated version of rationalism. Thus, we are informed not only that we have a 'new linguistics', but that we also have a 'new psychology'. Therefore, the question facing the language teacher is whether we should also have a 'new pedagogy'. The supposed trinitarian unity of the fifties, involving structuralism in linguistics, behaviorism in psychology, and the oral approach in language pedagogy, has been partially reshaped in the sixties by replacing structuralism with transformationalism and behaviorism with cognitive psychology. With our sense of symmetry, therefore, we seem to expect that the replacement process must inevitably continue to completion. The trouble with symmetry, however, as we learned from our wrestlings with Trager-Smith structuralism, is that, while it may be an expectation, it is rarely a reality. The danger lies in assuming that symmetry is a necessary condition—that, in our present context, a new trinitarian unity is a logical necessity.

Suppose for a moment that, because of our sense of symmetry, we choose to complete the replacement process. What alternatives do we have as possible replacements for the oral approach? With some facetiousness, and with little probability of acceptance, we might suggest the 'written approach'; but this smacks too much of a return to the largely discarded grammar-translation approach of yesteryear. Still, an updated version of the grammar-translation approach would have the merit of paralleling Chomsky's formalized return to traditional grammar and his suggestion that contemporary psychology should take its cue from the seventeenth and eighteenth century rationalists. I suspect my teacher of Swahili, who was happy to see the return of analysis to respectability in language teaching, would be quite pleased with this conclusion. Wardhaugh too, in speaking of the future direction of the intensive language course, gives us pause to wonder, when he says: ' ... there will be more concentration on skills such as comprehension, oral and written, on reading and writing, on spelling, and so on. The students we have are mature students and we cannot put them back to a dependency on oral language alone. "Become as little children again" and learn through the ear is too limited a principle today' (1967: 7). My reaction to this statement is (1) that the course content goals suggested have never been inconsistent with the oral approach, (2) that the students we have had in university ESL programs have always been mature students, and (3) that the principle of learning through the ear has always been too limited and was never in fact the sole learning principle of the oral approach. Be this as it may, however, I quite agree with Wardhaugh in his assessment of the possible consequences of our striving for a new trinitarian unity 'in which the new linguistics, the new psychology, and the new demands made of our educational system will find themselves welded into a new unity that will have as little theoretical justification as any past unity' (1969 : 5). This is an important point because it underscores the probable futility and possible irrelevance of ad hoc conclusions reached because of an overriding concern for symmetrical patterns of change.

A sense of uneasiness with the oral approach in the language teaching field stems largely, though not wholly, from a fairly widespread acceptance of the notions of 'competence' and 'performance' as they have been developed in transformational theory. Different from this proposal, but not wholly unrelated to it, was the 'communication-

manipulation' dichotomy suggested by Prator at least five years ago
(1964), a suggestion which also revealed a certain degree of dissatisfaction with the results of the oral approach. One could debate the
appropriateness of Prator's communication-manipulation model as an
analog of Chomsky's competence-performance model, but it is at least
clear that communication between speakers presupposes a shared linguistic competence and that relative ease of manipulation is a very real
feature of the performance aspect of language. Prator's concern was
with the apparent discrepancy between the manipulatory skill of the
classroom learner, characteristically in his response to pattern practice drills, and the frequent breakdown of this skill outside the classroom in actual conversational situations. Chomsky's concern has been
with the discrepancy between performance-oriented models of learning
and the nature of the linguistic phenomena which such models were supposed to account for. This is the position, of course, which underlies
his review of Skinner's Verbal Behavior.

Ultimately, in both cases, the concern involves the question of what
it means to know a language. Further, this question requires at least
two others: (1) what must be learned to say that one knows a language?
and (2) what human capabilities must be brought to bear in the learning
of a language? Answers to this second question have been proposed
much less readily than answers to the first, but the answers which
have normally been given to both of these questions by advocates of the
oral approach have, for the most part, been dismissed by the transformationalists and their followers. For example, we are told by
Wardhaugh in rather sweeping terms that 'the old intensive course was
based on an extremely dubious behavioral psychology which didn't account for the learning process in any interesting way. It had little of
interest to say about how either a first or second language was learned
mainly because the complexity of the learning task itself was completely underestimated' (1967: 5). Structuralist in their orientation,
most advocates of the oral approach have generally agreed with C. C.
Fries' frequent statements to the effect that the structural patterns of
the target language, arranged on the contrastive principle, constituted
what had to be learned in order to say that one knew a language—at
least in the first stage of learning. But the transformationalists have
demonstrated that these 'structural patterns' are no more than surface
representations of underlying structures and that, in numerous cases,
they do not adequately reflect the significant structural contrasts in the
grammar of the target language. Within the competence-performance
model, therefore, it is evident that the oral approach is under criticism for its failure to accommodate the competence aspect of language
and for its undue attention to the performance aspect. This is not unlike Prator's charge that the oral approach has been most successful

in its concern for manipulatory skills and least successful in its development of communicative abilities.

These criticisms are not unjust by any means, but we ought to be aware of the dilemma they pose for language teachers in their efforts to rectify inadequacies. Specifically, in the context of language pedagogy rather than of language theory, how do we assure that the learner of English as a second language emerges from his instructional program as more than just a well-trained parrot? How do we assure that the competence aspect of his language training is as successful as the performance aspect? My teacher of Swahili would have a quick answer: he would opt for greater attention to analytic detail. But this could easily be interpreted as a return to the more dubious aspects of the old grammar-translation approach. William Rutherford, in his text Modern English, has a more acceptable answer: a better organization and sequencing of the data to be learned. It should be perfectly apparent, however, that Rutherford's data are, for the most part, set within the accepted framework of the oral approach—that, in other words, they are just as amenable to an S-R behavioral presentation and learning approach as, for example, the Lado-Fries materials published by the ELI at Michigan. We might conclude that Rutherford's materials are better than the Lado-Fries materials; but, if we do so, we should at least recognize that they are better because the data are better organized (i.e. they reflect a better description of English syntactic structures), because they are more extensive in their presentation of these structures, and because they are more comprehensive in terms of the language skills they seek to develop. We should not assume they are better because they reflect, pedagogically, a psychological learning theory that is significantly different from, and superior to, the behavioral psychology of the S-R model. Rutherford's learning sequence of 'presentation, explication, and verification' is only terminologically different from the oral approach's 'presentation, explanation, and pattern drill'.

Clearly, though, the implications of the competence-performance model for second language learning run deeper than the restricted problems of textbook preparation or the relative emphasis that might be given to explanation and drill in the classroom situation. At issue, fundamentally, is whether or not the linguistic competence that Chomsky assumes for the native speaker of a language can be duplicated by that same speaker in his learning of a second language. The development of linguistic competence in Chomsky's sense, whether it is the competence underlying a first or a second language, would appear to be an absolute requirement, given the further assumption that the linguistic performance of a speaker, his verbal behavior, is an overt manifestation of this competence—that in fact it proceeds from this competence. Humans, just because of their humanity, are said to be

equipped with innate knowledge about linguistic structure in general—
an " 'hypothesis-formulating' ability of unknown character and complexity" (Chomsky 1959 : 57).   On the basis of this innate knowledge
and on the basis of 'the degenerate quality and narrowly limited extent
of the available data' (Chomsky 1965 : 58), the human learner acquires
knowledge about the utterances of his native language in the form of an
intermediate theory that accounts for those utterances.   This theory is
then applied to the interpretation and construction of utterances, which
include not only those that have been previously heard but also new and
previously unexperienced ones.   The verbal behavior, or performance,
of the learner is the overt manifestation of this application of the theory.   Thus, a theory of performance must be based, at least in part,
on a theory of competence.

      This, roughly, is the view of first language acquisition enunciated
by Chomsky.   As a hypothesis, it seems reasonable in its formulation,
and, at least with respect to the data available to the learner, true to
the realities of the learning situation.   Essentially the same hypothesis
has now been extended to the question of second language acquisition.
When this is done, the resulting formulation can assume deletion of the
initial stage, i.e. the 'hypothesis-formulating' ability, since this is
already a fact of the humanity of the learner.   The second stage involves the acquisition of knowledge about utterances of the target language, i.e. the construction of a theory to account for these utterances.
Once this theory has been built, in whole or in part, it would then be
applied to the construction and interpretation of utterances of the target
language, manifested overtly in the performance of the learner.   The
operative principle underlying this final stage has been stated by Ritchie (1967: 47): ' ... knowledge formation or acquisition (the process
of storing information, e.g. about utterances) must take place before
knowledge use (use of information already stored). '

      The extension of this hypothesis concerning first language acquisi-
tion to the second language learning situation leads to certain predictable conclusions.   The most obvious of these is that language learning
is primarily a cognitive enterprise rather than a behavioral one, and
that consequently the direction of learning is deductive rather than inductive.   It is easy to see how this conclusion could be interpreted as
an endorsement of the old grammar-translation approach.   Whatever
its faults may have been, the grammar-translation approach was
clearly deductive in its procedures and cognitive in its emphasis.
Moreover, the traditional grammar on which it was based was closer
in spirit to transformational theory than to structuralism in linguistic
description.   All the proper ingredients seemed to be present, including the attention to lexicon and the intuitive 'rightness' of orthographic
representations.   Yet the fact remains that Viëtor rejected it, and
Jespersen rejected it, and Sweet and Palmer rejected it.   The fact

also remains that the grammar-translation approach, at least as it was applied in this country, can claim no notable success in having produced <u>users</u> of second languages, whereas Wardhaugh (1967: 8-9) admits that, while 'we didn't really know why it worked,' ... 'the old intensive course ... was successful.'

It is not profitable to indulge in a kind of paranoia over the oral approach, or, for that matter, to adopt a status quo position on the oral approach for purely pragmatic reasons. Nevertheless, it seems to me equally unprofitable to seek a new pedagogy to replace the oral approach, just because we have a new linguistics and a new psychology, without first attempting to clarify some of the principal underpinnings of the oral approach as it was formulated by Fries.

For example, the oral approach is criticized because it is based on the notion that language is behavior and because it does not explicitly recognize that language is also knowledge. Language behavior presumably does not take place unless cognitive factors operate to produce such behavior. Yet, supposedly, the primary cognitive factor—the theory constructed to account for utterances—is developed on the basis of available data. In first language acquisition these data are degenerate in quality and narrowly restricted; but if, in second language acquisition, we insist that a similar theory must be constructed by the learner for the achievement of linguistic competence, we know very well that the available data is not degenerate in quality nor narrowly restricted. In fact, it is very well organized. Thus, the only modification in the oral approach which must be made to accommodate it to the competence theory is to insure that the already organized data are re-organized to reflect correct derivational histories for classes of utterances.

From a practical pedagogical point of view, there would seem to be no alternative to this except to concentrate more attention to matters of explication. This could involve an increased intellectualization of the teaching program—a pedagogical maneuver whose justification rests on an appeal to the intellectual capacities of the adult learner. This, of course, is what Wardhaugh has in mind when he reminds us that 'the students we have are mature students ... ,' but we should make no mistake that a greater intellectualization of the language teaching task is a natural requirement of linguistic theory, since no linguist, including Chomsky, holds that intellectual prowess is a necessary condition for the human capacity to learn languages. In any case, the oral approach has never denied the necessity for a certain amount of 'explanation' in the teaching situation. Our 'explanation' now should simply be better than it was formerly, just because the grammatical description we have now is better than the one we had previously. It is a moot question whether one develops the 'explanation' through inductive or deductive procedures. As always, the danger still remains that, in our eagerness to accommodate the notion of competence in our understanding of what it means to know a language, we will be tempted to underestimate and underplay the notion of performance.

Another underpinning of the oral approach that has been attacked as inadequate is the contrastive principle. The data derived from contrastive analyses are said to be insignificant because the analyses concern themselves only with surface structure representations, and because it is frequently claimed that the differences between languages are largely of a superficial nature. What is really important, it is often stated, is the fact that languages are remarkably similar to each other in their deep structures. The strong version of this theory of linguistic universals is held by Bach (1968), who maintains that 'the deep structures of sentences in different languages are identical,' that there is 'a universal set of base rules' (91).

The triviality of contrastive analysis as applied to surface structures and the significance of recognizing similarities in deep structures are readily apparent in Chomsky's example of French le monde visible and English the visible world, involving the derivation and surface placement of adjective modifiers. A parallel interpretation of Persian mixahæm benævisæm and English I want to write could also be demonstrated, with morphemic elements like English to and Persian mi-, be-, and -æm introduced in transformational rules to provide the surface concatenators for the underlying constituent sentences. Such rules would be not unlike those required to secure gender agreement in French. In these cases, the differences between English, French, and Persian are indeed superficial.

Along with this view of deep structure, there is Bach's interpretation of the base component as similar to the logical systems proposed by Carnap and Reichenbach. This interpretation, according to Bach, provides a way to express directly 'the idea that it is possible to convey any conceptual content in any language, even though the particular lexical items available will vary widely from one language to another' (122).

Interpreting the notion of 'deep structure', therefore, becomes a matter of how deep is deep. Bach's 'deep structure' is clearly far more abstract than the 'deep structures' suggested by the English, French, and Persian examples. But, if it is the case that the base component rules of the grammar function as input to the semantic interpretation component, as has generally been proposed in transformational theory since Chomsky's Aspects, and if it is the case that some form of the Sapir-Whorf hypothesis is still viable, then it would seem that, at some intermediate level of deep structure, languages probably differ significantly in their deep structure constituents. Bach's interpretation of deep structure, if it is correct, may truly deny the strong version of the Sapir-Whorf hypothesis, but a weaker version of that hypothesis still seems to be credible. If this is so, then contrastive analysis should continue to function as an important underpinning of the oral approach,

the required modification being that it would apply usefully to an intermediate level of deep structures rather than to surface structures.
Thus, rather than witnessing 'the demise of the contrastive analysis
hypothesis', as Wardhaugh (1967 : 5) has suggested, I would think that
contrastive analysis might be one of the most exciting areas of future
linguistic research.

An interesting, though highly speculative, application of this point
of view might be made to the contemporary second dialect situation.
In transformational-generative theory, regional dialect differences
may normally be accounted for by minor differences in low-level rules,
or in the ordering of such rules, especially those which specify the
phonetic shape of utterances. It is assumed, with obvious justification,
that regional dialects share the same set of base and transformational
rules. These assumptions seem to be reasonable and valid in the case
of regional differences in Standard English. But some of the recent
work on so-called 'Black English', particularly the work on the verbal
auxiliary, suggests that these assumptions may not be entirely valid in
the case of this variety of nonstandard English. I refer specifically to
a recent analysis by Loflin (1968) of the base rules which expand the
verbal auxiliary constituent for one dialect of 'Black English', recognizing that his description is at one extreme of the current research in
this area. Since Loflin's work is extreme in its formal description and
also in its implications, I do not wish to make a strong case for it.
Nevertheless, his argument is interesting, provocative, and deserving
of comment. Briefly, and without detail, it is this: the rules which he
sets up for the expansion of the verbal auxiliary in the base component
are decidedly different from those that would ordinarily be set up for
the verbal auxiliary in Standard English. In particular, his rules are
different because he posits certain verbal categories for 'Black English' that are not posited for Standard English, e.g. Generic vs. Non-
generic, Indefinite Past Imperfective vs. Definite Past Imperfective,
etc. He argues that he must do this because not all possible expansions
of the verbal auxiliary behave identically in passive transformations or
in certain embedding and conjoining transformations. His analysis, he
claims, is compelled by the simplicity criterion for the evaluation of
grammars. Thus, he attempts to justify his analysis on purely formal
grounds.

Suppose, for the time being, that his analysis is correct in terms of
formal criteria for the evaluation of grammars. The implications, I
think, would be far-reaching, though my speculations about them are
possibly quite outlandish. At some intermediate level of deep structure, the categories posited as formatives in the expansion rules of
the verbal auxiliary are different from those of Standard English. Regional dialects of a particular language are assumed to share identical
base rules, the differences between the dialects accounted for only in

low-level rules. The differences between Standard English and this particular variety of 'Black English', at least with respect to the verbal auxiliary, would be comparable to the differences one might expect between different languages. Indeed, Loflin guesses that the differences between 'Black English' and Standard English are probably greater than those, for example, between Danish, Norwegian, and Swedish. Again, if it is the case that the semantic component operates on the base rules as input, then it would be reasonable to conclude that real semantic differences exist between 'Black English' and Standard English. Loflin refers specifically to the handling of <u>time</u> in 'Black English' as one instance of this difference. The reference to <u>time</u> is reminiscent of Whorf's statements about Hopi and English (1940). If, as I said, Loflin is correct, we might conclude that the difference between 'Black English' and Standard English is greater than the expected difference between dialects—perhaps closer to the expected difference between languages. We might also speculate that Loflin's conclusions provide a kind of formal correlate to the claims of some black Americans that 'whitey's language' is not their language.

My own speculations on this matter are not Loflin's, and I would not be offended if they were summarily dismissed. Loflin's conclusions, however, deserve consideration, primarily because they seek to be justified on the basis of an appeal to formal criteria. They represent a test of the simplicity criterion for the evaluation of grammars, and should at least be debated on that basis. Moreover, if there is merit to his analysis, his conclusions should raise interesting questions about the relationship of languages and dialects to the mutual intelligibility criterion. It is quite probable, for example, that certain nonstandard dialects of Scottish English conform very closely to the syntactic component rules for Standard English, yet are totally unintelligible to speakers of Standard English because of considerable differences in the lexicon and in low-level phonetic rules. In the 'Black English' situation, however, we may have a form of speech which is intelligible to the speaker of Standard English, but which differs from it in part of its deep structure—comparable to the difference that we would assume for different languages.

In conclusion, transformational theory in general, and its notions of competence and performance in particular, can, and should, exert a significant influence on the teaching and learning of English as a second language and as a second dialect. But it may be suggested that, out of this new linguistics and the new psychology which accompanies it, should come not a new pedagogy, but a reformulation of our present one. The oral approach may have been too behavioristic in its theoretical basis, but it need not be. Neither, on the other hand, should we take our present preoccupation with language as knowledge to be an invitation to forget that language is also behavior.

REFERENCES

Bach, Emmon. 1968. Nouns and Noun Phrases. In Universals in
Linguistic Theory, Emmon Bach and Robert T. Harms, eds. New
York: Holt, Rinehart and Winston, 90-122.

Chomsky, Noam. 1959. Review of Verbal Behavior by B. F. Skinner.
Language 35: 26-58.

_____. 1965. Aspects of the Theory of Syntax. Cambridge, Mass-
achusetts: MIT Press.

_____. 1966a. Linguistic Theory. Northeast Conference on the Teach-
ing of Foreign Languages, Reports of the Working Committees.

_____. 1966b. Cartesian Linguistics. New York: Harper and Row.

_____. 1968. Language and Mind. New York: Harcourt, Brace and
World, Inc.

Fries, C. C. 1960. A New Approach to Language Learning. Reprinted in Teaching English as a Second Language, Harold B. Allen,
ed., 1965. New York: McGraw-Hill, 84-87.

Lado, Robert. 1964. Language Teaching: A Scientific Approach. New
York: McGraw-Hill.

Loflin, Marvin. 1968. Competing Transformational Generalizations
in the Auxiliary Structure of Afro-American English. Paper presented at the NCTE Annual Meeting, 29 November.

Prator, Clifford H. 1964. Development of a Manipulation-Communi-
cation Scale. NAFSA Studies and Papers, English Language Series,
Number 10, 57-62.

Ritchie, William C. 1967. Some Implications of Generative Grammar
for the Construction of Courses in English as a Foreign Language.
Language Learning 17: 45-69, 111-131.

Rutherford, William. 1968. Modern English. New York: Harcourt,
Brace and World, Inc.

Wardhaugh, Ronald. 1967. The Intensive Course: A Reexamination.
Paper presented to the ATESL section, Region V NAFSA Meeting,
2 December.

_____. 1969. Linguistics, Psychology, and Pedagogy: Trinity or
Unity? English Teaching Forum 7, 2: 2-6.

Whorf, Benjamin Lee. 1940. Science and Linguistics. Reprinted in
Readings in Applied English Linguistics, Harold B. Allen, ed. New
York: Appleton-Century-Crofts, 58-69.

DISCUSSION

David DeCamp, University of Texas: I am somewhat concerned that
you see the relevance of the generative approach being exclusively, or
at least primarily, confined to deep structures. It seems to me that a

lot of the interesting things that have been done in applying generative linguistics to language teaching and many of the interesting things that could be done tend to be exactly the opposite, tend to be putting things in the transformational component and, even more importantly, in the phonology.

Now this is brought up very clearly by this Loflin study that you are speaking of, which was extremely interesting in that it occurred almost simultaneously with Bill Labov's study of the English auxiliary which covered many of the same phenomena, that is, the same data. Loflin, as you correctly pointed out, dealt with this as a fundamentally-different deep structure, assuming that his Negro English was fundamentally very different, more different than Danish, whereas the Labov approach to the same thing was able to deal with it simply as a phonological rule. I think we know enough about contrastive analysis to know that the one thing that we do not want the contrastive analysis to do is to exaggerate and create language differences where they do not exist; that is, in general, when you have a choice, that a description in a contrastive analysis which in no way exaggerates, that is, which minimizes the amount of difference between the two grammars, is probably preferable.

It certainly is simpler, because in an approach like Loflin's, it is necessary that all the way through the whole derivation of a sentence, the whole thing from the very top is all very, very different; and this does not isolate and pinpoint the exact point in the concept of the language, the concept of the sentence where the difference occurs and enable you then to build a pedagogical technique around it; whereas if you can isolate it at a particular point as a phonological rule, you can produce some sort of a practice drill on this.

Now the use of generative phonology in teaching is something that long, long antedates Chomsky. There are many good, solid, tried and true principles of this that were being used by language teachers a very long time ago. We are not talking in terms of items in arrangement, but process terminology like voicing, shortening, all kinds of other terminology, even such an item as 'g-dropping'. We have found now that good ol' Miss Fidditch was right in her treatment of 'g-dropping'. I can well recall, I spent fourth grade in a community where there were a lot of second-generation German immigrant children, and there was a lot of difficulty with words like longer coming out [lɔŋɡer] and singer coming out [siŋɡer], and so on. This fourth grade teacher who was, I am sure, innocent of any formal reading in linguistics, developed this little memonic poem for the proper form before different -er endings:

When -er means 'more than', sound your g,
But when it's 'one who', no-sir-ee!

I think that we could quarrel with her literary merit as a poet, but

I think that linguistically and pedagogically she was very sound.

   Scott: Just very briefly, I think that I agree with most of what you said. I was aware of the difference between Labov's statement and Loflin's statement earlier this morning, the reference to the phonological rules. I am not claiming, of course, that Loflin's analysis is a correct analysis. I am merely saying that it is an interesting and provocative one. And I am only saying that if it turns out to be correct—if it does—then it suggests, at least to me, that if also there is some viable notion of the Sapir-Whorf hypothesis, and if it is part of the general transformational theory that base rules function as input to the semantic component, then I would think that this would be a way of formally correlating the Sapir-Whorf hypothesis with a contemporary description. I don't know.

   William A. Stewart, Education Study Center: Without disagreeing with DeCamp's point that there is a lot more to be contributed from generative theory in the realm of low-level rules and surface structure than has been really pointed out, I think it was unfortunate that he picked for comparison an apparent conflict between the Loflin and the Labov descriptions of the Negro-dialect, be/is. In fact, if you look at these descriptions carefully, they are really dealing with two different auxiliaries. Labov's contribution is primarily an attempt to explain Negro-dialect utterances of the type he tired, as having an underlying auxiliary which is deleted through low-level rules based on standard-English contraction (so that the Negro-dialect sentence is he is tired—or something like it—at one level, he's tired at another level, and he tired with deletion of the auxiliary, as the final form.) Loflin, on the other hand, was not dealing only with Negro-dialect sequences like he tired, but rather with the kind of distinction which I have repeatedly pointed out between he tired and he be tired. Now, in the Labov study, this invariant be, although it is mentioned, is not really dealt with adequately from a semantic point of view. Thus, I think that there is very little of the kind of serious consideration of the deeper difference between these two kinds of constructions that would validate a comparison of the Labov study with the Loflin study on that basis.

   Sister Dolores Burton: This is just a terminological point, but I have been rather disturbed since the conference began last night by dichotomies like 'Appalachian white' and 'Negro speech', implying in one case that there is a social class distinction for the whites, but that the other label belongs to all black. And also the distinction just made between Black or nonstandard English and white speech, which seems sort of subtly racist to the effect that all blacks or all Negroes speak a nonstandard dialect, and I just think that we could be a little more sensitive to the terminology here.

Scott: I hope I didn't give the impression that I was lumping all Negro English together. I think we all would obviously recognize that there are dialect differences there and, in fact, Loflin in arriving at his particular analysis is quite clear in saying that this is one variety of what some people have come to call 'Black English' and, in fact, he refers to his analysis as an idiosyncratic grammar based on data really just from one informant.

William Labov, Columbia University: In response to that last comment, the speaker should realize that the issue of defining what the dialect is has been considered at great length by the literature, and eventually everyone has to find one term to use to talk about it. I happen to use 'nonstandard Negro English', other people use 'Black English'. If every discussion of the dialect is to be prefixed by the seven or eight paragraphs that are necessary to deal with this topic adequately, we won't get very far.

Let me say that I found Mr. Scott's paper very interesting; I think that the points he was making are very penetrating. But there is one problem that I think we should comment on: many of us are disturbed by the fact that data are treated very casually in many recent papers of the best generative grammarians. Examples are cited from one person's 'idiolect', and we have no notion of whether anyone else agrees with them. Now when you hear Stewart talk about Negro speech, you are listening to citations from a large body of knowledge gathered from a great many speakers. When you listen to Fasold or Wolfram or myself, you are listening to data gathered from a study of an entire speech community by many field workers, many born and raised in the area. We study the language as it is used. On the other hand, we have Loflin's study based chiefly on the speech of one 14-year old Negro boy who sat face to face with the interviewer for about a year. When we read the examples of sentences judged grammatical or ungrammatical, they bear no resemblance to the patterns that we can hear on the tapes recorded in the same research project. There is no way for the readers to check this; there is no way to actually compare any of these statements with those of any other speakers. So we are dealing not with the idiolect of the investigator, but the idiolect of one isolated boy whose position in the community is quite uncertain. We read that sentences such as the following are ungrammatical: The dude, push from the chair, fell on the floor. Instead we should have: The dude, pushed from the chair, fell on the floor—supposedly a statement in nonstandard Negro English. Obviously it was manufactured for the occasion to prove that one is not allowed to delete the -ed in attributive participles. Anyone who would make judgments on the grammaticality of such obviously unspeakable sentences is a very poor informant indeed. But it is not the informant—it is the method which is at fault.

Last night Wolfram presented data on phonological conditioning of deletion of the -ed suffix. Wolfram pointed out in his dissertation a statement by Loflin that no one has discovered any basis for phonological conditioning of -ed. If Loflin had listened for five minutes to his own speaker or any other speaker of nonstandard Negro English, the phonological conditioning of the -ed suffix would have leaped out at him. I think that we have to take a resolution to draw our examples from serious linguistic studies, and these serious linguistic studies must be based upon an earnest effort to present checkable data and arguments based upon linguistic reality.

Walter A. Wolfram, Center for Applied Linguistics: With all due respect to Loflin, who did his work at CAL, I should mention several things concerning his data. In the first place, some of the things he says about his data are not actually supported in the data. For example, one of the things he maintains is that there is no has auxiliary in the dialect he is describing; yet in the CAL data, which he certainly had access to, we have found instances of have and has. These, then, are completely contrary to what he is saying.

The second comment has to do with his categorical type of approach to his data. When he is talking about the nonstandard English of his informant, for example, he mentions the zero realization of the copula, paying little or no attention to the fact that this particular speaker is fluctuating between the absence and the presence of the copula, which puts the whole thing in a completely new framework in terms of variability. Now, I realize that some of us who have counted things have been criticized quite severely for our 'non-qualitative' approach to the matter. However, in terms of the whole notion of variability in language and of particular importance in sociolinguistics, if you do this type of analyses, you come out with a grammar which cannot represent the linguistic and sociolinguistic facts about how grammar is actually used.

Robert Rainsbury, New York University: As a teacher of English as a second language, I am delighted to hear Mr. Scott's sentiments, because it is not the kind of thing we usually hear from the transformationalists. I would like only to rise somewhat in defense of Dr. Rutherford's book, which I happen to be teaching this semester, in that I think there is more to say than simply that the explanations are different but the methodology is more or less the same. I think there is one component that everything from now on will have to have in increased quantities, and that is those exercises where the speaker is to generate his own sentence following a certain formula. I would guess, without making a count, that a good one-third, at least, of Dr. Rutherford's book is devoted to this kind of exercise, very often very skillfully prepared, with things like the construction of parallel sentences, or 'make a statement about this, using this kind of construction.' There is a great deal of that in the book, and the emphasis on it is, I think, somewhat new.

Scott: I think that is quite true. I'd only remark that as long as I have been involved with ESL work in awareness of the oral approach, I've always been under the impression that notions of controlled conversation and what have you have always been very much a part of the oral approach too, allowing for this sort of thing.

Tsung Chin, Georgetown University: My question is not directed immediately to the speaker, Mr. Scott; rather a general question, it has something to do with the commentary by Mr. DeCamp, since we are on the subject now about method. Now I don't think that either the oral approach, audio-lingual, or the grammar translation method, has been clearly defined, as you all know from reading the literature. Also, when we open up a book on teaching methodology, almost invariably at the very end of it we will see this declaration: 'Teaching is an art. What has been dealt with in the book is not enough. The teacher has to do the job.' So what I want to say is that pedagogy and linguistic ability are entirely different things. In a classroom situation if, say, we teach a Chinese speaker the distinction of b and p in English, how we do the job is a different question. But to say that the teacher has applied transformational theory as Mr. DeCamp has pointed out, or as what he wants to do as shown in the article he published in the latest issue of TESOL, for instance, or to say that by doing this the teacher has applied even as far as the distinctive features 'voiced' vs. 'voiceless', —I think that probably is too much.

Richard Thompson, Georgetown University: Along quite the same lines as Professor Chin, I would like to comment on the statement that you made which I will try to quote. 'To reflect the new linguistics and psychology, we need only to reorganize materials to reflect the correct derivational history of an utterance.' I think that this makes certain assumptions that are not true.

In the first place, this assumes that speakers somehow really use transformations. I think it not inappropriate to point out that the transformational model uses transformations, it has yet to be proved that speakers of languages use transformations.

Secondly, this assumes that first and second-language learners should acquire language in a way which reflects the derivational history of an utterance. While some evidence can be presented for first-language acquisition, the presence of a fully-developed language in second-language learning suggests that contrastive analysis is of greater value in the organization of materials to permit the introduction of a more complicated structure similar to the native language at an earlier stage than a transformational history might allow.

Scott: I don't think, first of all, that I said this is all that had to be done to reflect the new linguistics. What I am getting at is simply what seems to be a very, very widespread acceptance of the notion today that the oral approach in our previous approaches to teaching English as a Foreign Language is inadequate because it is strictly behavioristic, strictly manipulatory, and this has been its only success. People are saying today that what we have to do is to insure somehow that the individual emerges as more than just a manipulator of certain structured forms; he has got to reflect a competence. As far as I know, the only way that one gets pedagogically at the notion of how the learner is going to reflect some sort of linguistic competence in the language that he is learning is to reflect somehow or other in the pedagogical materials the fact that sentences, for example, like John is easy to please and John is eager to please—this sort of thing—are not identical, that they come from different derivational histories; and Rutherford has reorganized his text material to reflect this sort of thing. That is all that has been said here.

Robert J. DiPietro, Georgetown University: I'll make it very short. I detected in the talk that surface structure and deep structure somehow had the connotation of superficial and profound, and I think this should be avoided. It is of no great use to an English-speaking student of Arabic, say, to tell him that the differences between Arabic and English are superficial. I don't think that similar statements help at all in language teaching. So I am happy to hear you defend contrastive analyses. The matter of surface structure and deep structure probably should be rephrased anyway in terms of specific grammar and universal grammar.

LINGUISTICS AND LITERACY

DAVID W. REED

University of California, Berkeley

Abstract. Presumably linguistics is relevant to learning to read
and write, primarily insofar as it can specify the relationship between
the grammatical system of a language and the phonological and orthographic systems by means of which the output of the grammar is
actualized as a string of physical signals. Different descriptions of
the phonological and orthographic systems will be of greater or less
value for this purpose according to whether the purpose was taken into
account in their formulation.

By far the best statement of the phonological system of English is
that in Chomsky and Halle's Sound Pattern of English; there is no remotely adequate description of the system of English orthography. Chomsky's system seeks to account for morphophonemic alternations and, in
the process, indicates that segments at the lexical level, on which the
alternations are based, are psychologically real, or items of unconscious knowledge for the native speaker. This formulation is inadequate
in two ways for the purposes of instruction in literacy: (1) the lexical
segments can scarcely be real to a six-year-old child if his vocabulary
does not yet include many of the items in which the morphophonemic
variations are manifested, and (2) the orthographic system of English
indicates many facts about the language in addition to morphophonemic
variations, and these facts are presumably part of the unconscious
knowledge of the highly literate user of the language; yet they are not
usually represented in Chomsky's segments at the lexical level. Among
such facts are morpheme (or formative) discrimination, dialect variation, and etymological source.

To make a maximum contribution to instruction in literacy, linguists
should describe the phonological system that can be abstracted from

the vocabulary of the average six-year-old child (the 'native language') and the orthographic and phonological systems of the most highly literate speakers (the 'target language').

Probably the most successful efforts to apply the knowledge gained from scientific analysis of languages to practical concerns have been made in the field of second language instruction. It has been recognized that effective instruction should be based on a detailed understanding of both the native language that the learner has already acquired and the target language that he seeks to acquire. Contrastive analysis sets up a general frame of terminological reference within which the similarities and differences between the two languages may be stated. The similarities that are noted are then used to outline the basic stages of the instructional process, and the differences to identify the emphases that should be maintained.

It does not seem to have been generally recognized as yet that there is a close analogy between second language learning and learning to read and write one's native language. In both situations the learner approaches the task, having gained particular attainments: in the one case he understands more or less of the structure of his native language; in the other he understands the structure of a limited vocabulary that he represents by purely oral symbols. In the first case he sets out to acquire what is, from a certain point of view, a totally different system for representing meanings with which he is already familiar; in the second case he seeks to acquire a totally different—i.e. graphic rather than vocal—system of representing a grammar with which he is largely familiar. Paradoxically, although every child whose mental and physiological equipment is remotely normal acquires, without noticeable effort, 'perfect' control of a native language by the age of five, many children still fail utterly in the acquisition of a second language and of perfect control of the writing system employed to represent their native language.

In a field of endeavor where more educational energy and funds are expended than in perhaps any other—namely, the skills of reading and writing one's native language—it is shocking that so little is known about the preparation that the child brings to the task and about the goal of instruction. Research in children's acquisition of language has been largely restricted to the earliest ages. To learn what the vocabulary of a typical five or six-year old is like, we have nothing more up-to-date than the results of a study compiled in the 1920s (Horn 1928), and even this is a bare list of words with almost no indication of how it was compiled. Linguists have been content to assure us that by age five, or some other magic preschool age, the typical child has acquired a perfect mastery of the grammar of his native language. If this were indeed true, would it not be surprising that he experiences so much difficulty in learning what ought to be a far simpler thing——to represent this language in graphic symbols equivalent to the vocal symbols he has already learned? Quite clearly neither the typical first-grader nor the most intelligent and highly literate adult knows all there is to know about the English language. Once the matter is put in these terms, we should recognize that we have been deluding ourselves, in that we have used the word language in two different senses. To say that the child has acquired perfect mastery of his native language is to say that he has acquired an idiolectal phonological system for representing the grammar of that language as it is manifested in a limited vocabulary that is entirely adequate to his childish needs. He will almost certainly be more naïve than the highly literate adult in attempting to answer such questions as the following: (1) How is one supposed to pronounce an unfamiliar word that has been formed by suffixation from a familiar word? (2) Are two linguistic forms that have the same phonological representation for all speakers of the language different words or one word with different meanings? (3) If two linguistic forms have the same phonological representation in the speaker's idiolect, do they have identical representations for all speakers of the language?

So much for the kind of deficiency we should expect to find in the first grade child's knowledge of his native language. It has been at least implied that the highly literate adult is better off in all these regards. If this is indeed the case, we may ask what there is about the process of becoming literate that provides the learner with some unconscious knowledge of morphophonemics, dialect geography, and etymology, even though he has probably never heard of these abstruse subjects? Presumably there is information in the writing system, beyond mere phoneme-grapheme correspondence, that he picks up unconsciously in the process of learning to read and write. This possibility can be examined by studying the writing system itself.

Information on morphophonemic alternations of the sort described in Chomsky and Halle's Sound Pattern of English (1968) is embodied to a large extent in the English system of writing. Dialects of American English employ up to 16 vowel nuclei in stressed syllables (these nuclei correspond approximately to the 'morphophones' identified by Henry Lee Smith in 'English Morphophonics' (1968). Yet only two to four contrasting vowel nuclei occur in unstressed syllables in the same dialects. Dialects that make a maximum number of distinctions in unstressed syllables (and therefore most closely resemble the abstract system of the language) generally have a high front tense vowel or diphthong in words like Rosie's (genitive form of the name Rosie), a high central lax vowel in roses (plural of rose), a mid central lax vowel in Rosa's (genitive form of the name Rosa), and a mid back tense vowel or diphthong in window. In dialects like Standard British or some Southern United States varieties the opposition between the first and second nuclei is neutralized. In many scattered areas the contrast between the second and third units is neutralized. In much of the Middle West the last pair of nuclei are pronounced alike. Any one of these neutralizations alone produces a system with three vowels in minimally stressed syllables. If two neutralizations occur, only two vowel nuclei remain. I have not encountered any dialects in which all three possible neutralizations take place, which would have the effect of reducing unstressed vowels to one.

The dialect differences that have been observed can be accounted for by low-level rules that take effect after more general morphophonemic alternations have been explained. The important point is that as many as sixteen vocalic nuclei in stressed syllables are reduced to no more than four nuclei in minimally stressed syllables of related words. I have previously used (Reed 1965) the words legality, rebellion, civilian, Mongolian, and cherubic to illustrate a similar point. If the word-forming suffixes are removed, there remain a series of disyllabic bases in which the second vowels are all pronounced the same in some dialects: legal, rebel, civil, Mongol, and cherub. Even in such dialects, the fact that the second vowels are all different segments at the lexical level is apparent from the pronunciation of the derived forms. This kind of morphophonemic variation abounds in the more learned, Latinate segment of English vocabulary. Presumably, highly literate adults have an unconscious knowledge of the rules that account for such variation. The vocabularies of six-year olds, on the other hand, probably contain only a few of the sets of words in which the rules are exemplified. It seems highly unlikely that such children have even an unconscious knowledge of the rules. The knowledge is acquired partly from enlarged contact with spoken English and the vocabulary expansion that accompanies it, but probably to a much greater extent from reading, and employing the skills of literacy. This is true, not only because written vocabulary is more formal, but also because the spelling system constantly reinforces identification of the morphophonemes.

The spelling system likewise aids the literate adult in identifying and distinguishing between morphemes that are phonologically identical. I recall hearing David DeCamp make this point most effectively in a lecture given at the Linguistic Institute in Austin in the summer of 1961. He indicated that as a result of interviewing illiterate adults in Jamaica he had reached the conclusion that their identification and discrimination of morphemes differed in important respects from that of literate speakers of the language. One example that I quote from memory was that the sale conducted in a store and the sail of a ship were identified by many illiterate informants as the same word. In a manner familiar to students of folk etymology, they had found semantic rationalization for the supposed identity: The sail of a ship is a large sheet of canvas, and a sale held in a store is announced on a large sheet of paper. It may be assumed that as soon as the learner becomes aware that sail and sale are spelled differently, he begins to think of them as different words rather than different meanings of the same word, and dismisses the fancied semantic resemblances that may become quite real for the illiterate speaker.

English spelling, however, does not always supply such helpful information about morpheme identification. There is the familiar case of corn on the cob and a corn on the toe. Although native users of the language who have not studied the effect of Grimm's Law and who are unfamiliar with the specific etymology of the words in question might without such conscious knowledge suspect that these are two different words from the fact that the first is a mass noun, the second a count noun, I have often verified the contrary fact that more than half of a typical college class will indicate their feeling that the two corns are different meanings of the same word. When I ask what leads them to this conclusion, they usually inform me that the two kinds of corn are approximately the same shape. This explanation, although coming from literate adults, is, because of the lack of specific clues in the spelling system, remarkably like the semantic rationalization of illiterate informants in Jamaica regarding the identity of the two /se:lz/. (An interesting footnote to this discussion is that, although we have just observed that English spelling is deficient in not indicating that the two corns are different words, it is deficient in precisely the opposite manner in providing no means of writing the phonological form /se:lz/ in my last sentence, which referred to the 'identity of the two /se:lz/.' I have overcome this difficulty in writing my manuscript by employing a more-or-less standard phonemic transcription of the phonological form. The example gives confirmation, however, of the fact that English spelling usually identifies lexical rather than purely phonological entities.)

Let us consider one final example of the relationship between English spelling and the identification of English lexical units. Suppose we are asked whether board is one word with several meanings or several entirely different words in the phrases on board the plane, the actor trod the boards, the festive board, fifty dollars board, and board of education. Lacking specific knowledge of the semantic history of the word, we could note that it is always spelled the same, which suggests that it is one word. We noted in the instance of the two corns, however, that spelling is not an infallible guide to morpheme identity. The contemporary semantic evidence would seem to support the conclusion that several different words are involved, since it is difficult in the absence of earlier records to imagine any connecting links between several of the semantic entities. In the instance of board, of course, English spelling is an adequate guide to lexical identity, since contemporary meanings of board have become isolated from one another through the obsolescence of some meanings like 'deck of a ship', which, if still alive in the language, would indicate the nature of the relationship between all of the current meanings.

Up to this point the argument has sought to demonstrate that the very process of becoming literate changes what is for the speaker psychologically real in his native language. The example of board suggests that even further changes in psychological reality will occur for the literate speaker who takes up the study of the earlier literature written in his native language or, even more particularly, who takes up the study of linguistics, both synchronic and diachronic.

It may be objected that the knowledge acquired by such persons is scarcely 'naïve' and, in the case of the linguist, it isn't even 'unconscious'. Presumably because all speakers of a language from an illiterate adolescent from the southern mountains to the greatest living author or the editor of an unabridged dictionary of English share much naïve, unconscious knowledge of the language, it is of some interest to isolate and explain this common factor in the linguistic competence of everyone. Such a worthwhile pursuit, however, should not lead us to overlook or minimize the very real differences in competence between the two. It is presumably the responsibility of contrastive analysis to describe and explain these differences, and the job of educators to design programs of instruction, informed by the findings of contrastive analysis, that will go as far as possible toward enlarging the learner's knowledge of his native language whether conscious or unconscious.

Turning to the last of the three questions we set out to explore, we wish to determine the extent to which English spelling represents phonological differences that occur in some dialects but that may be unknown in the idiolect of a particular first-grade child or in the dialect of a class of children. William Labov has shown (1967) with reference to the dialect of Harlem, that many phonological rules that operate to drop final consonants, simplify final consonant clusters, and otherwise neutralize the endings of words, produce numerous sets of homonyms from what are contrasting sets in standard dialects. The phonological distinctions that are maintained in standard dialects are, almost without exception, represented in English spelling. The relative nearness of standard English to English writing in these respects makes the task of learning to read and write somewhat easier for the child who has acquired the standard distinctions than for the ghetto child in whose speech the distinctions are missing. On the other hand, as the ghetto youngster acquires literacy, he gains unconscious knowledge of the phonology of other dialects, even if his own speech patterns remain largely unaffected.

Phonological neutralizations which increase the amount of homonymy in a dialect are by no means confined to the dialects of the socially dis-

advantaged. Two recent and extensive vowel changes have added greatly to the stock of homonyms in most dialects of English. As to the first
of these, I am unaware whether Standard British English has been affected but am under the impression that it has not. In any event, the
situation described by Daniel Jones (1937) for that dialect earlier in this
century may be taken as representative of the original distribution of
low back vowel phonemes in the language. These were three in number:
(1) a lower mid back tense round vowel or diphthong /ɔ:/ as in law, (2)
a low back lax slightly round vowel /ɒ/ as in hot, and (3) a low central
unround vowel usually described as long, /a:/, as in pa. Correlation
between the incidence of these vowels as indicated in Jones' Pronouncing Dictionary and the spelling patterns of the language are so close that
a very short set of rules is adequate to describe the situation compre-
hensively and accurately.

At some point in time before the Linguistic Atlas survey began in the
eastern United States in the 1930s, neutralizations of this threefold
distinction appear to have been well underway. The most common pattern of distribution of low back vowels by this period was that of a two-
fold contrast between a low back round and a low central unround vowel.
This loss of one contrasting unit took place when words of the second or
'short o̲' class were realigned with the first and third classes. The re-
alignment was usually worked out in terms of phonetic environment, although details differed from dialect to dialect. Thus, in the Northern
dialect area, 'short o̲' before /g/ generally aligned itself with the low
central unround vowel type; whereas in the Midland and Southern areas
it became aligned with the low back round type. Not only were there
dialect differences of this kind as regards the incidence of phonemes,
but also there were differences in the phonetic norm of phonemes that
were sometimes appreciable enough to cause one man's low central unround norm to approximate another man's low back round norm and vice
versa. The dialectal situation was sufficiently complicated to cause
marked difficulties in training field interviewers in the consistent recording of low back vowels, as attested by Hans Kurath in the Handbook
of the Linguistic Geography of New England (1939).

By the late thirties there were already areas such as western Pennsylvania in which the interim two way contrast among low back vowels
had been further neutralized to a single phoneme, usually with a fairly
wide range of phonetic actualizations. Although there is a chronological
lacuna in our evidence occasioned by World War II, the earliest postwar
surveys done in the West suggest that neutralization to a single low back
vowel had been underway for some time in areas like Utah, Idaho, Arizona, and Southern California (unpublished materials in the Linguistic
Atlas of the Pacific Coast). A telephone survey conducted more recently by William Labov suggests that the one-vowel system is becoming
rapidly established in the speech of younger persons all over the coun-

try. This finding is strongly supported by the difficulties normally encountered today by professors of phonetics in teaching college students to make the auditory discrimination between /aː/ and /ɔː/ in listening to dialect recordings of older speakers.

In short, within a period of perhaps no more than fifty years, what was once a set of three contrasting vowels have been telescoped into one in most American dialects, with the creation of a substantial number of new homonyms. If Standard British maintains the three contrasts, youthful speakers of that dialect should enjoy a definite advantage in this regard over their American counterparts when both approach the task of learning to read and write. For the American child, the problem of spelling words with low back vowels becomes one of memorizing an apparently arbitrary correct spelling from a number of possible spelling patterns for each word. It may be supposed that the older spellings are worthy of being maintained, since, once they have been learned, the speaker acquires unconscious knowledge of the phonological patterns of other dialects.

If it should appear from this set of sound changes that British English constantly maintains closer contact between its phonology and the system of English spelling, this notion can be dispelled by consideration of a second set of developments that are partially related to the first. I shall introduce this discussion with a personal example. When I listen to advertisements for a particular British razor blade, I always hear the announcer refer to it as the Wilkinson 'sawed' blade, when he is trying to say sword. I am amused at these homonyms in British English, because my naïve knowledge of English phonology tells me that the first word has a low back round vowel without following /r/, while the second word has a mid back vowel that is more round and more tense and that is followed by /r/. This makes the two words about two and a half miles apart in my phonology. British English has, in this case, undergone two sound changes that are responsible for such homonyms as sword vs. sawed: The mid back vowel has been lowered before /r/ and then the /r/ has been lost.

I first became aware that there was something special about my pronunciation of words like sword when I was introduced to the study of English phonetics in the early 1940's. Whenever I was asked to transcribe such words, I was invariably told that I had used the mid vowel where I should have used the low vowel. It was several months before I discovered that I contrasted the low and mid back vowels before /r/ and indeed could adduce numerous minimal pairs among quite common words such as four vs. for, hoarse vs. horse, and mourning vs. morning. My instructor was unimpressed, saying that my minimal pairs sounded like homonyms. It was only some years later—too late to use as evidence in the classroom discussion—that I discovered that John Kenyon had made my identical error throughout the second edition of

Webster's New International Dictionary (1934), in recording the pronunciation of such words. At any rate, I have been unable to discover
a single word in which his marking of the pronunciation differs from
my own.

More recently still, I have learned that the spellings of the two sets
of words, which seemed largely chaotic because I had not bothered to
classify them carefully, are in fact highly consistent with the earlier
pronunciations which my dialect still maintains. Briefly stated, if a
word belongs at all to one of these two sets and is spelled with <o> plus
another vowel letter such as <a> (boar), <o> (door), or <u> (four) or if
the <r> is followed by 'silent <e>' (fore), the word is invariably pronounced with the mid vowel. If, however, such a word is spelled with
<wa> (warn) it is always pronounced with the low vowel, and the same
is true with rare exceptions of words spelled with simple <o> not preceded by a labial consonant (nor). One common exception to this last
rule is (torn), pronounced with the mid vowel. The only sizeable group
of these words whose pronunciation is not readily predictable from
spelling is those spelled with simple <o> preceded by a labial, particularly /p/ or /f/. Thus port, pork, and fort have the mid vowel, but
fork has the low vowel; import has the mid vowel, but important has
the low vowel.

Phonological neutralizations that have occurred in these words in
America are later than and different from those that occurred in England. In England, as noted above, the two classes of words fell together using the low vowel as phonetic norm, as one consequence of a
general tendency to lower vowels before /r/. In America, with the extensive neutralizations that were occurring between low back and low
central vowels, there seems rarely to have been neutralization of these
vowels before /y/ or /r/. That is to say, buy and boy, barn and born
do not usually become homonyms. There being no dialect with contrasting sets of words distinguished by a mid back vowel versus a low
back vowel before /y/, it was perhaps natural for words like boy to
develop a mid vowel or at least to be reinterpreted idiolectally as containing somewhat lower allophones of /o:/. Words like born followed
suit and fell together with borne rather than with barn. Only relic dialects like mine retain the advantage of closer correspondence to English
spelling.

In conclusion, to make a maximum contribution to instruction in
literacy, linguists should describe the phonological systems of six-
year old children from a variety of dialect areas and socioeconomic
classes. Each of these is a 'native language' that some children bring
to the classroom. All are about equally sophisticated, although some
vary more than others from the total structure of the language represented by English spelling. Certainly none differs so widely as to be
termed 'a basically non-logical mode of expressive behavior, ' (Ber-

eiter 1966) nor is any so fully developed that we can say that its speakers have acquired perfect mastery of the grammar of English. Linguists should also describe the 'target language'—the full phonological and grammatical system of English as it is represented by English orthography. This is much more complex than we seem yet to have realized. It includes not only the morphophonemic variations explained so well by Chomsky and Halle, but also the lexical identities and distinctions, dialect variations, and etymological facts represented by the orthography. My conclusion is an obvious platitude: Teachers can do a better job of teaching if they have a better understanding of where the child starts and where society hopes he will arrive.

REFERENCES

Bereiter, Carl. 1966. An academically oriented preschool for culturally deprived children, in Hechinger (ed.) Pre-school Education today. New York: Doubleday.

Chomsky, Noam, and Morris Halle. 1968. The sound pattern of English. New York: Harper-Row.

Horn, Madeleine (ed.) 1928. A study of the vocabulary of children before entering the first grade. Washington, D.C. International Kindergarten Union.

Jones, Daniel. 1937. An English pronouncing dictionary on strictly phonetic principles (4th ed., rev. and enl.). London and New York: Oxford University Press.

Kurath, Hans. 1939. Handbook of the linguistic geography of New England. Providence: Brown University Press.

Labov, William. 1967. Some sources of reading problems for Negro speakers of nonstandard English, in New directions in elementary English, 140-167. Champaign: NCTE.

Reed, David W. 1965. A theory of language, speech, and writing. Elementary English 42, 847-51.

Smith, Henry Lee, Jr. 1968. English morphophonics: implications for the teaching of literacy. Monograph 10. Oneonta, New York: New York State English Council.

Webster's New International Dictionary. 1934. 2nd edition.

DISCUSSION

David DeCamp, the University of Texas at Austin: I think this idea is of immense importance, that the child has a considerable part of the learning process to do and that he continues it on for a good number of years; that is, this does not end in childhood years. It has been a relatively short period of time ago that people were saying very knowingly and very securely that a child has completely and utterly learned all his language by age five or six or some such nonsense. Exceptions were made, but they tended to be only lexical exceptions. He might not know certain vocabulary items.

I think that there is enough evidence now that there are a good number of rules that he doesn't learn until later, or at least he doesn't learn the regular application of them. The stress-rule examples that you use are very apt on this. The child presumably learns something like a stress rule by means of hearing and theory construction. The child learns microscope and he knows that if you use a microscope, you are performing micróscopy; if you use a cystoscope, you are performing cystóscopy; if you are using a proctoscope, you are performing proctó-scopy. But, on the other hand, as Haj Ross has pointed out, if you use a snooperscope you are not performing snoopérscopy; in a submarine when you use a periscope, this is not períscopy, and if you look through a kaleidoscope, this is not kaleidóscopy.

Now these are things which people get thrown on even at adult years. Monday morning I was listening to the radio. A commercial message for a local business college announced that that week they were beginning new classes in 'stenógraphy and stenótypy', whereupon he immediately stopped and there was a long silence, and he corrected himself to steno-typing. The remarkable thing is not just that the child is able to learn rules (this would be remarkable enough in itself, as language acquisition), but the fact that in spite of all these indecisions and the odd behavior of the applicability of rules to particular examples, that there is so remarkably little uncertainty about stress placement.

As you pointed out, apparently totally independently Kenyon had come to the same conclusions you have in exactly the same lexical items to which these phonological rules applied. The fact that the child is able to do this, and even then if there is a stylistic shift involved, if there are stylistic differences involved, he learns to adapt to these also. There is an immense amount of human competence involved in adjustments of this sort above and beyond what the human child is normally given credit for.

THE BASIC INGREDIENT

HAROLD B. ALLEN

The University of Minnesota

Abstract. Within the past ten years two areas of English language teaching in the United States have come into sharp focus as their social, economic, and political implications have arrested the attention of educational and political leaders. Institutes, workshops, and in-service courses have suddenly been set up for teachers of students whose first language is not English and for teachers of students whose first dialect is not standard English. Graduate programs have been created to prepare future teachers of non-English speaking students; and already a few special graduate courses have been created to help prepare teachers of the students who control only standard English.

But much of what now must be included in a good institute or program would not be required if the training of all English teachers contained the basic ingredient without which there can be no real discipline of English. That ingredient is concern with the English language itself. It is all very well to establish crash programs in this time of emergency; it is, of course, desirable to make available specialized graduate training. But we who have these concerns are short-sighted if we do not at the same time strongly support a language-oriented restructuring of the English curriculum in elementary and secondary schools. We are short-sighted if we do not ask for a curriculum that will have the English language as its central content.

One day about fifteen years ago the then chairman of our Romance languages department left a classroom and came up to me in the hall, obviously rather disturbed. "Harold, " he said, stabbing me in the

chest with a forefinger, "why don't you people in the English department teach students the subjunctive?"

I looked at him innocently. "What subjunctive?" I asked.

He exploded.

That was the beginning of what now we would call an intermittent
dialog, held over the next few months in his office, in my office, in
the hall, and even in the men's room. Most of his students, he com-
plained accusingly, had never heard of the subjunctive before taking
French; most of the others couldn't associate the term with any linguistic phenomenon known to them. I remarked from time to time
that English has only vestiges of the historical subjunctive, identified
only in the third person singular of the present when used in fairly formal contexts after verbs of fearing, doubting, hoping, and the like, and
also in the form <u>were</u> of the unique verb <u>be</u> in contrary-to-fact conditions in the past, as in <u>If he were here</u>. But my friend in Romance languages never quite grasped, I'm sure, just why a student who in his
own language would say, <u>I walked to the campus</u> and also <u>If I walked to</u>
<u>the campus I wouldn't be here now</u>—with the same verb form in each
sentence—might have trouble with a language in which the corresponding verb forms would not be alike. The chairman had had too long an
indoctrination in Latinate grammar to accept the objective picture of
the state of the English verb; and the student had gone through school
under English teachers who, frustrated by the inapplicability of Latinate grammar to English, apparently had just given up talking about
grammar at all. Most of us here this noon could, I am sure, volunteer
similar anecdotes. Not everyone teaching a foreign language in this
country has yet accepted the principle, argued nearly thirty years ago
by the late Charles Carpenter Fries, that an objective contrastive analysis must precede a sound program for teaching one language to the
native speakers of another language. Certainly not all foreign language
textbooks are yet based upon that principle.

But it was primarily with respect to teaching English as a foreign
language that Fries had enunciated that principle; and increasingly
since the founding of his English Language Institute in 1940 the leaders
in the field, and the textbook writers, seem generally to have come to
realize that a modern scientific description of English must underlie
its being taught to nonspeakers of English. This realization, indeed,
was a focus of the Georgetown Round Table only a year ago.

The English Language Institute and the various later institutes and
teacher-training programs recognized that the preparation of ESL
teachers to use the new materials must include at least one course in
the structure of modern English as well as other recommended courses
in phonetics, American English and even the history of the English language. Now these are not specifically courses in English as a second
language—in either its theories or its practice. They are simply

courses in the English language. These institutes and programs had to offer this work for the plain reason that their students had never acquired an adequate knowledge of their own language in either school or college.

Regrettable as the situation was, institute and program directors grimly accepted it. They assumed the responsibility of including these courses in their programs then intended principally for the comparatively few students being trained to teach English abroad or to foreign students here.

Today the focus has drastically changed. The social and economic disadvantages of several million Americans, children and adults, for whom English is not the first language, have received national attention. Of course, the earlier need to prepare a small number of English-as-a-foreign-language teachers for work abroad and with foreign students is still a need. But the great public emphasis suddenly has been placed upon the critical requirements of ESL teaching and bilingual teaching in this country, with English as the target language. We have become aware of the extraordinary human values involved in the need to teach acceptable English to speakers of Spanish, of French, of Chinese, of an Indian language.

Two important facts have appeared. First, the English-as-a-foreign-language textbooks were seen to be less than perfect for teaching English as a second language in an American environment. Already some immediately relevant textbooks have appeared for use in the United States and others are in the making. Second, and particularly pertinent here, is the fact that the many thousands of elementary and secondary teachers involved with this problem in the classroom had not only received no training in second language teaching but also enjoyed not even a minimal background of information about the nature and structure of their own language, English.

I need not review how the existence of NDEA opened the door for the funding of the first summer institutes in teaching English as a second language. Now it was not prospective teachers who participated. The participants were teachers already concerned with the problem of non-English-speaking children in their classes. Yet the institute planners found it necessary to deal not only with language teaching methods but also with the essentials of English structure and English usage and English varieties.

Other in-service retreading projects—municipal, state, and federal —likewise have been compelled to face this inadequacy on the part of teachers already in the classroom. As yet no satisfactory solution has been found; there exists no method, widely applicable, by which all the involved teachers can be brought into the area of language knowledge-ability. We still have only ad hoc approaches. Even what are called teacher-proof materials will not quite do the job for teachers whose background predisposes them to resist materials that are linguistically and sociologically oriented. This is not to say that such materials are not to be prepared and used; this is not to say that every available type of sound in-service training should not be employed. But it is to say— and I say it with emphasis—all this is not enough.

Yet while this huge problem still occupies our attention we have been forced to keep within focus another rapidly developing and in certain ways perhaps more formidable problem of English teaching. This is the problem, also complicated by social and economic issues, presented by the existence of conspicuously divergent social dialects, especially but not exclusively those of the black ghettos. It is a more formidable problem than that of TESL, because it is not only the passive language inadequacy of the teacher that must be overcome. A teacher's acquisition of a sound attitude toward the teaching of English as a second dialect can be thwarted by the competition provided by those who would inculcate other attitudes and persuasively offer other approaches.

One such specious approach is compounded of the traditional school prescriptive viewpoint toward matters of usage, on the one hand, and also the viewpoint of some speech consultants and speech therapists respecting deviations from a hypothetical speech norm. It is a viewpoint that considers deviations as errors, each of which is subject to individual correction. With the speech consultant this approach often entails the related assumption that the nonstandard speaker is a speech defective and hence in need of remedial therapy in a speech clinic situation.

A second approach is that of the psychologist, such as Carl Bereiter, whose studies purport to show that the black child is deficient in cognitive development, without power to think coherently and to form abstract concepts. The child, of course, has been tested in an alien adult environment, and with respect to ideas and things not characteristic of his home situation. Inevitably he shows up poorly in contrast with the white middle-class child accustomed to the concepts and materials and vocabulary used in the testing. So would the white middle-class child show up poorly if tested with ideas and objects found in the life of the black ghetto.

A related approach is that of the sociologist, such as Basil Bernstein, whose studies of British lower-class children have demonstrated to his satisfaction that they suffer from having what he has termed a 'restricted' language code. Again, the restriction, if there is one, is in terms of contrast with a quite different environment. The British middle-class child might well be found to have a restricted code, too, in terms of the communication demands of the slums.

All these approaches ignore the seemingly obvious fact that, whatever the causes may be, the specific problem in question is a language problem, one of language contrast and language teaching. They have ignored the work of people who are specialists in language and in language teaching. Since in ignoring this research they could not at the same time ignore the fact of language itself, they have been influenced by the popular notions and inherited misconceptions about language that characterize prescientific awareness of what language is and how it functions.

Happily, such a conference as this Georgetown Round Table can help to expose the weaknesses of these approaches. The forthcoming national conference on English as a second dialect, to be held in this city next year with the joint sponsorship of the Center for Applied Linguistics and the National Council of Teachers of English, and with the support of the Ford Foundation, should make even more widely known the primary validity of an attitude based upon sound linguistic knowledge. I trust that the summer NDEA Institutes on English for the disadvantaged will similarly offer sound information to the teacher participants. But, unhappily, this is not enough. Institutes and workshop and in-service training simply cannot reach all the teachers whose students confront them with the social and linguistic challenge of nonstandard English. Currently I am teaching a class in social dialects for thirteen Minneapolis inner city teachers. But I have no easy way to reach the scores of other teachers who also need new information and new insights but who for various reasons cannot or will not take an extension course outside of school hours.

Do not mistake me. A sound language component should be part of every institute or workshop or other program for helping teachers now in service to deal understandingly with the second dialect problem and with the second language problem—the bidialectal and the bilingual. Every ad hoc means should be used. But this is the short range view. This is the crash solution. If this and this alone is what we ask, then we will be acting in one continuing state of emergency—year after year —for the problems are not going to disappear with this generation of teachers. It is not enough to put up a tent for the night; we'd better start the foundation for a house.

I propose that while we support all sound ad hoc programs, we also support action that ultimately can make unnecessary the teaching of basic information about English sounds, English structure, English usage to teachers in service. I would point out that this information is not of exclusive concern to the teacher of English as a second language or English as a second dialect. On the contrary, this information every professing teacher of English should have in order to do a professional job. Within the past few years more and more leaders in the field of English have come to realize that without such knowledge the teacher of English is handicapped in literature and composition as well as in what he does with the language component in the curriculum. Already states have begun to insist upon adequate English language instruction in the preparation of teachers of English. New York led the way. Minnesota followed last year with new regulations that now are in effect.

Other states are moving to a requirement that the secondary school
teacher of English be prepared both in the history and the structure of
the language. The national English Teacher Preparation Guidelines,
published last fall after a two-year study, asked for this minimal component, for elementary teachers as well as for secondary school teachers.

As more and more teachers move into the classroom with an adequate knowledge and hence a sound attitude toward matters of dialect
and language variation and language learning, fewer and fewer teachers
will require such elementary information in special workshops and institutes. The new teachers will be ready to move ahead with the special
problems of bilingualism and bidialectalism without having to stop on the
way to acquire that elementary information.

I propose, then, that all of us concerned with these special problems
adopt the long view by doing everything possible to raise the standards
of English teacher preparation throughout the country through the inclusion of an English language requirement in the certification specifications. You have a personal responsibility to assume. Ascertain what
the situation is in your state. If it is not up to the Guidelines standards,
help the state English council in its fight to improve the situation. I can
tell you how we did the job in Minnesota, but your case quite likely will
be different. Whatever it is, the job can be done—with your help. I
can ask you to do this on the basis of improving the English profession
as a whole, but today I am being deliberately practical if not selfish. I
ask you to do this on the ground that, when all English teachers are wise
in the ways of their speech, the problems we here are concerned with
will be sharply reduced. The situation will no longer be a frustrating
one for the teacher.

I propose also that you support a related cause, the drive to make the
English language the central core, the bedrock, of the entire English
curriculum. It is the locus ab quo for the successful teaching of composition and literature. It is the linguistic birthright of every student
to have the chance to learn about the history of his language and its vocabulary, about its amazing structural complexity, about how meaning
is conveyed from one person to another, about the relationship between
language forms and their typical context including social status, about
the paralinguistic features that accompany language use. Only an adequately trained teacher can deal with these new elements of the language
arts curriculum. And only such a teacher can help fit these elements
into the bidialectal and the bilingual programs. I submit to you that
when such a teacher operates within such a curriculum many of the serious questions we are asking ourselves here this week will be answered.
For sound language knowledge is the basic ingredient.

LANGUAGE INSTRUCTION AND THE SCHOOLS

PETER S. ROSENBAUM

Thomas J. Watson Research Center, Yorktown Heights, New York

Abstract. It can be argued the growing dissatisfaction with native language instruction in the schools arises inevitably from the fact that the facts of life about classroom instruction do not mesh well with the key features of successful language instruction. Effective language instruction presupposes the construction of a learning environment in which is provided properly supervised practice of relevant learning tasks. Such practice should provide individualization of remediation and individualization of work assignment. Classrooms are structured around the needs of teachers rather than the needs of students. From the fact that a teacher can only do one thing at a time follow a number of system features of classroom instruction which are incompatible with learning environment criteria for good language instruction. A most crucial task of language instruction today, therefore, is to devise a new classroom regime capable of satisfying all major language learning environment criteria.

Ideas about how to improve schools in general and language instruction (native or foreign) in particular are not in short supply: paying teachers as much as you can and getting only the best, master teachers on television, new equipment, better classroom techniques based upon linguistic or psychological research. Many of these proposals, and others, warrant consideration; but it is very doubtful that most of them will lead to a truly important improvement in language instruction unless the current patterns of classroom practice are changed. The problem is simply that the facts of life of classroom instruction do not mesh well with the key features of successful language instruction. Let me illustrate this point and then go on to discuss a problem in linguistic engineering: namely, how to convert the classroom into an effective environment for language learning.

The central issues in the design of a learning environment are (1) the nature of learning, (2) the goals of learning, and (3) the features of the learning environments that support the attainment of these goals. Let me begin with some very general observations about learning.

First, any organism is continually learning whatever seems relevant to it through its interaction with its environment. Generally speaking, a learner perceives something as relevant, hence learns it, only to the extent that it seems to have some favorable emotional consequences, either direct or indirect, hence that there is some advantage to learning. Thus, learning is made possible by, and is contingent on, the organism's ability to perceive and weigh potential advantages, to identify and evaluate contingencies involving the behavior to be learned. These thoughts give rise to universal definitions of learning and teaching. Learning means acquiring new or improved control over one's environment. Teaching means structuring or manipulating an environment so that a learner through experience in this environment can with facility acquire the desired control.

Now let me make an observation that may sound trivial: the tasks through which learning is acquired should be in some sense pertinent to what is learned. I say 'in some sense' because the relation between the goals of a learning activity and the learning tasks involved in it may be far from obvious and quite complex. While we might all agree that most activities in the first year of elementary arithmetic do not lead in any efficient way to a knowledge of how to spell, we are all aware of the great controversies surrounding the effectiveness of various learning activities proposed for different methods of, for example, reading instruction, and we must conclude that no one really knows how to evaluate these learning activities or even whether, within reasonable bounds, they differ very much in value. However, I suggest that there is a criterion of evaluation for learning tasks that is not purely subjective; the feature of the learning task that presents the highest challenge should be such that it is overcome only by acquiring and demonstrating that skill that is the goal of learning. This is the only sense in which a learning task needs to be related to the goals of learning.

Another crucial point is that a good learning environment must be responsive, since only to the extent that the environment highlights the difference between an actual performance and a desired performance does it permit the learner to perceive needed changes in his own behavior. Many seemingly attractive learning environments fail on this count: they provide an environment that always appears the same no matter what the learner does. He cannot discover a productive learning strategy and he will not even try since there's just nothing in it for him.

An effective learning environment is not merely responsive, but the contingency structure of its responses is such that in performing learning tasks the learner will voluntarily choose those options that will lead to desired patterns of mastery. Crudely put, an ideal learning environment permits the learner continually to 'beat the system', and indeed insures that his most advantageous approach to doing so involves adopting and mastering the desired terminal behaviors.

I could sum it all up by saying the essence of a learning environment is the structure of the behavioral contingencies for the learner. What the learner learns is not spelling, or arithmetic, or French, but how the whole environment reacts to him and in what way his behavior in relation to spelling, French, etc., acts to control the environment. This mode of thinking is not an easy or natural one for all those whose attention is on what the learner will know when the course is done. On the other hand, for the learner, who doesn't yet know what he will know when he is done, the focus of attention is necessarily on the immediate activities in the environment and the relative advantages and disadvantages of operating in it in various ways. Even though he may desire abstractly to acquire the subject matter practically, he can only do this as a by-product of living in his learning environment with its rewards and punishments as he can perceive them.

In analyzing and evaluating a learning environment or system, we find it useful to distinguish three essential components of the system: (1) a content component, (2) a mediation component, and (3) a supervision component. Content concerns the topics to be presented, their density, their order of presentation, and the like. Mediation comprises the set of procedures, the procedural language if you will, by which the learner and the environment communicate, including the form of learning tasks, the system of instructions, the communication of remedial messages and reports on progress to the student. Supervision involves those control activities to achieve the environmental responsiveness that effectively implement a supervisory design policy. Examples of such actions are the assignment of practice time and task types on the basis of individual performance measures. A good language learning environment must be at least adequate in each of the three aspects.

The architecture of a learning environment may be varied in these three aspects either individually or jointly. For example, the idea of teaching remedial English as a second language is a methodological departure primarily in the mediational and supervisory areas. The appeal of such an approach derives from the supposition that, since the behavioral goals of foreign language and remedial language instruction are so similar, the key features of successful foreign language instruction should be appropriate for remedial language instruction.

The basic principle of all effective language instruction systems is to provide properly supervised practice of relevant learning tasks.

Moreover, properly supervised practice should provide 'individualization of remediation' and 'individualization of work assignment'. Learning tasks themselves should satisfy two general criteria. First, such
tasks should be capable of addressing both aspects of linguistic knowledge, 'competence' and 'performance'. Competence involves an implicit understanding of how sentences are constructed, what the words
mean and how they are spelled, and how the meaning of complete utterances is extracted from these utterances. Performance refers to the
production and comprehension of sentences, in speaking, writing, listening, and reading. The concepts are valid equally for remedial as
for foreign language instruction, although the content and exercise mix
will clearly differ for the two. Second, learning tasks should be 'creative' rather than analytic, requiring the learner either to generate an
utterance or to produce a response based upon the comprehension of an
utterance rather than select it by a process of elimination from a known
set. Creative tasks are important because of their close relation to
the desired behavioral objectives of language learning, namely, the
ability to produce and fully comprehend well-formed utterances in all
modes.

Creative language learning tasks are, generally speaking, complex
tasks that demand responses of the learner which can be incorrect in
any number of details. In responding to a student in regard to a complex task it is often educationally valueless to merely tell him whether
he is right or wrong, since he may well not be able to judge where the
error is, and thus not know how to improve his performance. Of far
greater value would it be to pinpoint the student's errors so that he will
be able to observe exactly those respects in which his performance falls
short of the desired performance. Thus, for the complex learning tasks
typical of almost all aspects of language instruction, correction simply
must be individualized to be efficient.

As is understood by all, some students are weaker than others. An
effective system for supervised practice must provide for and assign
the amount of practice required on a differential basis, in much the
same way that a good classroom teacher allocates her time to students
differentially in accordance with an intuitive or objective estimate of
their needs. It is a fundamental problem of classroom work that such
individualization of work assignment is not efficiently realized, with
the result that poor students don't get enough practice and good students
will do redundant practice or even simply let their minds wander.

Indeed, when we address the question of how to change classroom
instruction to make it more compatible with the fundamentals of effective language instruction as I have outlined them, we see that the basic
fact of life about classroom instruction is that all activity is structured
around the teacher's needs rather than around the student's. Teachers
feel, by and large, that this is the way things have to be, and this feel-

ing is surely not just a rationalization. The plain fact is that a teacher can do only one thing at a time, and from this plain fact a number of features of classroom instruction follow inevitably:

(a) The classroom is activity rather than proficiency oriented, because the one thing the teacher can do conveniently is conduct a group activity.

(b) All students do the same thing in class, regardless of special needs, because if they do different things, the conditions for any learning quickly disappear.

(c) A single disruptive student can easily stop the entire educational process for all students, (in fact, in some schools teachers say that the classroom problem is the problem of the disruptive child) simply because of the impossibility of ignoring any dramatic occurrence in the classroom.

(d) The classroom is time and not task oriented. Nothing is as recurrent in classroom life as the bell. And the lesson the bell teaches is this: nothing a student does is so important but that he should stop it when he hears a bell ring.

(e) Social relationships in the classroom tend to be jail-like. Attendance, punctuality, and deportment are mandatory and are given central attention. The inmates can talk to the jailor but not to the other inmates; small group and team work are often frowned upon rather than encouraged.

In making these observations I am, of course, not talking about your schools or the ones you are familiar with, but about the schools that have problems, about precisely those schools where achievement in the language skills is so minimal, that is to say, the vast majority of public schools.

We can summarize the problems of typical classroom instruction by saying it's impossible to give students very much supervised practice, even under the most ideal circumstances. Because the classroom is time structured, it rewards time serving rather than achievement. Since assessment is not thorough and continuous, the periodic evaluations of students function to mete out failure rather than to ensure success. And finally, since classrooms are teacher centered, hence presentation oriented, communication between the teacher and the student tends to be poor simply because the teachers do not know how much the students have heard and understood. We could characterize the deficiencies of a teacher-centered, presentation-oriented environment as essentially 'mediation failures'. Even in very good schools this mediational deficiency makes a classroom, as it is currently organized, a fundamentally poor learning system for language instruction.

It is not an easy matter to improve language instruction in the schools particularly when we stipulate that improvements, to be effective and worthwhile, must be consistent with the larger system of class-room operations and the people who run them. To adapt an observation made by the provost of a large university, classroom reform encoun-ters the same emotional and technical problems as are involved in mov-ing a graveyard. Still, the challenge is clear and important: we really need to design a better learning environment for language instruction, one which, on the one hand, adheres to the basic criteria for success-ful language instruction and which, on the other, is manageable by teachers in the classroom context.

I cannot propose a comprehensive solution to these problems but there is one direction in which I feel we should go, one which is more like the language laboratory in making use of student active learning, but which is much more of an 'interactive learning environment' than the present language laboratory. In such an environment a student learns primarily by practicing individually, and receiving individualized remediation, somewhat as though he had a personal tutor. Such an en-vironment is not easily realized in a completely satisfactory form. In experimental computerized versions of such an environment being de-veloped by IBM Research, the tutor is a computer itself, communicat-ing with a student by means of a terminal station equipped with a type-writer, tape recorder, and image projector. At the terminal station, the student practices language learning tasks and receives individual-ized correction of his errors. Further, the computer monitors the student's performance, continually computing indices of proficiency, and allocates accordingly the amount of practice that the student will have to do in a certain topic or skill area.

Such a laboratory in today's technology has many limitations. Nev-ertheless, such laboratories can now be made. A large experiment conducted at Stony Brook (SUNY) last year employed such a computer-ized interactive learning environment as an adjunct to a first year Ger-man course. The results of this study suggest very strongly that stu-dents who received such individually supervised practice learned a great deal more than those who did not. Even more important, poorer students tended to be helped more than better students, exactly the ef-fect one would both expect and hope for from extensive individualized practice.

Whether we can devise other methods not requiring such big ma-chines, and what will be the optimal combination of man and machine, is too large a subject for me to undertake here. However, the key to devising new systems will be to conceive of environments that can pro-vide some form of correctly supervised practice of relevant learning tasks to an extent which greatly exceeds what could be provided in the conventional classroom.

It may not be an easy job to design such systems, but because the need is great I believe we should seriously undertake to invent and develop them.

Let me close by reiterating a key point. No truly important improvement in language instruction, remedial or otherwise, can be realized without an alteration in the logistics of classroom learning, for current classroom practices do not mesh with the environmental requirements for effective language instruction. Therefore, the most crucial task of language instruction today is to devise a new classroom regime capable of satisfying all major language learning environment criteria.

DISCUSSION

Anneliese Altmann, graduate student, Georgetown University: Mr. Rosenbaum, you sound to me like a hippy in a business suit. The problem here is that the taxpayer does not have enough money to pay for a teacher-student ratio of one to one. Also, what you outlined about the Stony Brook experiment—I have heard the whole report at Simon Fraser University—it seems to me that this is no solution, because we use the oral method nowadays. The experiment at Stony Brook was more or less restricted to writing and reading. As far as I know, not all aspects—for instance, the oral aspect—were provided separately. The test results here were not as good as those in the control group, although the reading was better.

I admit that much of the technical equipment and the environment in the language-learning situation is poor and could be improved upon. During the last couple of weeks I have been reviewing Russian, and tried to use the language laboratory. These labs are really inefficient technically. You put a headset on your head which is very heavy and sturdy so that it wouldn't be ruined by students who do not like their heads squeezed by the sets. (Note that headsets come in one size only; heads do not!) You'll just try to hold the headset to one ear, and even with this you have problems. What you would like to have is a pair of earphones as big as a dime. You would also like to have a bigger booth to take your shoes off to be comfortable, to absorb something. I must give credit to Georgetown University, though, for letting me take some tapes home. In my living room my responses were loud enough for the neighbors to hear.

Although a student-teacher ratio of one-to-one is infeasible, so that one cannot have a purely student-oriented environment for learning a language, it seems that, nevertheless, a teacher can do much to come along the student's way by having a personal session with him, also by having more teaching assistants to help him. Consequently, the student gains a better control of the language because he hears and responds to various speakers.

Rosenbaum: Well, I really didn't want to talk today about machines, and I really brought up the Stony Brook study primarily to illustrate a direction. But I meant explicitly to say that in fact I don't view this to be an ideal solution at all, for precisely the reasons you raise. And I'd say that you see the challenge in exactly the same place as I see it. It seems almost impossible to design a system that would simulate a one-to-one environment. However, I am not so sure it is all that out of the question; but it is hard to say right now what form it is going to take.

One other point: let me correct your understanding of the Stony Brook experiment. It was largely textual, and the terminal tests administered were the Foreign Language Cooperative sub-tests. On speaking and listening, the two groups were virtually indistinguishable, the CAL group being slightly but not significantly better. We were surprised at this because we expected the audio-lingual group to be very superior in these skills, precisely because they used the language lab. Our supposition is that the language lab was not being used optimally, so that no student in either class improved his speaking and listening skills beyond what would have been acquired in the classroom period itself. So that is why we think that both groups did equally well on the speaking and listening. On the reading and writing sub-tests, the differences were very great, and these tests are not generally considered to be spelling tests. We could talk about this, but the fact of the matter is that, on whatever it is that the set of sub-tests tests, there were very great differences.

Bernard Penny, FSI: I would like to ask you a bit further on this environment that you present in the classroom. Is this environment to be the real world, or some analogous situation of real life?

Rosenbaum: That is a very good question. The only thing that has to be real in the environment are the contingencies. Did you ever read the Saber Tooth Curriculum? I've got to tell you about the Saber Tooth Curriculum; it is worth it. It was written in the early thirties, and it was a satire on the then progressive education. It attempted to contrast various curricula, and the first school that it talked about was Classical Fish-Grabbing; Classical Fish-Grabbing was taught in prehistoric times, when people lived on fish. In the Classical Fish-Grabbing curriculum, students in a classroom would go through fish-grabbing motions, and that was classical fish-grabbing. Then there was a Reform School of Fish-Grabbing, and the Reform School of Fish-Grabbing was Real Creek Fish-Grabbing School. And in that school, of course, kids went down and waded in shallow waters going through fish-grabbing motions in a real creek. And the ultimate reform school was the Real Fish Fish-Grabbing School, where students would stand around in a little pool grabbing stunned fish that had been thrown in. Now to come to your point: all three schools flourished at a time after the coming of the first Ice Age, at which time everybody caught fish in nets!

TEACHER TRAINING FOR ENGLISH AS A SECOND DIALECT AND ENGLISH AS A SECOND LANGUAGE: THE SAME OR DIFFERENT?

BETTY WALLACE ROBINETT

The University of Minnesota

Abstract. The overlapping areas in training teachers of English as a second dialect and teachers of English as a second language are explored: for example, the development of sound attitudes toward language learning, an understanding of how languages operate, and a knowledge of English phonology, morphology, and syntax. The areas in which differences in training are necessary are pointed out: for example, the development of extreme sensitivity in handling the socio-economic implications of nonstandard language, and the discovery of techniques to overcome the relatively difficult problem of changing language habits which show much similarity to those being learned (as against the seemingly easier task of changing habits which are very different). We know too little about the many second dialects of English; for just as contrastive analyses of English and other languages have made ESL teacher training easier, systematic analyses of these second dialects of English is a prerequisite for enlightened ESD teacher training.

Many references have been made recently to the appropriateness of employing English-as-a-second-language techniques to teaching English as a second dialect (Allen 1967, David 1968, Robinett and Bell 1968, Slager 1967, Stewart 1964). It seems worthwhile, therefore, to explore the implications of these suggestions from the point of view of teacher preparation. That the need for specialized preparation in teaching English as a second language is an accepted fact is evidenced

122 / BETTY W. ROBINETT

by the teacher training programs throughout the country. According to the Center for Applied Linguistics publication University Resources in the United States for Linguistics and Teacher Training in English as a Foreign Language (1966), some twenty-nine institutions offered degree programs with a major or minor in TESL. Although the training of teachers in ESL has had a relatively short history in the United States (Marckwardt 1967), some consensus has been reached as to the subject matter of such programs. If the recommendation is now being made that techniques similar to those learned in ESL training be employed in ESD teaching, it follows that the ESD teacher may need similar training in order to understand these techniques and to use them effectively.

Let me emphasize my use of the term effectively. There are some who claim that if instructional materials are well designed, any teacher can use them, whether or not he has had special training. But these teachers are usually 'text bound'; they are inflexible. When they are forced to deviate from the text because of something that arises from the classroom situation, they often make egregious errors in judgment in terms of linguistic information and language-teaching methodology. The effective use of materials depends upon the teacher's knowing the principles behind the textbook design: i.e. the reasons for presenting items in certain ways, the reasons for selecting certain items and omitting others, and the reasons for a given sequence of items. Only with this kind of background will the teacher ever be flexible, self-reliant, and capable of reacting intelligently to problems for which the text provides no ready answer.

It seems appropriate, then, to describe in general terms what might be the content of a typical teacher preparation program in English as a second language. In terms of such a description we can then decide how much might or might not also be useful or necessary for the ESD teacher.

The program I will describe is a composite gleaned from three major sources: (1) descriptions of programs in the Center for Applied Linguistics' A Survey of Twelve University Programs for the Preparation of Teachers of English to Speakers of Other Languages (1966), (2) descriptive brochures of recently developed programs, and (3) my own experience as a trainer of teachers. Such a program can be said to contain three basic components: linguistics, English language, and professional education. These components may be arranged in various ways and may overlap; but for the sake of discussion let us assume that they are organized into five separate courses. We shall arbitrarily name these courses Introduction to Linguistics, Applied Phonetics, Modern English Grammar, Methods in Teaching English as a Second Language, and Practicum in Teaching English as a Second Language.

One additional feature should be a requirement fulfilled either within the program itself or as a prerequisite to entrance into the program: the knowledge of at least one foreign language. There are several reasons for this requirement, but probably the most important is the sense of a greater objectivity in looking at one's own language which results from having another with which to compare it.

Dependent upon a given institution's particular resources and bent, additional subjects, which will not be discussed as part of the basic program, appear in TEFL programs presently offered; e.g. testing, cultural anthropology, English and American literature, history of the English language, American English, contrastive analysis, use of the language laboratory, and materials preparation. The survey reveals no unanimity in the subject matter area responsible for the administration of ESL programs; but eight of the twelve programs are administered through departments of linguistics and four through departments of English, foreign language or education (Ohannessian 1967).

Let us now look at each of these five courses as they might be conceived of for preparing ESL teachers; then we shall discuss their relevancy to ESD teacher education. Naturally, the content of the individual courses is of my own making and may bear no relationship to any program now existing or about to be born (except possibly that at the University of Minnesota).

1. The course entitled Introduction to Linguistics should include general information about such things as system in language; what constitutes phonological, morphological, and syntactical descriptions; the relationship between language and meaning; linguistic change. At the end of such a course, students should be expected to have a relatively sophisticated attitude toward language and its operation. Following the format of the study guide developed by Plaister (1966) for the use of master's degree candidates in TESL at the University of Hawaii, students should be able to discuss questions such as the following upon completion of this course in a TESL program:

What is the relationship between speech and writing?
What is complementary distribution?
How is redundancy in language an aid to communication?
What are some devices used in languages to signal grammatical relationship?
What is the relationship between language change and standards of usage?

It seems to me that the ESD teacher needs a course with much the same kind of general content but with much less emphasis upon exotic languages and much more emphasis upon English. The teacher should come out of the class with a basic understanding of how language operates.

2. The Applied Phonetics course on the ESL program should enable a teacher to recognize and produce a variety of sound types which are different from English, and to react to the varieties of sounds in English which are at the allophonic level. The course should also include practice in suprasegmental features of stress, pitch, and juncture. The basics of articulatory description and a familiarity with differing phonetic and phonemic notations should be a major requirement of the course. Students should be able to discuss questions like these:

What is intonation?
What is the difference between a vocoid and a vowel?
What two kinds of 'l' sounds occur in English?
How does the Trager-Smith analysis of English vowels differ from other analyses?

The ESD teacher, on the other hand, needs a phonetics course which presents a thorough analysis of the English sound system. Only as much time would need to be spent upon the recognition and production of sound types found in languages other than English as to give the teacher flexibility in articulation techniques. Primary emphasis should be upon varying sounds within the standard and nonstandard dialects of English (McDavid 1968). Some time could also be profitably spent upon errors in spelling which may reflect dialect pronunciation.

3. The course in Modern English Grammar should include a description of the morphological structure and the syntax of English with some attention to its historical development. Because of the varying points of view in the present-day analysis of English structure and in the instructional materials available for teaching English to speakers of other languages, the course should probably present both the structural and the transformational-generative approach toward grammar. Sample questions of the type which students should be expected to discuss competently are the following:

How many tense forms does English have?
What are possible allomorphs of the English plural morpheme?
Which is more powerful in English, word order or inflection?
What is aspect and how is it signalled in English?
What is the rewrite of auxiliary in transformational-generative terms?
What are some restrictions in prenominal modification?

The course in Modern English Grammar for the ESD teacher would contain the same basic information except that the structure of standard English would be continually contrasted with the grammatical systems of the nonstandard dialects. Special attention might be focussed on the nonstandard features which are remnants of an earlier period in the history of English.

4. The course in TESL methods should probably include a bit of the historical background of foreign language teaching; but the majority of time would be spent upon the oral or audio-lingual approach with its sequence of listening, speaking, reading, and writing activities. The importance of contrastive analysis as a basis for selection and sequencing of materials should be explored. Varieties of techniques and the use of audio-visual aids should be discussed in terms of grade level, class size, and available materials and facilities. The elements that constitute good pedagogy should be openly discussed and not left to chance: i.e. a variety of activities; the involvement of all the students in the classroom; a challenge for each student geared to individual performance so that the best students are not bored and the poor students are not frustrated; a sense of accomplishment, no matter how small, on the part of each student at the end of each session.

Here the student should learn about the many kinds of activities which are the hallmark of foreign language teaching: minimal pair drills and backward build-up exercises, simple substitution and transformational exercises, question and answer activities, dialogues. Here also he will become familiar with the sequencing of activities from those which are highly controlled to those which are free, or from what Clifford Prator calls 'manipulative' to 'communicative' kinds of language practice (1965).

Questions which a student might be expected to answer at the end of the methodology course would be:

What would you characterize as a 'correct model'?
What is the purpose of teaching dialogues?
Of what importance is 'pace' in the language classroom?
What use is made of rules in teaching grammar?
How can the audio-lingual approach be used with large classes?
If a student makes errors in pronunciation while you are drilling grammatical structures, what should you do?

The ESD methodology course must be approached from the knowledge that the speakers of these nonstandard dialects do not themselves believe that they speak a language 'foreign' to English. The emphasis here should be upon adding a dialect of a basic language already known, although there is some evidence, at least in the case of Negro nonstandard, that certain dialects have developed from a pidgin to a creolized form of English (Stewart 1967). ESD and ESL must be carefully differentiated in the mind of the teacher for this reason, but the irony of the situation is that the teaching method can be much the same. For example, the suggestion that nonstandard speakers learn to read first in the vernacular (Labov 1969, Baratz 1969) is a commonly accepted premise of second language teaching. The use of oral pattern practice is probably one of the most well known features of second language methodology; therefore, it is not surprising that its use be recommended for ESD (Slager 1967). These techniques should always be employed, as they are in second language teaching, from the 'additive' rather than the 'replacive' point of view. So often, those concerned with substandard speakers think of the work as 'remedial', a matter of 'improving' language. For this reason, also, instructional materials should be carefully selected to focus attention only on areas which clearly deviate from the standard language, not on items which are 'disputed usages' within the standard system itself.

Motivation is always pedagogically important, but it seems an innate part of ESD methodology. I believe that good language-teaching pedagogy can itself be a motivating factor. A student who is not inwardly motivated to acquire the standard dialect by the enticements of 'doors that will open' or by the picture of himself floating or swimming in the 'mainstream' of American life can sometimes become so involved in participating in a class that has been carefully and excitingly structured that he will be motivated by the classroom activities themselves. He may even be said to learn in spite of himself. Once his interest is aroused, the inward motivation may come.

Implicit also in an ESD methodology course is the principle of contrastive analysis, but contrastive analysis is most useful when it is thoroughly done. Beginnings have certainly been made in the contrast of nonstandard with the standard dialect, but they are just beginnings. Detailed information of the various nonstandard systems as a basis for instructional materials will preclude such reactions to nonstandard speech as its being primitive or as its being the product of the mentally inferior. All of the ESL techniques combined can never make up for the harm done to students by any teacher who exudes such provincial attitudes toward language.

Ohannessian has made some pertinent statements regarding teacher training for ESL which are worthy of consideration for ESD teacher education:

> It seems to me, therefore, necessary to give the trainee not
> only competence in linguistics but an understanding of the psy-
> chological, pedagogical, and perhaps cultural and sociological
> factors that may enter into the making of instructional mater-
> ials suitable to the age, level, aims, and needs of the learn-
> er. Since all these tasks require specialized training, pro-
> gram planners should perhaps take into consideration the de-
> gree of competence necessary for each of these tasks and

should provide the requisite emphasis during the general training period. (Ohannessian 1967: 6).

I think the word <u>perhaps</u> in regard to cultural and sociological factors should be omitted when talking of ESD. These are very much a
part of what makes for difficulty in working with nonstandard speakers.
  5. The TESL practicum should provide the participant with the kind
of classroom experiences which will prepare him for assuming the
responsibility of his own class. There must always be sufficient time
set aside both before and after observation and/or practice teaching
for the supervisor to prepare the participant for the practicum experience and to discuss in detail what he has seen or what he himself has
done in the classroom. Some of these experiences can be achieved
through the use of films or video tapes, but nothing really takes the
place of standing in front of a class and having the opportunity to feel
how students react to what you are doing. It gives one insights that can
never be gained by talking about what happens or by seeing it on a film.
  Questions of the evaluative type in relation to a particular class or
series of classes would be a useful measure of the student's grasp of
the pedagogical factors which have been stressed in the practicum.
Examples of these might be:

Was there enough choral repetition? Too much?
Did the teacher involve all the students?
What is wrong with the way some specific item was presented?
Why did the teacher have trouble at a given point?

  The same kinds of observation and practice experience should be
provided for prospective ESD teachers. One of the ways in which ESD
practicum experiences may differ from ESL experiences is in terms
of what we know about what the student knows. In the English as a second language class the teacher usually assumes that the students know
little because it is obvious that they speak a foreign language. In ESD
classes, on the other hand, the teacher may assume that since these
children speak some kind of English, they understand much more than
they really do. We need more of the kind of information that Labov has
given us about the perils of simple classroom language for nonstandard
speakers (Labov 1969: 46). He points out, for example, that the use of
the directive <u>Ask Albert whether he knows how to play basketball</u> instead
of <u>Ask Albert if he knows how to play basketball</u> posed a problem for
certain nonstandard speakers who were unfamiliar with the word <u>wheth-
er</u>. Perhaps we need much more emphasis upon listening activities
than has been thought necessary before.
  Another area of research which might have pertinence both in ESL
and ESD is the hierarchy of difficulty in perception. Such a study as

that which Brière (1966) made of the perception of sound types might lead us to find out which phonological or grammatical problems need the most emphasis in terms of difficulty, and materials could be designed with these hierarchies in mind. I am reminded here of what my colleague Walter Lehn says about the difficulties which Arabic speakers encounter in learning English. They find it much more difficult to gain automatic control over the distinction between /n/ and /ŋ/ than they do over that of /p/ and /b/, even though both of these distinctions are missing in Arabic. Is it merely because the /p/ vs. /b/ contrast occurs in all positions in English—initially, medically, and finally, whereas the /n/ vs. /ŋ/ does not?

At the phonological and at the grammatical level, might there be certain items which are more difficult for nonstandard speakers to learn? If so, this would carry definite implications for the preparation of instructional materials; such items could be introduced early and reviewed constantly.

Finally, let me select the major points of difference which I think exist between ESD and ESL teaching. Whereas the ESL teacher requires a rather general knowledge of English dialects, the ESD teacher must be extremely knowledgeable about those dialects which are sociologically differentiated as well as about those which are regionally distributed. The ESL teacher needs 'language versatility'—a knowledge of sound types and grammatical structures from a variety of languages. The ESL teacher needs 'dialect flexibility'—a knowledge of and tolerance for phonological and grammatical systems which differ within the various dialects of English.

In all probability, greater emphasis in ESD professional education must be placed upon motivation techniques: how to make the class experience attractive withal accomplishing the desired linguistic performance. Foreign language students are accustomed to practicing linguistic forms which sometimes bear no relationship to their present environment, indeed perhaps to any environment; but ESD students balk at such practice (Carroll and Feigenbaum 1967: 39). Instructional materials must be pertinent.

The ESL teacher is not often bound by the puristic attitudes toward language so often common to many teachers. The ESD teacher, however, may be tempted to fall into the 'speech improvement' trap and may tend to confuse problems which are those of disputed usage with those of interference from the system in the nonstandard dialect. Although Loban (1966: 3) says his study is 'not concerned with disputed items of usage, ' he lists in one of the categories which has a high incidence of deviation from standard usage, the lie-lay choice. And Golden (1960) includes can and may among her pairs of troublesome verbs. These kinds of 'errors' are so generally confused in the minds of otherwise standard speakers of the language that they should not be classified as the same kinds of language deviations as those found in the typical nonstandard speech, as evidenced by the fact that in Loban's study the deviation among the high (Caucasian) speakers in the use of lie-lay was more than twice that of any other item listed (18). Time and effort should be expended on items which have undisputed status in the standard language: e.g. standard forms of the verb be or the standard forms of possessive nouns.

Vocabulary will not need as much attention for an ESD speaker, who already has considerable vocabulary at his command. Nor will the ESD speaker have trouble with many of the phonemic contrasts of English: seat vs. sit or cut vs. cot, for example. Nor does intonation seem to be much of a problem. The relatively few phonological items in nonstandard speech which deviate from the standard can be dealt with systematically with the help of such publications as NCTE's Non-Standard Dialect (1967) in which very specific information is given as to how to teach certain sounds. Unlike ESL materials, where the entire phonological system needs to be presented, only those items which deviate from the standard need be drilled.

The grammatical aspects of nonstandard dialects seem most obviously different from the standard, but even here the major structural devices are those of standard English. Word order is basically the same, although differences do occur in such Negro nonstandard sentences as I ask do he want to go instead of standard I asked if he wanted to go. Function words are present but are distributed differently: a apple for an apple, or I don't got any for I don't have any or I haven't got any. Inflectional forms appear to be the most deviant from the standard: e.g. the lack of a possessive designation on nouns so that it is common to hear John cousin instead of John's cousin, and a confused set of verb forms resulting in She have a book and They was going. But here again, it is clear that a total attack on the English grammatical system does not appear to be necessary as it is in ESL.

In the light of all that is still to be discovered about second dialects, let me conclude by saying that while ESL techniques may improve ESD teaching, I believe that it is the totality of the impact made by what might be called 'sociolinguistic orientation' that will effect the most good. ESL techniques are only one part—although a pedagogically useful part—of this total orientation toward what language is, how it operates, and how we react to it in our social setting. However, the field of ESD needs to develop teacher education programs of its own, implementing the many sociolinguistic factors which are peculiar to its realm, all the while utilizing whatever may be helpful from ESL. It will then produce teachers who can unselfconsciously accept nonstandard dialects for what they are—a perfectly good means of communication—and who can then proceed to add to the child's inventory of skills another means of communication—the standard dialect of English.

REFERENCES

Allen, Virginia French. 1967. Teaching standard English as a second dialect. Teachers college record 68. 355-370.

Bailey, Beryl Loftman. 1968. Some aspects of the impact of linguistics on language teaching in disadvantaged communities. Elementary English. 45. 570-578, 626.

Baratz, Joan C. 1968. Language and cognitive assessment of Negro children: assumptions and research needs. Unpubl. paper delivered at a meeting of the American Psychological Association, San Francisco, 1968.

_____. 1969. Linguistic and cultural factors in teaching reading to ghetto children. Elementary English 46. 199-203.

Board of Education of the City of New York. 1967. Nonstandard dialect. Champaign, Illinois, National Council of Teachers of English.

Brière, Eugène J. 1966. An investigation of phonological interference. Lg. 42. 768-796.

Carroll, William S. and Irwin Feigenbaum. 1967. Teaching a second dialect and some implications for TESOL. TESOL quarterly 1 : 3. 31-39.

Davis, A. L. 1968. Dialect research and the needs of the schools. Elementary English 45. 558-560, 608.

Dillard, J. L. 1967. Negro children's dialect in the inner city. The Florida FL reporter (Fall 1967).

Golden, Ruth I. 1960. Improving patterns of language usage. Detroit: Wayne State University Press.

Labov, William. 1969. The study of nonstandard English. Washington, D. C.: Center for Applied Linguistics.

Lin, San-su C. 1965. Pattern practice in the teaching of standard English to students with a nonstandard dialect. New York: Teachers College, Columbia University.

Loban, Walter. 1966. Problems in oral English. Champaign, Illinois: National Council of Teachers of English.

Marckwardt, Albert H. 1967. Teaching English as a foreign language: a survey of the past decade. The linguistic reporter, supplement 19.

McDavid, Raven I., Jr. 1967. A checklist of significant features for discriminating social dialects. Dimensions of dialect, ed. Eldonna L. Evertts. Champaign, Illinois: National Council of Teachers of English.

_____. 1968. Variations in standard American English. Elementary English 45. 561-564, 608.

Ohannessian, Sirarpi. 1967. Preparation for TESOL: needs and university programs. On teaching English to speakers of other languages, ed. Betty Wallace Robinett, 3-7. Washington, D. C.: Teachers of English to Speakers of Other Languages.

Ohannessian, Sirarpi and Lois McArdle. 1966. A survey of twelve
   university programs for the preparation of teachers of English to
   speakers of other languages. Washington, D.C.: Center for Applied
   Linguistics.
Plaister, Ted. 1966. Study guide: linguistics and TESL for MATESL
   students. Mimeographed, University of Hawaii.
Prator, Clifford H. 1965. Development of a manipulation-communica-
   tion scale. The 1964 conference papers of the Association of Teach-
   ers of English as a Second Language of the National Association for
   Foreign Student Affairs, ed. Robert P. Fox, 57-62. New York.
Robinett, Ralph F. and Paul W. Bell. 1968. Teacher's edition to ac-
   company English: target 1. New York: Harcourt, Brace and World.
Shuy, Roger W. 1968. A selective bibliography on social dialects.
   The linguistic reporter 10: 3.1-5.
Slager, William R. 1967. Effecting dialect change through oral drill.
   English journal 56.166-175.
Stewart, William A. 1965. Foreign language teaching methods in
   quasi-foreign language situations. The 1964 conference papers of
   the Association of Teachers of English as a Second Language of the
   National Association for Foreign Student Affairs, ed. Robert P.
   Fox, 23-35. New York.
_____. 1966. Nonstandard speech patterns. Baltimore Bulletin of
   Education 43.52-65.
_____. 1967. Sociolinguistic factors in the history of American Negro
   dialects. The Florida FL reporter 5 : 2.1-4.
_____. 1968. Continuity and change in American Negro dialects. The
   Florida FL reporter (Spring 1968).
University resources in the United States for linguistics and teacher
   training in English as a foreign language. 1966. Washington, D.C.:
   Center for Applied Linguistics.

DISCUSSION

Joan Baratz, The Education Study Center: One of the things that has
not been delineated in terms of second language learning versus second
dialect learning is the fact that when a teacher is standing in front of a
class and teaching English to non-English speaking students, she knows
(and the students know) that, no matter how well or how poorly they perform, they are at this point speaking or attempting to speak English.
Now, when a second dialect is being taught, the difference is not always
clear. That is, the student isn't always sure when he is speaking standard English and when he is speaking his dialect. This confusion has
to be eliminated. Stewart gives the example of He workin' vs. He be
workin', the former dealing with immediacy and the latter dealing with
a continuing state. If the teacher instructs the child to say He is work-

ing, she may feel that she has now taught the child standard English.
The nonstandard speaker, however, may really be using He is working,
not in terms of standard English, but in terms of his dialect form He
workin', which has a meaning of an immediate state. Consequently he
may hypercorrect and say He bees working in order to deal with the
continuing state. This whole aspect of what is going on with the child,
and the problem of whether he can clearly distinguish between standard
and nonstandard English has to be dealt with. In addition, teachers'
attitudes vary towards dialects as opposed to foreign languages. One
finds that foreign languages are usually associated with a legitimate
culture and an accepted national heritage. However, with nonstandard
dialects, there may in educational circles be a kind of tolerance for it,
merely because the linguist says it has a grammar; but this is about
the extent of the tolerance. There is no real respect for the social integrity of the nonstandard speaker's linguistic and cultural system.

Robinett: I can only say that I agree wholeheartedly with everything
she said.

Hugh Buckingham, Center for Applied Linguistics: You mentioned
grammatical difficulty as one criterion for the introduction of certain
grammatical items in the standard dialect. I think we should also remember, as pointed out last night at the Washington Linguistics Club
meeting at Georgetown by Walter Wolfram of the Center for Applied
Linguistics, that the social diagnosticity of certain grammatical forms
should also be used as an additional criterion for the sequencing of exercises for certain grammatical patterns.

TESTING ESL SKILLS AMONG AMERICAN INDIAN CHILDREN

EUGENE J. BRIERE

University of Southern California

Abstract.   This report discusses the activities of the English
Language Testing Project which have occurred during the first part
of the first year of the three-year project.   The purpose of the project
is to develop a series of tests of proficiency in English as a second
language for the 56,000 American Indian children attending Bureau of
Indian Affairs' elementary schools throughout the nation.   Samples
from five different language families, Choctaw, Eskimo, Hopi,
Navajo, and Sioux, have been tested on multiple choice written tests
and on several different instruments designed to elicit segments of
spoken language.   Underlying psycholinguistic theory, testing and
correction techniques, and statistical analyses of data are discussed
in detail.

Approximately 56,000 American Indian children are attending Bureau of Indian Affairs' schools on several reservations in the United
States ranging from Alaska to the East coast.   Some of the schools are
boarding schools while others are day schools.   The medium of instruction in all of the schools is English.   The children attending these
schools range from monolingual speakers of their native American Indian language to rather proficient bilinguals in English and in their native language.
   One of the very real problems which the principal and classroom
teacher must face is to determine a placement level for these children
in terms of their proficiency in English.
   This is obviously very difficult to do.   As is the case in any other

situation in which placement at the proper scholastic level is the goal, a variable (or variables) considered to be predictive of success or failure at different scholastic levels, say sixth grade, high school senior, or freshman in college, must be quantified, measured, and assessed. Ideally, this assessment is made in terms of an empirically determined scale which indicates a range of the amount of the variable which must be mastered in order to perform successfully in the particular subject area of interest at the various levels.

Frequently the predictive variables of interest are identified by a team of subject area experts and these variables are then tested among hundreds or thousands of students at the various levels of interest. The scores on the test are correlated with measures of success (usually grades) received in the subject of interest at the various scholastic levels.

Unfortunately, in spite of the agreement reached among the linguistic experts concerning the identification of the linguistic units comprising linguistic competence, there is no widespread agreement as to which linguistic categories should be tested as variables predictive of 'proficiency' in a language. Furthermore, in spite of the empirical observations of Hunt (1965), Loban (1963), and Strickland (1962) we still do not know, in any convincing empirical sense, just 'how much' English is necessary to be a 'successful' student at various scholastic levels such as the first or third or seventh grades.

In short, we do not even have a clear empirical description of the level of linguistic or communicative competence which exists (or is needed) at the various grade levels for the various native American English speaking groups attending our schools. The same lack of information is even more obvious for our non-Anglo groups, confronted with an ESL situation, attending the same school.

The works of Jakobovits (1968), Spolsky (1968a;1968b) and Upshur (1968) have shown us that our knowledge of the skills involved in knowing and speaking a language is at best limited to a knowledge of linguistic categories but devoid of any knowledge concerning the many so-called exolinguistic variables involved in any act of communication, such as situational context, role and intent of speaker and listener, etc.

Furthermore, it has become increasingly apparent that even the definition of a 'successful student' varies from ethnic group to ethnic group, from language group to language group, and from one socioeconomic class to another.

In addition to the psycholinguistic considerations which complicate the assessment of various aspects of communicative competence, language testing among the American Indian children is further complicated by the fact that several different native languages are used by the population of interest. Presumably, a contrastive analysis of the individual language groups with American English might indicate different kinds of interference for each group, thereby indicating that each group should have its own individual ESL test.

Unfortunately the immediate urgent need for instruments to evaluate the proficiency of the American Indian child in American English, however imprecisely, precludes the possibility of stopping all activity on language testing until (a) a contrastive analysis is made of every American Indian language and English and (b) an adequate theory or model of language performance or communicative competence is developed.

The English Language Testing Project has contracted with the Bureau of Indian Affairs to develop a series of tests of proficiency in English as a second language for the American Indian children attending BIA schools. The target population consists of children assigned to grades three through seven. An attempt is being made to develop a set of instruments which will evaluate both passive and active skills. This paper is an interim report of the first nine months' activities on the proposed three-year contract. The first part of the paper deals with the mechanical or practical aspects of the project. The second part of the paper discusses the rationale for some of the procedural decisions made in relation to some of the psycholinguistic variables involved in language testing.

In June of 1968 a meeting of the project consultants was held in Los Angeles. Those present were Mr. Tom Hopkins and Mrs. Evelyn Bauer from the Bureau of Indian Affairs, Mr. John Upshur from the University of Michigan, Mr. Harry Osser from San Francisco State College, Mr. Leslie Palmer from Georgetown University, Mr. Robert Wilson from UCLA and, later, at a subsequent meeting, Mr. Robert Jones, testing officer at USC. The purpose of the two-day meeting was to rely upon the special competencies of each member to establish guidelines for the entire project. Thus, the resulting design was a product of specialized knowledge in the fields of test and measurements, child psychology, transformational linguistics, item construction and computer routines needed to compute the many correlations involved in analyzing test results in item analysis, reliability and validity criteria. All forms of all tests developed on this project were first administered to English-speaking children in Los Angeles, Spanish-speaking children in New York and Los Angeles and Pima-speaking children in Arizona before the tests were taken out to the reservations for administration to the populations of interest.

On the basis of some previous work done with the Navajos during the year '67-68 (see Brière 1969) one form of written multiple choice item test which had been administered to 650 Navajo children in grades 3-7 was reviewed by the consultants. As this test was revised on the basis of an item analysis of a previously administered form, the consultants decided to (a) administer this form to other language groups and (b) to write an additional parallel form with items designed to test the same grammatical categories present in the first form of the test. A total of twenty-four grammatical categories were chosen on the basis of the difficulty scores computed from the first administration. The two written tests (forms 1 and 2) contained eighty-eight items of two basic types. A question type such as:

How often do you see movies ?
__ a. Next week.
__ b. Every month.
__ c. Right now.

and a fill-in-the-blank type such as:

John doesn't have . . . books.
__ a. Much
__ b. Many
__ c. A little

These paper and pencil tests were group administered to five different language families in grades three through seven. The sample population consisted of 137 Choctaws, 122 Eskimos, 200 Hopis, 136 Navajos, and 171 Sioux for a total of 766. The results of the Fall administration are currently being computerized for analysis. (A more detailed discussion of the computer activities is given below.)

Three techniques to test oral production were decided upon. The first, used by Osser to analyze Negro speech in Baltimore, was a repetition test. Two forms of the test were developed. The first form consisted of twelve sentences ranging from the linguistically simple to the linguistically complex. ('Linguistic complexity' was first defined theoretically in terms of the number of nodes in the underlying tree plus the number of transformations necessary to produce the terminal string. However, on the basis of the analysis of the results of our pre-test administrations, we reordered the hierarchy on the basis of the children's actual performances.) The second form consisted of twelve sentences representing the same grammatical categories as in the first form, but randomly presented.

The procedure was as follows: The examiner met with one child at a time. Directions and examples were given to the child until it was clear that the child understood what the desired terminal behavior was. The examiner read each sentence only once, and the children's responses were recorded on tape. (Scoring procedures for the various techniques used will be discussed in detail below.)

Another technique used to elicit oral speech was a 'transformation test'. In this technique the examiner would give the child the following instructions: 'I'm going to say something to you. Then I want you to say the opposite. Like this—I'll say, <u>Our friends are here</u>. Then you say, <u>Our friends aren't here</u>.' A series of examples followed, and then the subjects were given five declarative sentences upon which they were to perform the negative transformations.

A final technique for eliciting oral responses consisted of a series of twelve sets of pictures. Each subject was given a set of four pictures. Each picture in the set was different from the others along some dimension. For example, one set of pictures consisted of a bear standing on the bank of a stream watching a fish in the water. The second picture showed the bear with his two front paws in the water apparently going after the fish. The third picture showed the bear with all four paws in the water in closer proximity to the fish. The fourth picture showed the bear with his head under the water, attempting to catch the fish. The child looked at all four pictures and then was shown a stimulus picture which was exactly like one of the four pictures in the child's set. The child was asked to point to the picture that was the same as the stimulus picture. He then was asked 'Tell me about this picture. How is it different from the others?' The ensuing response was recorded on tape.

All of the oral techniques were administered to twenty subjects from grades three through seven from the five language families stated above. This represents five hundred subjects tested on the oral techniques.

Each technique involved its own scoring procedure. For the responses made on the repetition test a quasi-morphemic analysis of the responses was made. For example, in the stimulus: <u>We haven't seen the doctor yet</u>, a total of twelve points were possible. Two points were allotted for each noun—one for correct noun, and one for presence or absence of plural markers; and one point for everything else including a word order category, and an 'additive' category, i.e. did the child add anything that was not present in the stimulus.

The scoring procedure for the transformation test was as follows: Three major categories were isolated for investigation, the auxiliary, the negative, and the main verb. The auxiliary was analyzed in terms of four subcategories: (a) presence, i.e. whether the auxiliary was present in the response or not, (b) tense, i.e. whether the correct tense was used, (c) number agreement, i.e. whether the auxiliary agreed in number with the subject of the sentence, (d) substitution, i.e. whether a completely different auxiliary was substituted for the one required. The negative was analyzed in terms of three subcategories: (a) presence or absence of the negative, (b) form, i.e. was the correct form used, (c) word order, i.e. was the correct word order used. The main verb was also analyzed in terms of three subcategories: (a) presence or absence, (b) form, (c) substitution. Each category was scored in terms of a plus-minus system.

The responses made on the picture test were analyzed in terms of four categories: (a) an intelligibility category, whether the responses could be understood by the scorer, (b) a discrimination category, whether the response discriminated the stimulus picture from the others in the set, (c) a grammatical category, whether the response was grammatical, and (d) a vocabulary category, whether the subjects used the proper vocabulary to identify the items in the picture. By using a plus-minus marking system for each category it is obvious that any combination of plus-minuses could occur.

An attempt was made to identify external criteria which could be correlated with the results of each individual test or with the total results from all of the tests. Teachers were asked to rate the subjects who took the test on a five-point scale ('five' meaning 'native-like fluency') from the standpoint of comprehension and production.

A second set of external variables were the grades received by the subjects on the previous academic year in arithmetic, reading, English, and social studies.

A third set of external variables were the scores received (in terms of grade placement) on previously administered California Achievement Tests. Scores were recorded for Reading Comprehension, Arithmetic Reasoning, Mechanical English and Grammar, and total test score. Multi-variate correlations will be computed for all of these variables with the scores received on our tests.

In addition to the tests described, two additional equivalent forms of a multiple choice written test, forms 3 and 4, have been developed. The eighty-eight item test is based on forty-four grammatical categories (some of which overlap with the categories tested on forms 1 and 2) which were chosen as being probable good predictors of proficiency in English. The items that are included in our pre-tests have been chosen on the basis of an item analysis which we made on the data gathered in Los Angeles with our Spanish-speaking group and our Anglo group. For the most part, discrimination scores (phi coefficients) were used as the primary criteria, though, admittedly, at times, certain grammatical categories were considered as paramount, in spite of low discrimination scores.

A listening comprehension test was written based on one of the formats used in TOEFL. Speaker A makes a statement, Speaker B responds to this statement, and Speaker A completes the mini-conversation. A third voice is heard by the subject which asks, 'Where did this conversation probably take place?' Another type of question asked after the conversation is a factual one which requires an understanding of the conversation in order to answer the question correctly. After the child has heard the question he chooses the correct of three choices which he has printed in front of him but which are read by the third voice.

Based on the Dade County, Florida, testing materials another testing technique we are investigating is a series of three pictures differing from each other along some dimension, e.g. one item on the test shows a girl pulling a boy in a wagon in the first picture, a boy pulling a girl in a wagon in the second picture, and a boy and a girl pulling an empty wagon in the third picture. Each child is given a set of pictures and hears an oral stimulus on a tape, e.g. <u>The girl was pulled by the boy</u>. The child then crosses out the picture just described in the oral stimulus.

On the basis of our first administration the four picture test to elicit oral responses is being revised and additional sets of pictures are being developed.

Before developing the written test, arbitrary decisions as to which grammatical categories would be tested were made by the group of linguists working on the project. The rationale for this was that it seemed reasonable to assume that some categories must be mastered for a person to be fluent in English, consequently should be predictive of 'proficiency' in American English. We realize that this method of using selected linguistic items as an indicator of communicative competence is, perhaps, dangerous. But until we have a complete theory or model of linguistic performance, we decided to rely on this age-old method in order to answer the urgent need for instruments. We are fully aware that the arbitrariness of selection of items to be tested can have serious limitations. However, we feel that the instruments we are developing can have a great deal of use especially after a considerable amount of base-line data have been gathered from each language group.

Although we do not have a computer output concerning the two forms of the repetition test, i.e. one form arranged in a hierarchy of difficulty versus another form which was randomly ordered, a cursory glance at the data indicates that the scores received on both forms will probably not be statistically significantly different. Furthermore, it is interesting to note that at the moment it seems as if some of the scores received on the stimulus sentences are not necessarily related to a linguistic definition of complexity. In other words sometimes the so-called 'most complex' (defined theoretically) received higher scores than the so-called 'least complex'.

We had another surprise in which performance did not altogether uphold a theory. I mentioned earlier that we administer our tests to English speakers first. The purpose of this is to discover ambiguous items. The assumption was that native speakers of American English in grades three through six have mastered the grammatical categories being tested. Any item having a difficulty score of less than 90% was immediately suspect and rewritten or rejected. Unfortunately, it has become increasingly clear throughout the project that elementary school children do not, in fact, always know the grammatical categories being tested and a poor performance on one item may indeed indicate a lack of knowledge of the category rather than the result of a bad item. Furthermore, we have reason to believe that on some of the items with extremely low difficulty scores, say P=.500, (a) sixth grade children perform no better than third grade children on some categories but (b) other categories seem to fit into the maturational process (e. g. the comparative more deeper) and that sixth graders do better than third graders. We have just completed our experimental design and will soon be gathering base-line data from approximately 600 English speaking children in grades three through six in order to check out some of our findings from this year.

A thorough analysis will be made of the scoring technique used on the transformation test. To the extent that the three major categories and ten subcategories correlate quite highly we may be able to collapse this complex matrix into a plus-minus technique using only one category, i.e. right or wrong.

One point should be noted concerning the administration of the transformation test. We initially attempted to elicit the passive transformation, but discovered that, even among Anglo children, the responses were frequently not those which we desired. In other words, it seems as if the children either understood the 'rules of the game' completely or not at all. (This bi-modal distribution was evidenced in Miller's experimentations with embedding.) We would hardly be willing to say that the fact that an Anglo child did not 'play the game' necessarily means that he somehow lacks the linguistic competence for forming passives. For this reason, until more sophisticated techniques are developed for eliciting passives we feel that this method is extremely limited in its usefulness in evaluating proficiency in English for the non-native-speaking child.

The complexities involved in using a set of pictures to discriminate a stimulus picture are obvious to all of us. At what point are we measuring some psychological parameter involved in concept formation versus a linguistic parameter involved in speaking ability? On many occasions we found that Anglo and non-Anglo children would choose a picture on the basis of some noisy attribute of the category rather than to identify the actual criterial attribute. It would be extremely useful, if not crucial, if one of my learned colleagues at this conference could find the time and finances to design an experiment which would clearly isolate the variables of concept formation versus the variables of linguistic competence.

It is worth emphasizing the fact that no attempt was made to isolate scoring the production of individual segmental phonemes. For one reason, it is extremely difficult (if, at times, not impossible) to distinguish, from a tape, sounds which are phonetically similar. For example, the Navajo has a tendency to substitute glottal stops in word final positions. It becomes an enormous task to decide, say, if a Navajo child has indeed produced a velar voiceless stop versus a glottal stop in word final positions. Secondly, I personally am not convinced that the barriers to communication are the highest at the phonemic segmental level. There probably isn't a linguist in this room who has not learned a great deal from the Russianized English of one of our living legends in linguistics. In other words, speaking English with a foreign accent only becomes a problem when the phonological substitutions interfere with the message itself. In fact, there may be some very compelling social reasons for <u>not</u> sounding exactly like the white man, e.g. ostracism from other members of the tribe. For these reasons, we have not been too concerned with the segmental substitutions which did not completely distort the message.

The activities of this project make no pretense whatsoever of solving some of the more crucial problems facing the discipline of language testing today. For example, we fully well realize that the external criteria which we are investigating are the traditional approaches which language testers have been using for years. I personally am not convinced that a high correlation between the scores received on a multiple choice test in English Grammar with the scores received on a standardized test of English mechanics tells us very much about the validity of using multiple choice tests to measure proficiency in English in the first place. (It may well be that the ability to ride a bicycle is far more predictive of ability in language than any other single factor.) Furthermore, this project makes no pretense whatsoever at attempting to answer the problems in assessing the many psycholinguistic variables involved in 'communicative competence'. A very compelling argument for accepting Jakobovits' (1968) insistence on separating linguistic competence from communicative competence is the problem that occurs in life's little embarrassing moments. For example, for those of us who are less talented diplomatically than the rest, we have all faced the problem of knowing, at one time or another, what to say, when to say it, or how to say it. Clearly, the psycholinguistic variables which restrict the codes used in a given situation are not contained in a narrow definition of linguistic competence. Yet, we know that these restrictions are ever present in any social contact. As designers of language tests how do we begin to measure these variables if, by remaining within the constraints of the narrow definition of linguistic competence, we refuse to admit that they are important or even existent?

The primary purpose of this paper was to report the language testing activities which have been occurring with the American Indian children this year. Obviously, none of the techniques currently being investigated are new, original or, in light of the psycholinguistic consinderations of validity, perhaps even adequate. We do feel, however, that we are furnishing a series of instruments, however imprecise, that will be an aid to the school administration in placing the American Indian child at a level at which he can operate with the greatest degree of success. A secondary purpose of this paper, based on the limitations of the activities of the project, is to present a plea to my colleagues for some basic research which will enable us to stop defining the elephant in terms of its tail alone and permit us to move around in order to get a better understanding of the whole situation.

REFERENCES

_____. 1967. Dade County Test of Language Development (Receptive) Test 1—Elementary. Miami, Florida: Dade County Board of Public Instruction.

Brière, Eugène J. 1969. ESL Testing on the Navajo Reservation. TESOL Quarterly, III, 1, March.

Hunt, Kellogg. 1965. Grammatical Structures Written at Third Grade Level. Champaign, Illinois: National Council of Teachers of English.

Jakobovits, Leon A. A Functional Approach to the Assessment of Language Skills. A paper presented to USC Conference on Problems in Language Testing.

Loban, Walter. 1963. The Language of Elementary School Children, NCTE Research Report No. 1. Champaign, Illinois: National Council of Teachers of English.

Osser, Harry. A Study of the Communicative Abilities of Disadvantaged Children (forthcoming).

Spolsky, Bernard; Benzt Sigurd, Mashito Sato, Edward Walker, and Catherine Asterburn. 1969. Preliminary Studies in the development of techniques for testing overall second language proficiency. Problems in Foreign Language Testing, Language Learning, Special issue No. 3, 79-101.

Spolsky, Bernard. 1968. What does it mean to know a language, or how do you get someone to perform his competence? A paper presented to USC Conference on Problems in Language Testing.

Strickland, Ruth. 1962. The Language of Elementary School Children. Bulletin of the School of Education, Indiana University, 38:4, July.

Upshur, Jack. 1968. Measurement of Oral Communication. A paper presented to the USC Conference on Problems in Language Testing.

LINGUISTICS AND LANGUAGE PEDAGOGY—APPLICATIONS OR IMPLICATIONS?

BERNARD SPOLSKY

The University of New Mexico

Abstract. Much of the disagreement over the relevance of linguistics to language teaching has been caused by a failure to distinguish between the application of linguistics and its implications. On the one hand, linguistics and its related fields especially psycholinguistics and sociolinguistics help lay down the basis for a theory of second language acquisition; on the other, linguistics (especially that part of it concerned with language description) may be applied in the preparation of teaching material. But the applications and the implications are distinct.

In his luncheon address to last year's Round Table, Kenneth Mildenberger (1968) called for restraint in the public debate over linguistic matters. He asked linguists not to enlarge the credibility gap that he feared was growing between them and language teachers. He urged calm discussion rather than the intemperance that might frighten teachers back to the bad old ways. With full recognition of this, I shall do my best to avoid exacerbating any controversy. But of course I cannot avoid stating what I have come to believe. One of my own teachers always pointed out, when he was attacked for the 'complexity' of modern linguistics and its consequent unsuitability for pedagogy that it would be easier to teach that there are four elements, earth, air, fire, and water, than to get involved in the intricacies of the periodic table. But get involved we must: whatever simplifications are to be made in the interest of ease of teaching, they must surely be based on our best knowledge of the truth. And the truth is seldom simple.

When you look carefully, you find, in fact, that if there is one thing that the applied linguist has been successful at, it has been in his publicity campaign. No publisher today will risk a book in the field of language teaching without linguistics or a linguist on the title page. And the recent study conducted by Hayes and his colleagues has shown that whatever effect NDEA money has had on teacher qualifications and teaching quality, it has certainly been successful in setting up the ALM gospel as the popular wisdom. In under thirty years, then, the 'applied linguists' have won their public debate with the 'traditionalists', and even more importantly have captured the sources of power—textbook purchasing and federal funding. For most of that time, the attacks on them came from the right wing: from old fashioned teachers who argued to be left alone with their translation and their reading. But just as the battle seemed won, a new assault came from within, as other linguists started to say 'your linguistics is wrong' and even 'It's got nothing to do with language teaching anyway.'

While there had been earlier statements of the new position, the clearest and most disturbing publicity for it came in Noam Chomsky's address to the 1966 Northeastern Conference on Language Teaching. Here he shocked the applied linguists in his audience, and obviously confused many of the language teachers, by stating that neither the linguist nor the psychologist yet knew enough about the process of language acquisition to tell the language teacher what to do. Shocking and confusing, because for the last twenty years, people had been standing up and saying 'These are the linguistic principles of language teaching'. Where can we go now, if we are left without principles? Who will tell us what to do if the linguists won't?

The picture I have painted so far is over-simplified, of course, because the actual effects in classroom practice have never been as strong as the theorists have wanted. Many a teacher believes firmly in the principles laid down for audio-lingual teaching, but in his classroom, stops to explain at length the rules of the tense system, or writes on a blackboard, or gives vocabulary lists to memorize . . . methods, however detailed, must be interpreted and implemented by teachers, and as long as we use human teachers, each sets up his own criteria for what he will accept and what he will modify. But up till now, he has done this guiltily, fearing criticism for his incorrect method or approach. One of the most important results of the present controversy is to make possible what del Olmo (1968) refers to as the 'intellectual independence of the foreign language teacher'.

In this paper, I shall consider the meaning of this independence, arguing that there is a field of language pedagogy, a field that derives its theory from other 'pure' fields, one of which is linguistics. For language pedagogy to develop freely, it must be free to draw its assumptions from all relevant disciplines—linguistics, psychology, and pedagogy are the most important—and to test the assumptions for consis-

tency and applicability. Language pedagogy is limited and sterile all
the time it is considered to be a field in which the assumptions, methods, and findings of a single discipline are to be applied. A good deal
of difficulty has been caused by the use of the term 'applied linguistics'
as a free synonym for 'language pedagogy'. The term 'applied linguistics' is not a particularly happy one: in one way, it is too broad, failing
to suggest what linguistics is applied to; in another, it suggests a level
of practicality that lacks the dignity of 'pure linguistics'. The term itself is grammatically derived from an underlying 'Someone applies linguistics to something'. The 'someone' is an 'applied linguist', the
'something' is a field outside linguistics—language teaching usually,
but sometimes translation, lexicography, computer work, etc.

When one admits to the profession of linguist, one is usually forced
to point out that this does not mean that one spends all one's time learning languages, but that it involves a scientific study of language in general and specific languages in particular. Once this hurdle has been
surmounted, the next question one faces is, 'What's the use of linguistics?' One possible answer to this might be, it makes it possible to describe languages. Such an answer leads to a second question, asked
probably in a more hectoring tone: 'And what's the use of that?' Well,
we say, these descriptions can be used in language teaching, translation,
making dictionaries and grammars.

The approach implicit in these answers suggests a model that looks
like Figure 1.

FIGURE 1.

Language theory and description

Applied linguistics
Language teaching, translation, lexicography, etc.

That is to say, the findings of language theory and descriptions of languages are taken over as they stand, and applied directly to translation,
language teaching, and any other relevant field.

But it is clear that in spite of the many claims that have been made,
a description of a language is not in itself a set of directions as to how
to learn or teach the language. If it were so, we would only need to
give our students a grammar book and wait for them to start talking
the foreign language. In the same way, it is clear that a grammar book
does not tell us how to go about teaching the material. It specifies the
material to be taught, but not the way to present it. To this description,
then, there must be added a set of specifications as to how teaching
should be done. Let us for the moment suggest that this will be the
function of another discipline called Education, which itself is an ap-

plied field drawing on the findings of a pure science concerned with a
theory of learning and teaching. Our model then needs to be revised
(See Figure 2).

FIGURE 2.

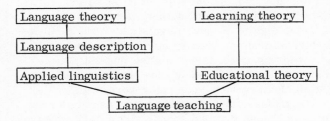

Now, we may ask, is there really any place in this model for applied
linguistics? If it draws all its knowledge from language descriptions,
what does it have to offer? In other words, what is the difference between the work of the descriptive linguist and the applied linguist?

It might be argued that there is a real difference between the sort of
description provided by the descriptive linguist and that passed on by
the applied linguist. This difference, it can be claimed, resides in the
fact that the descriptive linguist is simply describing the language,
while the applied linguist is adding to the description a comparison with
the learner's native language, a contrastive analysis. He is adding,
then, some sort of prediction of difficulties and suggestion as to hierarchy of difficulties.

At this point, it is only fair to ask in what way a contrastive analysis
differs from a normal description. If it is simply in the fact that it
sets out the two descriptions side by side, then we have defined the applied linguist's function as providing an indexing system. If, on the
other hand, in order to achieve the contrast, he is forced to change one
or both descriptions so that they are now in comparable terms, isn't he
really being a descriptive linguist? The general issue raised here was
discussed in some detail in last year's Round Table (Alatis 1968); the
point I am making here is clearly expressed in Professor Hamp's paper.

Look at the second model again. Note that on the top line we have
two theories, one of language and one of learning. Any linguistic description must be in terms of a theory of language. And there must be
consistency between the theory of language and the theory of learning
if the outcome of the teaching is to be successful. Indeed, one must
go further: a valid theory of learning must include a theory of language
learning, and a theory of language must face the problem of how language is learned. There is one case in which the two theories have
seemed to be consistent: the Skinnerian view that learning is the result
of operant conditioning, and the taxonomic view of linguistics (this con-

sistency admittedly depends on a sympathetic interpretation of the Skinnerian model). A result of this has been much of the current work in programmed foreign language instruction, where a generally accepted idea has been that the linguist will specify units and the psychologist-programmer will show how they may be established as habits. There are only two problems: neither theory is valid, and the method resulting from their application is not successful. (Spolsky 1966, Ornstein 1968).

So far, then, we haven't done very much for the claims of the applied linguist. But let's go back to our original question, and see if we might find a better answer.

'What's the use of linguistics?'

'To understand more about man, through a clearer insight into his competence in language, which seems to be one of the main things that distinguishes him from the animals.'

'What are the practical applications of this understanding?'

'To various forms of human engineering, such as language teaching ...'

Now a clear result of this set of answers is to put more emphasis on the 'theory' of language than on the 'description': to give the theory a place not just in linguistics, but in a unified theory of man (I avoid the term 'human behavior' advisedly, for I often feel like being a mentalist). From these answers, we can construct a model that is very different from the earlier ones (See Figure 3).

FIGURE 3.

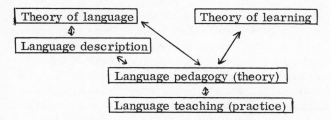

In this model, all boxes are connected with bidirectional arrows. The theory of language and the theory of learning must be consistent. The language description must be based on a theory of language; the theory must remain consistent with the data found in describing languages, and language pedagogy has clear relations with each of the other parts.

Let us consider these in turn. First, the relation with language description. As was suggested earlier, language pedagogy makes certain specific demands on descriptive linguistics for the provision of what is best called a pedagogical grammar, a grammar that may be readily adapted to the varying demands of the teaching situation. It offers to descriptive linguistics a method of checking the completeness of such a grammar. For example, language pedagogy demands of the language description that it include the basis for contrastive analysis: it might thus suggest the need for a number of different transfer grammars, and call for a description of a language in terms that permit of contrast. The textbook writer will often come to the descriptive linguist and ask him to give a specification of an area that might not normally be treated. And he will constantly be evaluating the descriptions against his own criteria: completeness, clarity, and ability to suggest a hierarchy of difficulty, the basis for an order of teaching. That he will usually be asking for rules does not necessarily mean that he will want to present these rules to his students, but rather that he will want to be able to organize the materials he teaches according to these rules. Of the descriptive linguist he will ask what can be called a 'pedagogical grammar for the teacher', namely a collection of statements about the language that specifies the linguistic behaviors involved in knowing the language; at the same time, he will probably need to be ready to prepare himself a 'pedagogical grammar for the learner', namely a consistent and simple set of rules about the language that may actually be given to the student. Thus, language pedagogy does not ask that linguistic descriptions be ready to be put into the hands of the student, but only that they be useful for the teacher and material writer.

Consider secondly the relation with the theory of learning. From this, language pedagogy looks to obtain hypotheses about the specification of the conditions in which learning will take place, and its activities will provide three types of empirical testing of the hypotheses. First, it will see whether they are consistent with natural language learning situations; for example, studies of bilingualism make clear that it is possible to acquire more than one language at a time, and give some ideas of the parameters involved in such learning situations. Second, laboratory tests will be carried out, setting up experiments in which as many of the variables as possible are controlled. Third, language pedagogy can test the hypotheses in normal classroom situations, realizing the general crudity of experimental design involved, but claiming the greater immediate relevance of its findings. Language pedagogy then will influence theories of learning in three ways: it will demand of them that their applicability to language teaching be clear, it will test their hypotheses, and it will provide an added connection between theories of language and of learning.

In just the same way, language pedagogy asks of the theory of language that it explain what language is in such a way as to imply how it might be taught. This demand must not be overstated: a theory of language cannot be expected initially to establish a model of production, but whatever model it does set up should have implications for language learning. Chomsky's work for instance raises the fundamental question of whether grammar is learned or innate. If the answer should be 'innate', we may be faced with the need to revise our teaching approach completely, perhaps even falling back on the much-maligned 'sunburn model' where it was assumed that exposure to a language was enough. But at the same time, the framework of transformational-generative grammar offers us a possible way of handling such previously nebulous concepts as analogy and imitation. It is not unreasonable to characterize the task of theoretical linguistics as the building of a machine (or model) capable of simulating the competence of the speaker of a language; but even when this is done, the task will remain of determining how this ideal model differs from the performance of human beings. The acquisition of a second language is an excellent laboratory for studying this problem. Language pedagogy then, must continually draw on language theory for implications concerning the acquisition of control of a second language, not expecting the answer, but looking for insights into the properties of language that may be taken into account in teaching. At the same time, it will make available to theorists the results of its experience, asking how the data it collects can be integrated with and accounted for by the theory.

Against this background, we may now consider the relevance of linguistics to language pedagogy. We have seen that a theory of second language pedagogy will draw its assumptions not just from theories of language, but also from theories of learning: it will need to take into account the work of the psychologist and of the pedagogical theorist as well. It is thus not reasonable for anyone to assert that language teaching methods be based on linguistics alone, nor is it fitting for a linguist to claim sole authority on how to teach language. This must be kept clear all the time: as a linguist, I recognize that my qualifications are limited; as one concerned with language pedagogy, I realize I must go outside my own field for a full picture.

When we ask what linguistics has to offer to language pedagogy, it is useful to distinguish between applications and implications. There are certain aspects of linguistics that may be applied directly in teaching. The most important one is the description of the language being taught. There is no question but that teaching needs to be based on the best possible description of the language being taught. And the better, the fuller, the more accurate the description is, the more chance the teacher will have to assist the learner in his growing mastery of the structure of the new language. Without such knowledge there will be no possibility of satisfactory sequencing of material, no chance of distinguishing 'mistakes' from the systematic errors that, as Corder (1967) has suggested, are the best evidence that language learning is taking place; no chance of useful explanation; no chance, in brief, of any meaningful control of the course of instruction.

But of course how this knowledge is to be applied is not a function of the language description. That a linguist describes a language in a given way, in a given order, or proposing a given sequence of rules, is not directly applicable; for it says nothing at all about the type of sequencing that might be used (Mackey 1965) or indeed whether linguistic sequencing is needed at all (Reibel 1968). That a linguist explains a phenomenon in a specific way does not tell a teacher how much he should use explanation in his class, or how this explanation should be given. These are questions to which language pedagogy must develop its own answers whether on the basis of linguistic theory, or from other sources.

A sound theory of language pedagogy will need to take into account the implications of three fields of linguistic activity. First is theoretical linguistics, whose task it is to explain the nature of language as a system. And modern linguistics is starting to do this, not yet conclusively, but suggesting a number of assumptions that should be taken into account. These assumptions may be summarized by saying that:

(1) Language use is essentially creative; thus, the notion of language as habit is not possible.

(2) The best explanation of this aspect of language is to say that the speaker of a language has available a system of rules to be used to produce and understand new sentences.

(3) The rules concerned are both intricate and abstract.

(4) The underlying intellectual organization required to acquire rules of this type suggests that there are universal properties of grammar.

With this in mind, let us consider a number of implications of current work in linguistics for language pedagogy. Take first the area of theoretical linguistics. Recent linguistic work has concentrated on the notion that language is creative. To explain this, it is necessary to propose an elaborate system of abstract rules that any speaker of a language develops as he acquires the language. From this, one may derive:

Implication 1. It is not enough to teach a language learner to respond automatically to predetermined stimuli: language instruction must lead to creative language use in new situations.

The acquisition of language has been shown to depend on two things: a human learner, and exposure to a language. Every normal human being acquires a language, the one he is exposed to. The kind of exposure doesn't seem to make too much difference. Operant conditioning can be used with animals, but they don't learn to speak.

Implication 2. Language can be acquired by active listening (listening and doing) even better than by listening and repeating.

Implication 3. Programmed language instruction will have limited results in language teaching.

The description of language has turned out to be an even more difficult and complex task than was believed before the problems of deep
structure and semantics were recognized. No one has yet succeeded
in describing any language with anything remotely approaching completeness.

Implication 4. The teacher or textbook writer will not be able
to find a complete grammar of the language he is teaching.
He will need to be able to draw on all available materials and
to prepare his own.

Studies of semantics emphasize the close relation of semantics and
syntax; and such studies as have been made of semantic systems of
different languages show that different languages have a different organization and labeling of the outside world.

Implication 5. When you learn a language, you have to learn
its semantic system too: accepting word-by-word translation
obscures this.

Syntax, the central component of a grammar, relates the content to
the expression. There are a number of basic relationships common to
all languages: function, transformation, agreement, and replacement.
Syntax is realized on the surface level by a number of structural devices:
function words, word endings, word order, and intonation; but there are
more fundamental processes involved: ordering, substitution, deletion,
and expansion.

Implication 6. The learning of fundamental syntactic relations and processes will not be accomplished by drill based
on analysis of surface structure alone.

Phonology is now conceived to be a matter of rules relating the underlying representation of sentences to their surface phonetic shape.
The importance of grammatical and semantic information in understanding speech has become clearer.

Implication 7. A language learner will need to be able to recognize the phonological distinctions made by speakers of the
language and to produce recognizable distinction. The more
he masters the language, the less important phonology will
be in this recognition.

Much work has been done in comparing descriptions of different languages. Such comparisons have been shown to be valuable in explaining

mistakes speakers of the one language make in learning the other, or in suggesting tactics that might be tried in presenting problem areas.

Implication 8. Knowledge of the structure of the learner's native language will help the teacher.

Turning now from theoretical linguistics, we can look at some recent work in psycholinguistics. Studies of how children acquire their first language have provided support for the hypothesis that such acquisition is a matter of developing rules rather than forming habits and generalizing.

Implication 9. Systematic errors (saying I goed instead of I went) are useful evidence to the teacher that the student is learning major rules.

Implication 10. Presentation of material should encourage formation of rules rather than memorization of items.

Studies of language and cognition have been inconclusive in establishing any causal direction, but it is clear that different languages classify and label the outside world in different ways.

Implication 11. When you learn a second language, you are also learning a second way of organizing your perceptions.

The third field to be considered is sociolinguistics. Studies of multilingual societies are showing the complexities in the way languages can have a different status, a different function, and a different proportion of bilingual and monolingual speakers.

Implication 12. The functional aim of a language course must be stated specifically.

Implication 13. It is not enough to learn a language: one also needs to learn how to use it.

Implication 14. Language use is closely tied to political, historical, religious, cultural, and economic factors.

An individual's language use is just as complex. Even a monolingual has several styles to choose from. Learning a language is significantly affected by the learner's attitude to speakers of the language. •

Implication 15. People are more likely to learn a language of high status than one of low status.

Implication 16. To learn a second language perfectly usually requires that one switch one's allegiance to the group represented by the language.

Implication 17. It is possible to learn enough of a language to use in a restricted domain.

These implications, I must make clear, are derived from work in linguistics. They need to be further refined, checked for internal consistency and for consistency with implications derivable from psychology and general pedagogical theory. They can then serve as a set of hypotheses for a theory of second language pedagogy, to be tested by empirical study of actual language teaching.

At this point, I should like to consider, in the light of the views of language pedagogy I have postulated, the possible relevance of second language pedagogy to work with standard dialect teaching. There is no reason to make the fuss that some do about the question of whether TESOD (if you will pardon the expression) and TESOL belong together. Matters of organizational jurisdiction are irrelevant to a scientific discussion. A brief glance at the vast differences involved in various language teaching tasks—differences of goal, learners, language, opportunity for teaching—makes it clear that there is no more difference between teaching a second language and teaching a standard dialect than there is between teaching Ewe to the Peace Corps and teaching French in a New York elementary school. Basic principles will be identical; actual methods will vary according to these principles. A sound theory of language pedagogy does not produce a method; it suggests implications that must be taken into account in developing such a method.

Given this, we can see how foolish it is to speak of taking over foreign language methods for teaching the standard dialect until there has been a new study, in terms of a sound theory of language pedagogy, of which methods are appropriate. The first task is clearly to have a reasonably clear view of how the standard dialect being taught differs from the actual dialect of the child. Without this, one runs the risk of running into the unfortunate position of such educators as Bereiter and Engelmann (1966) who start off with the rather surprising notion that disadvantaged children do not have a language at all.

The question is complicated by two factors: the urgency of the task on the one hand, and the difficulties linguists are having getting the question of language as opposed to language use straight. It is in this area that sociolinguistics is making its most significant contributions.

But this very controversy makes clear one of the basic limitations, not just of linguistics, but of language pedagogy itself. For while language pedagogy can make clear how teaching aims are to be described, and hopefully, even, how they might be obtained, it is, like most other social sciences, irresponsible in that it cannot decide which aims are best for society. We can describe bilingualism, for instance, or the standard language. We can study the effects of speaking two languages or speaking a nonstandard dialect. But our theories are unable to help us answer some of the most important questions: should we all be bilingual? Should all Mexican-Americans learn English? Should all disadvantaged children learn and speak standard English? In this area, we must be careful not to fall into the old trap, and say: 'A linguist does not make value judgments,' and then go on to make a value judgment: 'All languages and dialects are equally good.' For one of the most important things sociolinguistics is helping us to define is the sociological values of specific languages and dialects. Luckily, for those of us who believe in cultural pluralism, no one has yet shown conclusively that any language or dialect has clear cognitive advantages or disadvantages, but the social effects are quite clear. It is not as linguists that we decide whether it is better to change the language of the lower status groups or the attitudes of society to that language; but as responsible members of a society, we must be prepared to make such a choice. And as linguists, we should insist that such choice take into account what we know of language and its use.

Linguistics and its hyphenated fields have a great deal to offer to language teachers, but the fullest benefit can only come when their implications are integrated and formed into a sound theory of language pedagogy. Because linguistics is only indirectly applicable to language teaching, changes in linguistic theory or arguments among linguists should not disturb language teachers; in the same way, the growing evidence of the inadequacy of the pure ALM or the incorrectness of many of its assumptions does not threaten linguistics. Within this framework, and with language pedagogy independent of any one discipline and even more of any one school of thought within a discipline, we can get on with the theoretical study, the discussion, the experimentation, and the development that the language teachers ask of us.

REFERENCES

Alatis, James E. (Editor). 1968. Report of the Nineteenth Annual Round Table Meeting on Linguistics and Language Studies. Monograph 21, Georgetown University Monograph Series on Languages and Linguistics. Washington, D.C.: Georgetown University Press.
Asher, James J. 1969. The total physical approach to second language learning. Modern Language Journal: 53, 3-17.

Bereiter, Carl and Siegfried Engelmann. 1966. Teaching disadvantaged children in the preschool. Englewood, New Jersey: Prentice-Hall.

Chomsky, Noam. 1965. Aspects of the theory of syntax. Cambridge, Massachusetts: MIT Press.

_____. 1966. Linguistic theory. Reports of the Working Committees, Northeast Conference on the Teaching of Foreign Languages. 43-9.

Chomsky, Noam and Morris Halle. 1968. The sound pattern of English. New York: Harper and Row.

Corder, S. P. 1967. The significance of learners' errors. International Review of Applied Linguistics 5, 161-70.

del Olmo, Guillermo. 1968. Professional and pragmatic perspectives on the audiolingual approach: introduction and review. FL Annals. 2, 19-29.

Hamp, Eric P. 1968. What a contrastive grammar is, if it is not. Monograph 21, 137-47, Georgetown University Monograph Series on Languages and Linguistics. Washington, D.C.: Georgetown University Press.

Hayes, Alfred S., Wallace E. Lambert, and G. Richard Tucker. 1967. Evaluation of Foreign Language Teaching. FL Annals. 1, 22-45.

Hodge, Carleton T. 1968. BC=PS+AP. Language Science. 3, 17-20.

Mackey, William. 1965. Language Teaching Analysis. Bloomington and London: Indiana University Press.

Mildenberger, Kenneth W. 1968. Confusing signposts—the relevance of applied linguistics. Monograph 21, 205-13, Georgetown University Monograph Series on Languages and Linguistics. Washington, D.C.: Georgetown University Press.

Ornstein, Jacob. 1968. Programmed instruction and educational technology in the language field: boon or failure. Modern Language Journal 52, 401-10.

Reibel, David A. 1968. Language learning analysis. ms.

Spolsky, Bernard. 1966. A psycholinguistic critique of programmed foreign language instruction. International Review of Applied Linguistics. 4.

_____. 1968. What does it mean to know a language, or how do you get someone to perform his competence? Paper presented at the second conference on Problems in Foreign Language Testing.

IS A SOCIOLINGUISTIC THEORY POSSIBLE?

DAVID DE CAMP

The University of Texas

Abstract. Early formulations of generative linguistic theory, like
early formulations of empirical taxonomic linguistic theory, postulated
'an ideal speaker-listener, in a completely homogeneous speech-community.' By the 1950's many of the empirical linguists had grown dis-
satisfied with description of this mythical idiolect and attempted to
characterize a dialect or even a language. Thus we saw Hockett's
common core, Trager's overall pattern, and Weinreich's diasystems.
History has now repeated itself: a number of generative linguists are
no longer willing to rule all variability out of linguistics as a mere
performance factor. Although some variability is indeed only randomly idiosyncratic performance, many intra-speaker stylistic shifts
and many inter-speaker differences are rule-predictable. In fact
they may be subjected to a Guttman scalogram analysis, the cutting
points of which may function as binary features in the base component
of a grammar. These features not only block or activate the relevant
subsequent rules necessary to generate the grammatical sentences of
each speech variety; they also, like other features, are themselves
subject to semantic interpretation. 'Stylistic' or 'rhetorical' meaning
is thus rescued from the limbo of 'paralinguistics' and is treated at
the same level as lexical and syntactic meaning.

Both the sociolinguist and the 'pure' unhyphenated linguist are concerned with the linguistic relationships between the idiolect and the
language. The sociolinguist may also wish to study the social and
cultural correlates of these linguistic relationships and thus try to
deal with problems of individual performance and of linguistic change.
If he is to be a sociolinguist and not merely a sociologist looking at
language, however, his work must be based on linguistic theory, not

merely on manipulations of language data. An interpretation of generative theory which can accommodate both idiolectal and communal
competence and the interrelationships between them bridges the gulf
which for so long has divided our profession and eliminates both the
need and the excuse for non-theoretical sociolinguistics.

At present, sociolinguistics is at worst a poorly-defined interdisci-
plinary activity, at best an empirical discipline without a theoretical
basis. This is not to deny the real progress of sociolinguistics in the
last two decades. Consider, for example, the evolution of urban language surveys: From the pioneer surveys of New York speech by Yakira A. Frank (1948) and Allan Forbes Hubbell (1950) to my own study
of San Francisco pronunciation (1953) to William Labov's study of social stratification in New York (1966), there has been undeniable growth
in sophistication of method. This growth has been in the empirical
techniques for the collection and evaluation of data, however, and sociolinguistic studies of the 1960s are generally as isolated from linguistic theory as were those of the 1940s, or even those of Gilliéron.
The history of sociolinguistics, including dialectology, is largely a
series of technological innovations; and most of these were not really
new, but rather were belated applications to linguistics of techniques
which had long been standard procedures in sociology, psychology, and
economics.

I use the term 'theory' as it is used by the historians of science,
e.g. Thomas S. Kuhn (1962), to mean a postulated abstract model to
which all empirical data are referred and which provides the essential
paradigms to determine the normal scientific activity of the researcher
in that discipline, viz. the asking and answering of relevant questions.
This model must be formalized, or at least be formalizable, in explicit terms (usually mathematical) which at some fundamental level permit
meaningful dialogue with other disciplines. The weakest theory is a
'functional' model, which only relates outputs from the black box to in-
puts, e.g. a grammar which would generate all and only the sentences
of a language; the goal of much scientific research is to replace such a
functional model with a 'structural' model, one that makes the stronger
claim of describing what is actually in the black box. Mendel's 'genes'
were only a functional model of genetics; the research on the DNA and
RNA molecules has yielded a model that is much more nearly structural. Thus one branch of biology has at last become a true science; general linguistics is approaching that status; sociolinguistics is still in
the pre-theoretical, butterfly-collecting stage, with no theory of its
own and uncertain whether it has any place in general linguistic theory.

A theory may be validated either formally or empirically, but these
two evaluations are not exchangeable, for they relate to totally different

properties of a theory. It may be formally evaluated on such attributes as explicitness, internal consistency, external consistency (i. e. with the theories of related disciplines), simplicity, and productivity (i. e. the maximum number of theorems which may be inferred from the fewest initial axioms). A formally valid theory cannot be proved 'wrong' empirically, for the theorist creates his own imaginary universe, in which the data all conform to the theory by definition. The empirical fact that such entities as squares, circles, and straight lines do not exist in our 'real' world does not prove that Euclidian geometry is wrong. A theory whose imaginary universe more clearly resembles some relevant aspect of the real world may, however, be judged more 'useful'. Non-Euclidian geometries have been found more useful in certain scientific fields whose advanced technologies have revealed discrepancies between Euclid's model world and our real world. The sentences generated by a generative grammar are by definition all and only the grammatical sentences of the idealized language of the theory. Both the linguist and the layman, however, would normally prefer, ceteris paribus, whichever grammar whose set of grammatical sentences most closely conformed to his own intuitions of grammaticalness or to those of his informant.

Empirical data may prove a theory to be useless or irrelevant. They seldom prove it to be wrong. Nor is failure to incorporate every aspect of a large and complex field necessarily fatal to a theory. Astronomy does not attempt to tell us everything there is to know about the stars. One of the legitimate functions of a theory is to define the relevant questions which can be the basis of acceptable research. The thesis of this paper, however, is that for at least the third time in history, a prevailing linguistic theory has been suspected of failing to provide a place for sociolinguistics, that this lack was indeed a significant factor in the demise of the two earlier theories, and that it is therefore of great importance to general linguistics that we now examine current linguistic theory to determine whether it can indeed accommodate sociolinguistic questions.

The Stammbaum theory of the nineteenth century Neogrammarians was never rigorously formalized, but it was indeed a theoretical model of language. It assumed an idealized linguistic universe in which each speech community was completely homogeneous in language usage but not necessarily homogeneous in the initiation of language change. Each community was therefore liable to be split by a change which operated in one sub-area but not in another. Language change was assumed to be rule-governed behavior describable in purely linguistic terms. The linguistic universe was seen synchronically as a large mosaic of clearly-demarcated areas and sub-areas, and was seen diachronically as a sequence of innovations whose domain of simultaneous occurrence was either an entire homogeneous community (in which case the result would

be further differentiation from other communities) or a contiguous sub-
area of a community (in which case the result would be a bifurcation of
the community into uniformly innovating and uniformly conservative
subcommunities).

This theory was simple, explicit, internally consistent, and therefore very satisfying formally. It even seemed empirically valid when
applied to certain selected data. It was never disproved; it only became
less useful, less interesting, as dialectologists like Gilliéron, idealists
like Vossler, creolists like Schuchardt, and many others discovered
that the Neogrammarian model was too frequently incompatible with
those aspects of the real world which they wished to study. A theory
which dealt only with the initiation of a linguistic change and either
omitted or distorted the dispersion and subsequent history of that
change was unacceptable to too many linguists. Unfortunately, no viable alternative theory emerged. The so-called 'wave theory' of
Schmidt was never really developed and was more an illustrative met-
aphor than a theoretical model. In the school of Gilliéron we find a
complete rejection of theory, a haphazard inductive search for correlations between sets of empirical observations.

To the extent that post-Saussurean structuralism was really a theory and not merely a set of empirical procedures, it also assumed a
uniform idealized speaker, the 'idiolect'. Although it did not require
a homogeneous speech community as the Stammbaum theory had, it
made no provision for linguistic diversity beyond defining 'language'
and 'dialect' as collections of idiolects which share most of their features. Diversity within the idiolect was swept under the rug as 'free
variation' and ignored. Diversity between idiolects within the speech
community was acknowledged; but because no definition of larger group-
ings such as dialect and language was ever offered beyond merely calling them 'collections of similar idiolects', it was implied that a language
had no structure of its own and could be described only by a collection of
separate grammars, one for each idiolect. The term 'idiolect' was defined operationally as that span of language phenomena to which a single
set of rules could apply; but because intra-idiolectal free variation was
permitted, no explicit definition was possible. Even given a complete
grammar of X, one could not reliably determine whether, for example,
a noncontrastive variation between nasalized and nonnasalized vowels
in language X was intra-idiolectal or inter-idiolectal. Nor was it easy
to determine the real-world counterpart of the theoretical idiolect, for
one live speaker who shifted styles might correspond to several idiolects, and conversely two speakers might conform to the same rules
for a considerable span of speech. Although presumably la langue was
an empirical matter, to be determined by inspection of la parole, there
were no rules on the minimum length of two similar samples of la parole

which had to be examined before declaring that they represented the same langue.

The taxonomic structuralism of de Saussure and Bloomfield, for all its faults, was the nearest thing to a linguistic theory that we had for half a century, and a great deal of significant research appeared in that half century. Like the Stammbaum model, however, it was not suited to the questions which many linguists, especially sociolinguists, wished to investigate. In the 1940s and 50s, therefore, several modifications to the approach were suggested in the hope of escaping the idiolect trap and providing for the description of a dialect or even a language. Thus we saw Hockett's 'common core' (1958: 321-38), the Trager-Smith 'overall pattern' (1951), and Weinreich's 'diasystems' (1954). As I have elsewhere pointed out (DeCamp 1961, 1968), however, these attempts at theory-reform were too little and too late. The common-core approach merely relegated all linguistic diversity to the area of indeterminacy as if it were free variation. The overall pattern merely superimposed different idiolectal descriptions, obscuring the structures of the individual varieties without producing any generalizations about the 'language' except for a composite taxonomic inventory of potential grammatical devices which might be found in any or all of the varieties. And diasystems were only an arbitrary juxtaposition of separate descriptions, an elaborate system of notation to convey just the same information as would be found in a shelf of separate grammars of each variety, each in its own volume. None of these approaches described the functional correspondences between analogous features in different dialects. None of them enabled us to convert sentences in one dialect into equivalent sentences in another. If the ability to make such conversions is a part of the native speaker's competence, then it should be accounted for in the theory.

These innovations could not save taxonomic structuralism and perhaps only weakened it; certainly the emic-etic principle lost a great deal of the appeal which it had had in its much simpler Bloomfieldian version. The intellectual tide was turning against empiricism. Syntactic Structures was published in 1957, and the rest is history. But does history repeat itself? Of the various theories or quasi-theories which have appeared in linguistics, the generative transformational model has by now been the most thoroughly validated, both formally and empirically. Its early claims to validity, however, were at the expense of restricting its relevance to only a portion of the traditional activities and interests of linguists. Most of historical linguistics, stylistics, sociolinguistics, and ethnolinguistics seemed to be ruled out by Chomsky's assertion that the generative model was concerned primarily with the idealized 'competence' of 'an ideal speaker-listener, in a completely homogeneous speech-community' (Chomsky 1965: 3). At many linguistic centers today, only the area thus delineated by

Chomsky is called 'theoretical linguistics', or perhaps even 'linguistics'; other aspects of language study are thought of as ancillary fields or 'hyphenated disciplines'.

There is good reason to believe, however, that these restrictions are not essential to the theory and have been only a temporary phase of the development of generative linguistics, just as Newton's laws of motion were directly applicable only to bodies in a frictionless vacuum. Motion under our real-world conditions is not thereby ruled out by the physicist, but it does involve additional mechanical laws, complexities which had to be postponed until the elementary principles had been worked out first for motion under unnaturally simple conditions. Several linguists have already extended generative theory to diachronic description (e.g. Kiparsky 1968, Chomsky and Halle 1968: 249-89). Papers on generative dialectology have appeared (e.g. Keyser 1963, Labov 1968, Bailey 1969), and several of us are convinced that all aspects of sociolinguistics can be similarly accommodated. Despite the apparent initial hostility, the generative-transformational model is the most hospitable to sociolinguistics of any linguistic theory yet known.

Linguistic variability is the sociolinguist's stock in trade. Taxonomic linguistics provided only two treatments of variability: consider it intra-idiolectal free variation or consider it inter-idiolectal, i.e. the two alternative forms are in two different idiolects and hence in different grammars. Either recourse excluded the diversity from linguistic consideration altogether. Generative theory, on the other hand, can simultaneously represent a language, all of the dialects of that language, and all of the switching operations which interrelate the language and its dialects. I contend that it can do so without the necessity of such fundamental changes in generative theory as Labov has proposed.

'Competence' and 'performance' have too often been misinterpreted as mere revivals of de Saussure's 'la langue' and 'la parole', but the similarity holds only up to a point. Indeed the exact height of my tongue for the articulation of a diffuse vowel, the exact length and degree of complexity of the next sentence I will utter, the exact ratio of inverted to noninverted indirect objects in the total set of sentences which I will create tomorrow—these are random or at least idiosyncratic matters of performance and cannot be considered rule-governed behavior, at least not until the psycholinguists finally learn enough to create a genuine performance model. Not all variability is thus excluded, however. If I suddenly assume a pompous, stuffy manner, several changes will simultaneously occur in my speech. No one knows exactly what happens in my central nervous system to cause these changes; but the parallels within the theoretical model are clear enough: my negative contraction and palatalization rules are blocked, so that I say 'This is not literatyur' rather than 'This isn't literachur'. My relative-attraction transformation is reordered to follow, rather than precede, my case-assignment rule, so that I say 'Every linguist whom I met was inebriated.' Dozens, perhaps hundreds, of such changes simultaneously occur, as if I had suddenly thrown an enormous switch labeled 'pompous'. This is not random, idiosyncratic variation within the confines of some overall grammar. The switch itself is rule-describable and is a part of my linguistic competence, though the frequency with which I use it is a matter of performance. The number of predictable changes which make up a typical stylistic shift is too great for random coincidence. The molecules of water bouncing randomly about in Brownian movement do not suddenly all throw themselves simultaneously in one direction, thereby knocking the kettle off the stove.

It would be an even greater distortion to say that I switched to an entirely different grammar when I made that stylistic shift, as if I were to start speaking Chinese. We all have hundreds of stylistic levels and constantly switch from one to another. We certainly do not store hundreds of complete grammars in our heads. To so represent stylistic shifts in the theoretical model would be to force the theory so far away from empirical reality that it would lose all relevance to natural human language. We know that any normal schoolboy can learn Pig-latin much more quickly than he can learn French. He therefore must have some switching mechanism for changing prescribed subsets of his grammatical rules while leaving the remainder of the grammar undisturbed. The generative theoretical model provides such a mechanism in the binary semantic/syntactic features. A feature [+ pompous] could be inserted in a segment of a deep structure phrase marker by the same kind of rule that inserts features like [+ negative] or [+ declarative]. Once thus inserted, this feature would control all the prescribed changes throughout the remainder of the derivation. It could control the insertion of additional stylistic features by means of rules such as the following.

$$[+ \text{pompous}] \rightarrow \begin{bmatrix} \underline{+} \text{ petulant} \\ \underline{+} \text{ sarcastic} \end{bmatrix}$$

It could be included in relevant lexical entries in order to block or to permit the selection of that lexical item, to change the pronunciation (e.g. vahz and ayther instead of vase and either), or to change the syntactic behavior of the lexical item (e.g. to require learned Latin affixes: stadia and auditoria instead of stadiums and auditoriums. The [± pompous] feature could be included in the structure index of a transformation in order to trigger it or to block it or even to replicate the rule, thus producing the effect of permutation of rule order. And of course it could similarly affect the phonological rules. The strength of the generative model here is not just that it permits variability, for even the taxonomic grammars could indicate alternative forms at any level. Rather it is that the feature system provides a control mechanism over the variability.

Early formulations of generative grammar did not include syntactic features, depending instead on complicated systems of subscripts to identify and control the co-occurrence of lexical types (e.g. V_{t412}). When features were first added to the model five or six years ago, only a small number were used, and these generally had clear-cut semantic as well as syntactic implications, e.g. [$\pm$ human, $\pm$ abstract]. Since then, the number of features has greatly increased, with two important consequences: a drastic simplification of the branching rules in the base; and a reduction of the options available in the transformational component. All the optional transformations which had changed the meaning in earlier grammars (e.g. negative, interrogative) were made obligatory, under control of features which were optionally introduced in the base. Rosenbaum (1968) goes so far as to include features for extraposition and indirect object inversion, thus making the two relevant transformations obligatory, and he suggests the possibility of eliminating optional transformations altogether.

Extraposition and indirect object inversion are matters of style. If Rosenbaum's rule

$$[- \text{gerund}] \rightarrow [\pm \text{R } 13] \ / \ \begin{bmatrix} + \text{PRO} \\ \underline{\hspace{1cm}} \end{bmatrix}$$

is acceptable as the device for selecting and then controlling the 'extraposing style', there should be no objection to including features like [$\pm$ pompous] for similar purposes. Moreover, this procedure would permit the consideration of stylistic meaning. Semantics, which were at first simply excluded from generative grammars and then achieved a sort of second-class citizenship in the ghetto of a separate 'interpretive' semantic component, have now been incorporated into the base by most theorists. Consequently all syntactic features are potentially also semantic features. Features such as [$\pm$ pompous] and [$\pm$ R 13] (Rosenbaum's feature which triggers extraposition) are subject to semantic interpretation on the same basis as features like [$\pm$ Masculine]. Thus stylistic meaning can be rescued from paralinguistic limbo and included in the theory on the same basis as any other kind of meaning.

Up to this point my example has been a single binary stylistic feature [$\pm$ pompous]. There are many styles, however, perhaps a whole continuous spectrum of them, containing as many styles as there are stylistically significant features in the grammar. Must we then mark our lexical entries and our transformations to indicate the blocking, triggering, and other effects on them of fifty different stylistic features, perhaps a hundred? Because many, perhaps most, of the rules in a grammar will be sensitive at least to some stylistic shifts, an at-

tempt to incorporate all distinguishable styles would seem to complicate the grammar astronomically. Indeed it would, if it were necessary to write out at each style-sensitive point in the grammar a hundred
different stylistic features. However, there are not a hundred different
pronunciations of the word vase, only two. If the hundred different
styles could be linearly arranged, like children lining up to be assigned
numbers, with all of the vahz-speaking styles grouped at one end of the
line, it would then be sufficient to specify only one number, e.g. 85,
meaning that styles numbered 86-100 call for a pronunciation vahz, but
not styles numbered 1-85.

To a great extent, stylistic variation does constitute a linear spectrum or continuum. To the extent that a set of style characteristics is
part of such a continuum, they may all be arrayed in one linear series
on the basis of their co-occurrences, with no need for cross classification. That is, a speaker being sufficiently pompous to say vahz would
almost certainly also say It is I rather than It's me. Thus these two
characteristics would divide our hundred styles into three groups: those
with vahz and It is I, those with vase and It is I, and those with vase and
It's me. The fourth mathematical possibility—co-occurrence of vahz
and It's me—would occur only rarely and under exceptional circumstances, e.g. making fun of the establishment. A third stylistic feature, a fourth, a fifth, etc., are similarly considered and placed in
this linear series in the appropriate relative order according to their
co-occurrences. If the number of features were unlimited, the series
would approach a continuous spectrum. This technique is called the
Guttman scalogram analysis (Guttman 1944, Torgerson 1957) and is
widely used in psychology and sociology though not in linguistics. In
1959 I independently 'discovered' the technique and used it in the analysis of the post-creole linguistic continuum of Jamaica (DeCamp 1961,
1968). It has now also been applied to American dialect data by Walter
Stolz (1968) and by Charles-James Bailey (1969) with interesting and
useful results.

If linguistic diversity is linear, as it frequently is, then the cutting
points of a Guttman analysis can function as a useful binary feature
schema so that only one stylistic feature need be specified at any one
rule of the grammar ([+ i] implying [+1, +2, ... , +i], and [-i]
implying [-i, -(i+1), ... , -n]). If the diversity, or one component
of it, is nonlinear, then a similar approach might still be in order,
though if a given linguistic feature varies in two dimensions, the necessity of two simultaneous sets of indices would greatly complicate
the system. Note that linguistic geography is not necessarily two- or
multi-dimensional. It can also be simply linear, a function of the distance from an urban center, for example. As a contribution to a some-
day theory of sociolinguistics, I offer the following hypothesis: that the
linguistic diversity within any speech community may be factored into

a small set of sociolinguistic 'structures' each of which may be represented by a simple mathematical function (a line, a circle, etc.) and
by a corresponding schema of binary features which, if they are incorporated into a generative grammar, can result in the grammar's
generating those aspects of the linguistic diversity which are attribu-
table to that structure. If this hypothesis should turn out to be untrue,
then I cannot see how we could explain the fact that every adolescent
somehow learns to navigate through a fantastically complex sea of sociolinguistic situations. To develop the average adolescent's social
skills in language, despite the misinformation he receives from his
teachers, even if he somehow intuitively knows that the complex can
be factored into manageable structures, is a miracle of learning comparable to language acquisition itself.

Two final points to clear up: there are some linguists who will accept this incorporation of variability into a generative grammar, but
only to the extent that all varieties in the system are within the competence of one speaker. That is, they will agree to a generative stylistics but not to a generative social dialectology. Consider again a
linear system of one hundred speech varieties, each only minimally
different from its neighbors in the series. Suppose that Speaker A can
make sufficient stylistic shifts that he can command speech varieties
1-50 but not 51 or those beyond it. Suppose Speaker B similarly has
command of varieties 10-60, Speaker C of varieties 20-70, etc. The
entire linear series of a hundred varieties can be established on the
basis of the overlapping abilities of different speakers in the community. I contend that this entire series constitutes the linguistic competence which the theory should account for. The fact that no one speaker
has command of the entire range is merely an accident of performance.
No one speaker knows all the words in Webster's third edition either,
nor can he speak a trillion-word sentence. I suggest that linguistic
competence can just as well be communal as individual. The psycho-
linguist will presumably continue to prefer the latter interpretation,
the sociolinguist and ethnolinguist presumably the former. To arbitrarily and unnecessarily restrict the theory in order to exclude either
possibility would only be to reawaken an idiolectal ghost from the dark
ages of eme and allo.

A final point before summing up: What a speaker can say in a sentence is restricted by context, and his meaning is interpreted in terms
of context. The relevant context is not necessarily all verbal, however,
though only verbal contextual features have so far been considered in
generative theory. There is no compelling reason why the selectional
restrictions of a generative grammar could not be stated partly in
terms of kinesic or proxemic features. Susan Ervin-Tripp (1967)
formulated her presentation of comparative systems of personal address in the form of flow diagrams. These diagrams may be easily

reformulated into generative feature rules, however, and such rules are exactly what we will need if our grammars are to say anything meaningful about the syntax and the semantics of given names, sur- names, and titles. If the theorists are really serious about incorpor- ating the semantics in the syntactic base instead of segregating it in a separate interpretive component, then I predict that we will be seeing some mighty strange things showing up in the semantic/syntactic fea- ture rules, features which have long been familiar to the anthropologist and the sociologist but which we never thought we would see in a formal theoretical grammar.

The title of this paper asked a question, which is not yet explicitly answered: Is a sociolinguistic theory possible ? That depends. If a third and independent theoretical discipline is meant, separate from both linguistics and sociology, then I seriously doubt it. If we mean an extension of sociological theory to include social aspects of language, then definitely not. From that direction we will get empirical proced- ures for the handling of data, which will be very useful to us. Every sociolinguist should know more about experimental research design. But until sociology develops a theory of its own, it can hardly contrib- ute one to sociolinguistics. The opportunities to develop a sociolin- guistic aspect of general linguistic theory, however, have never before been so encouraging. Sociolinguistics simply cannot afford to continue its aimless drifting, collecting pretty butterflies and quaint word-lists in self-imposed isolation from the exciting things that are happening in general theoretical linguistics. Sociolinguistics has become too im- portant for us to tolerate that. For every competent linguist who steps back or slows down in the search for the truth about the social nature of language, a charlatan steps forward with mouth full of glib answers, hand outstretched to grab the federal grant. Problems such as Negro English and Spanish-English bilingualism have given our work an ur- gency which we did not choose but which we cannot deny.

REFERENCES

Bailey, Charles-James N. 1969. The integration of linguistic theory: internal reconstruction and the comparative method in descriptive linguistics. Unpublished.

Chomsky, Noam. 1965. Aspects of the theory of syntax. Cambridge: MIT Press.

_____ and Morris Halle. 1968. The sound pattern of English. New York: Harper and Row.

DeCamp, David. 1953. The pronunciation of English in San Francisco. Berkeley, dissertation, University of California. Abridged version published in 1958-59, Orbis 7: 372-91; 8: 54-77.

_____. 1961. Diasystem vs. overall pattern: the Jamaican syllabic

nuclei. Unpublished paper presented at the 1961 winter meeting of
the Linguistic Society of America. To appear in Studies in the language, literature, and culture of the middle ages and later, ed. by
E. Bagby Atwood and A. A. Hill. Austin: University of Texas Press.
1969.

_____. Toward a generative analysis of a post-creole speech continuum.
Unpublished paper presented at the 1968 international conference on
pidginization and creolization of languages. To appear in the proceedings of that conference, ed. by Dell Hymes. Cambridge: Cambridge University Press. 1969 or 1970.

Ervin-Tripp, Susan. 1967. Sociolinguistics. (Language-Behavior
Research Laboratory, working paper 3.) Berkeley, California.

Frank, Yakira A. 1948. The speech of New York City. Ann Arbor,
unpublished dissertation, University of Michigan.

Guttman, Louis. 1944. A basis for scaling qualitative data. American
sociological review 9 : 139-50.

Hockett, Charles F. 1958. A course in modern linguistics. New York:
Macmillan.

Hubbell, Allan F. 1950. The pronunciation of English in New York
City. New York: King's Crown Press.

Keyser, S. J. 1963. Review of Hans Kurath and Raven I. McDavid,
Jr., The pronunciation of English in the Atlantic states. Language
39 : 303-16.

Kiparsky, Paul. 1968. Linguistic universals and linguistic change.
In Universals in linguistic theory, ed. by Emmon Bach and Robert
T. Harms. New York: Holt, Rinehart and Winston, pp. 170-202.

Kuhn, Thomas S. 1962. The structure of scientific revolutions.
Chicago: University of Chicago Press.

Labov, William. 1966. The social stratification of English in New
York City. Washington: Center for Applied Linguistics.

_____. 1968. Contraction, deletion, and inherent variability of the
English copula. Unpublished.

Rosenbaum, Peter S. 1968. English grammar II. (Section 1 of Scientific report 2 on Specification and utilization of a transformational
grammar. RC-2070). Yorktown Heights, New York: International
Business Machines.

Stolz, Walter, and Garland Bills. 1968. An investigation of the stan-
dard-nonstandard dimension of Central Texas English. Unpublished.

Torgerson, Warren. 1957. Theory and methods of scaling. New York:
Wiley.

Trager, George L. and Henry Lee Smith, Jr. 1951. An outline of
English structure. (Studies in linguistics: occasional papers 3).
Norman, Oklahoma: Battenburg Press.

Weinreich, Uriel. 1954. Is a structural dialectology possible? Word
14 : 388-400.

DISCUSSION

Ralph Fasold, Center for Applied Linguistics: I found Professor DeCamp's paper extremely interesting and thought provoking; and it seems that what you have done, at least in part of what you said, is to come close to suggesting a formalization of what Gumperz called the linguistic repertoire. Would you care to comment on that?

DeCamp: I consider Gumperz one of the most productive and creative minds working in the field. I don't think that what he has there is as yet a sociolinguistic theory. Any more than what I have here now is. The thing is what we are doing here—this attempt to formalize these different sets of relations—is an extremely important thing. Now the kind of thing that Gumperz has been doing there is a different kind of a structure from what I have. I am not saying that this continuum concept that I have here and that I have found in Jamaican work is universal.

What I am willing to conjecture now on the basis of the success which he has had in India and what I have done here, and what various other people are doing in other work, is that rather than just being a completely unlimited number of possible different sociolinguistic situations, that this is very much like Fourier analysis of a wave. You know you can have a wave that can be infinitely complicated, but on the other hand you can factor it out into a relatively small number of simple forms. And I think what Gumperz found in his Indian village was a relatively simple one, that is, one in which one of these components was relatively pure, comparable to the linear array I found in Jamaica. I think that what we find in most complex communities is probably a combination which includes some factors of his type of material, some of what I have, and probably some others we don't know. I would conjecture that the number of such possibilities is small, entirely on the basis that otherwise I couldn't conceive how a child could learn to master them.

Sadanand Singh, Howard University: I disagree with your calling exploratory research collecting butterflies. Collecting data only leads to testing of hypothesis which leads one to building of a model and developing a theory.

DeCamp: The term 'butterfly collecting' or another synonymous term, 'botanizing', is used in the sciences. This has nothing to do with the fact that butterflies are pretty flighty things that flutter around, this isn't what is meant at all. It merely is referring to what people would usually call a prescientific stage of a discipline, which until very recently all biology was, which chemistry and physics left behind in the

17th century, which psychology is just starting to move out of, and
which linguistics has only very recently moved out of. That is the Ba-
conian type of empirical induction, which as most philosophers would
see it now is not a scientific method; that is, Bacon's inductivity is not
a scientific method, it is a prescientific method.

'Butterfly collecting' is simply the collection of a whole lot of information toward the day when somebody can produce a formal theory.
Now this is valuable, this is useful. We need a lot of empirical data
collection also. I certainly would not want to imply by this that in this
I'm saying that there is not an importance to the kinds of things that
the Urban Language Survey is doing at CAL, or Bill Labov's work in
New York. This is immensely important. What I am saying is that
although it is necessary, it is not sufficient. We've got enough data
now; it is about time to guide further research by means of some sort
of a theory. The chemist wouldn't even think of operating in the way
that he's pictured in the movies, simply going into the laboratory and
sort of pouring things back and forth out of bottles and waiting to see
if an explosion occurs. Now in the early days of chemistry, yes, exactly this was done, and it was a very valuable kind of research. We
are ready to evolve into another stage now, that is all.

Bob Cromack, Hartford Seminary and the Summer Institute of Linguistics: I found this paper very interesting. I would like to make one
feeble objection to a questionable statement. You are saying that transformational-generative grammar is the only theory at present offered
which can handle stylistic shifts. I've found that with stratificational
grammar, as it is being developed by Gleason and some of us up there
in the cold north, we can handle this type of thing very neatly without
having to postulate several different grammars.

One illustration of what we feel we can do with stratificational grammar is that we can handle a whole utterance, a whole discourse, stylistically or according to these variants. Our input would say that the
whole discourse, all the sentences in a given discourse, will be gov-
erned by a certain stylistic feature. The stylistic impulse can be relaxed and later reintroduced, in order to bring in the other thousand
features you are talking about. But the point is that we can handle
style in a context beyond the simple sentence.

DeCamp: This is a subject that I would just as soon not discuss.
I would say only on this, that it is hard to take seriously any so-called
theory which will not admit itself to evaluation either formal or empirical. At such time as any representative of the stratificational theory
will be willing to openly debate this on logical grounds, that is, the
formal mathematical basis of the theory, or will produce empirically-
verifiable results from it, that is, actual grammars of languages, so

that you can look at them and compare what such a grammar has done with grammars that have been formed in another manner, at such time I will start taking it seriously. So far, unfortunately, this has not happened.

William Labov, Columbia University: I appreciate your concern for a more abstract theoretical approach and for the amplification of our data by formal means. We agree on the fact that a purely descriptive approach doesn't really lead anywhere—it only succeeds in making the sociolinguistic situation seem more and more complicated. The implicational scale is certainly an important idea.

But I don't think we agree on the role of theory here. It seems to me that you want to extend generative theory to a wider area by simply adapting the current terminology and rule forms to your data, and I think there are two ways in which your presentation represents a step backwards.

In the first place, you are using categorical, invariant rules as if speakers always used a particular form in a given system, and relying on the old notion of code-switching to explain the variation that you find. I know you will find this simply doesn't work when you come to apply it to a real body of speech. You'll be faced with dozens of code-switches in the middle of a sentence, for no apparent reason. Anyone who works with the language that people actually use finds that there is inherent variation that can't be disposed of.

I think you are familiar with the formal treatment we've developed for variable rules within the generative framework; the paper on 'Contraction, Deletion, and Inherent Variability of the Copula' was distributed at the Jamaica Conference. You may have seen the implicational scale developed by Stolz and Bills in their sociolinguistic work at Texas; they found that they couldn't stick to invariant rules: some of the points on their scale depend on whether the speaker uses a given rule for over a certain proportion of the cases.

In the second place, your general approach to theory seems to me essentially one of reducing your data into a form that will fit Chomsky's model. I think it would be a shame if you Creolists take their very rich knowledge of the language and the community and try to squeeze it into an inadequate theoretical framework. Our own approach to theory takes the reverse approach. One of the reasons that we work in the speech community is to enrich the data available to linguistics, and to refine theory so that it can account for change and variation.

DeCamp: Well, there are two questions here. First, I indeed agree that you often get stylistic shift several times within a sentence. The way in which I have been handling this I didn't present in a handout today, a set of formal rules or anything of this sort. The stylistic binary features, however, will be presented as a part of the type segment of each sentence within the sentence, that is each S̲ in the phrase marker. Now this would provide for as many different stylistic segments of a sentence as you have embedded S̲'s within. Now not only in my own data, but in Stolz's Central Texas data, I have so far not been able to find any situation in which this would not be adequate, that is, the span of every stylistic segment of a sentence has been at least of a length which would represent a sentence, that is, an S̲ in the deep structure.

Now on your other question, comparing my work with what you are doing. I've followed your work with great interest. One of the principal differences I see here is that you are incorporating matters of probability, percentages, proportions, and so on, into the rules, that is the probability of use of something where you are comparing what happens when you move from the Panthers to the Jets and so on. Now to do this requires really greater damage to the theory; that is, it requires a greater theoretical justification.

In other words, I would consider myself a conservative compared to you. I would say that you are considerably further out than I am. I would like to develop what there is here and see how far one can go without making your more radical changes, in order to see whether they are absolutely necessary. It may very well be that I will find situations which I simply cannot handle by remaining with a binary-feature system, but this has not happened so far. If it does, I would probably have to incorporate something like this. Until then, I would consider the frequency with which a certain style is used to be temporarily a matter of performance rather than competence.

Labov: Well, I would like to see the binary-feature notion given every opportunity to develop, and I hope that you will try to apply them to a good body of speech. One of the trends I hope will not develop in sociolinguistics is one that we see every time a journal appears: theories are conceived on the basis of tiny fragments of data and published without any further work. I'm tremendously impressed with the wealth of knowledge that you and other Creolists have about the languages you've been working with and the speech community; I'd hate to see all of that reduced to a few anecdotes because it didn't fit into the current model for analysis.

Charles Scott, The University of Wisconsin: My comment has been partially anticipated here. It strikes me that it's one thing to talk about optional stylistic features and to talk about the possibility of introducing options either in transformational rules or, more recently, introducing these options as features in the base. This is one kind of thing, I think. The other kind of thing is the question as to how these options, whether they are in transformational rules or as features in the base, are triggered in the first place. And I am wondering here just how your presentation, aside from the formalization procedures by means of the binary-feature notion and so forth, differs significantly, say, from Firthian context of situation or even perhaps from Pike's notion of language distributed in nonverbal matrices, language in relation to a unified theory of the structure of human behavior, and what have you. In other words, you've got to have, somewhere along the line, some set of features, whether they are established binarily or not, that somehow trigger the selection of options in the grammar.

DeCamp: The question that you are asking is essentially the question of what is it that urges us to produce sentences of any given type at all; that is, what is it that causes us to ask a question instead of making a statement, what causes us to make a sentence imperative rather than interrogative? The difficulty on this is that there is no such thing as a semantic theory—that is, a really viable one; there really never has been one. People have always talked about semantics since the Greeks, and we simply don't have a semantics. What we have is a whole lot of theories, is some place where everyone has said, 'Well, now, if and when we ever get semantics, this is where we will plug it in.' This is what it will hang on to in the theory.

I feel that by getting all of these materials, these dimensions of stylistic as well as simply extensional meanings as eraser, blackboard, and table and so on, getting these all into the same component of a grammar, at least enables us to deal with these things to the extent that we can talk about what these meanings are.

Now a stylistic shift is triggered obviously by something that goes on outside in the real world. That is, a third person enters the room or somebody leaves the room. I mean, you have these two little kids being tape-recorded and so on. Alright, here is this nice, big, friendly white interrogator that Bill was talking about who has been talking with him; and suddenly he leaves and walks out of the room. This is an observational fact which obviously triggers something. In a sense, that is the meaning of that stylistic shift in these kids. Just as the fact that we are here and I am here in the presence of an eraser and I talk about the eraser on the table. Somehow the thing that is here, and the fact that it is within my grasp, is a portion of that meaning.

Now we don't understand how all that works, but I would say that doing it this way at least we would be able to say that whatever happens stylistically we would know that we could at least put it on the same kind of basis that we could talk about things like erasers and blackboards.

SUBJECTIVE JUDGMENTS IN SOCIOLINGUISTIC ANALYSIS

ROGER W. SHUY

Center for Applied Linguistics

Abstract. Recent research into the sociolinguistic factors involved in speech identification and attitudes has revealed several things which bear on certain aspects of sociolinguistic theory. In this report it will be observed that linguists may successfully utilize peoples' subjective reactions to language data to support or supplement the more usual kind of data—the actual speech of informants. The study of such subjective reactions also yields further information on the controversy about how 'Negro speech' may be conceived and whether or not it exists. Thirdly, such research provides insights into the question of how standard and nonstandard varieties of English may be defined and discussed.

In general, this paper is a report on a recently completed project of the Sociolinguistics Program at the Center for Applied Linguistics (CAL). I will be concerned with several of the broad aspects of this project which bear on certain aspects of sociolinguistic theory. Specifically I will address myself to the issues of (1) how objective language data and subjective responses to such data are mutually supportive, (2) the controversy over whether or not there is such a thing as Negro speech, (3) the notion of social markedness, and (4) ways of compensating for the absence of a vocabulary of socially meaningful terms with which the general public can evaluate speech.

Although some of the earliest work which attempted to account for social variation in American speech was done by the Linguistic Atlas researchers, it was not until the present decade that linguists have shown concern for improving on the subjective impressions of Atlas fieldworkers, the vagueness of their social taxonomies as well as the errors of validity and reliability noted by Pickford in her 1956 criticisms of Atlas procedures. Recent concern for using a verifiable sociological model for rating the social status of informants is a relatively new aspect of sociolinguistic research, thanks primarily to the rigor of anthropologists (especially Gumperz, Hymes, and Bright) in differentiating the social groups to which they were relating linguistic variables.

The earliest work which considered social variation in American speech is found in the <u>Linguistic Atlas of U. S. and Canada</u> (Kurath, et al. 1939). Current research has attempted to deal with the methodological weaknesses of the <u>Atlas</u> such as (1) the vagueness and subjectivity of the Atlas fieldworkers' social taxonomies and (2) the errors of validity and reliability of their procedures (Pickford 1956).

Among linguists it is clearly the work of Labov that has best combined the insights of both sociology and linguistics. In his study of the social stratification of New York speech he utilized sociologically valid sampling procedures, he devised quantitative measurements of linguistic variables, he elicited speech in different contextual styles, and he explained some of the features which linguists frequently have dismissed as free variations as systematically correlated with social differences. The research of the Sociolinguistics Program at CAL, with its antecedents in the Detroit research formerly at Michigan State University, has incorporated many of the insights of all of its predecessors and, it is hoped, has launched out into some new directions as well. One of these directions, as this paper will bear out, is in the relationship between subjects' 'objective language data' and their subjective reactions to language data and concepts.

Objective language and social stratification

Although linguists have not been known, in recent years, to join linguistic forms with social context, there is a rather strong current movement to expand the focus on linguistic form in isolation (idealized language) to linguistic form in social context (realistic language). In an effort to set the linguistic data in appropriate sociological contexts, the staff of the Detroit Dialect Study used a modified Hollingshead scale to assign a social number to each person in that city (Shuy, Wolfram, and Riley 1968). The spectrum of assigned social status numbers, which ranged from the highest, 20, to the lowest, 134, was then arbitrarily quartiled.

Having established a tentative social population, the next task was to extract relevant linguistic data from the some 700 tape-recorded, hour-long interviews of randomly selected Detroit residents and to display some of these data with the social classes in which they occurred. Figures noting such displays are found in Shuy, Wolfram, and Riley (1967) and in Wolfram (1969). Figure 1, modified from Shuy, Wolfram, and Riley (1967) is illustrative of these displays.

FIGURE 1. Multiple Negation: Social Stratification

Percentage	UM	LM	UW	LW
100				
90				
80				
70				
60				
50				
40				
30				
20				
10				
0	1.7	11.1	38.1	70.6
Social Status Rank	20–49	50–79	80–109	110–134

For each informant all instances of negatives co-occurring with indefinites were tabulated. This procedure gave a total number of potential occurrences for multiple negation. From this total the number of actual occurrences of multiple negation was tabulated. The percentage of actual multiple negatives in relation to potential multiple negatives was then computed (see Figure 1).

Similarly, Wolfram has tabulated the relative absence of the final member of word final monomorphemic consonant clusters (e.g. test, mask, mind, cold, etc.) among Detroit Negroes by social class (Wolfram 1969). The data are presented in Figure 2.

FIGURE 2. Absence of final cluster member in Monomorphemic
clusters, Negroes

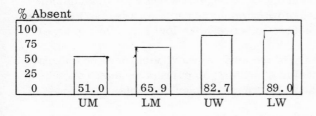

% Absent

100				
75				
50				
25				
0	51.0	65.9	82.7	89.0
	UM	LM	UW	LW

From Figures 1 and 2 our techniques of discovering relative frequencies should be clear. Equally clear should be the reasons underlying our belief that the major linguistic differences across social class are not a matter of the presence versus absence of a feature as much as the relative frequencies of their distributions. Further research may reveal, in addition, other structural differences across dialects relating, no doubt, to such things as different ordering of rules between social dialects.

Although the identification of social status was difficult to achieve, identification of race was relatively easy. Because of the nature of unequal opportunity in this country, it would be unfair to compare all Negro speech with all white speech, irrespective of at least the dimension of social status. Consequently Figure 3 displays both race and SES simultaneously. Figure 3 shows the percentage of noun phrases in which potential (grammatically possible) occurrences of pronominal apposition (e.g. 'me and my brother, we went to the park') were realized.

FIGURE 3.   Pronominal apposition

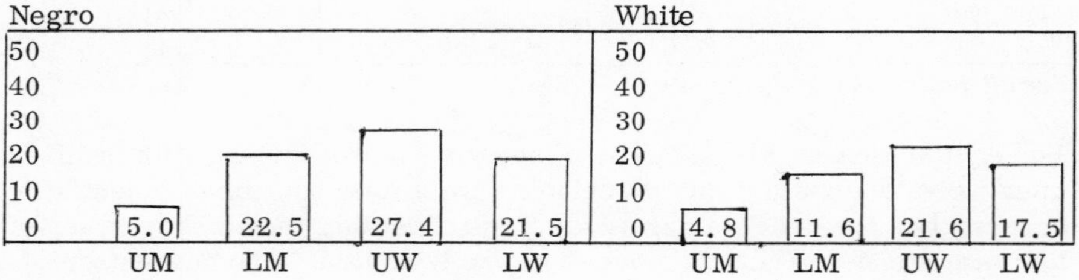

Of particular interest with respect to the racial contrast in the use of pronominal apposition is the point at which greatest contrast exists, at the margins of the lower middle class, and that whites apparently become more sensitive to this index than do blacks. One further observes that whereas multiple negation is a grammatical index for which rather high sensitivity exists (due largely to the schoolrooms of America), pronominal apposition does not seem to share this high sensitivity as an index of social stratification. It does seem to contrast racially, however, in that lower middle class Negroes sharply contrast with upper middle class Negroes in their use of pronominal apposition, whereas the sharp contrast among white speakers is between the lower middle and upper working classes.

With this brief summary of the kinds of work being done on objective language data, let us turn for a moment, to current research on subjective reactions to language data and language concepts.

Subjective reactions to language data and concepts

It is not uncommon for listeners to assign class status and ethnic identification of individuals on the basis of their spoken language (Putnam and O'Hern 1955, Lambert et al. 1960, Harms 1961, Berlin 1962, Nader 1962, Buck 1968). This is especially true in terms of identification of Negro and white speakers. Although we continually make assumptions about individuals from the manner in which they express themselves, there is very little systematic research concerning the psychosocial and linguistic variables which play a role for the listener in the identification process.

William Labov's pioneering efforts in the field provided a useful empirical model for further research (Labov 1967). Working with five phonological features, Labov found that the subjective reactions of his subjects were inarticulate and below the level of conscious awareness (Labov 1967: 405). He found that there is no vocabulary of socially meaningful terms with which the subjects could evaluate speech and that although New Yorkers often held strong views about the speech of their city, only a few could cite specific words, sounds, or phrases which adequately characterized what they meant. Labov's exploratory work revealed that for subjective reaction tests, natural utterances of native speakers were superior to synthetic representations made by experimenters.

It is not our purpose here to summarize the results of past research in this area. What is of major concern is that our research into subjective reaction revealed patterns quite similar to those yielded by our objective language data.

How the subjective data were gathered

The Detroit study (Shuy, Baratz, and Wolfram, 'Sociolinguistic Factors in Speech Identification' NIMH, Project No. MH 15048-01) used a tape stimulus which included 21 discourses of between 20 and 30 seconds each and 9 shorter discourses which were extracted from the speech samples of the longer utterances. The speakers were selected from the corpus of the Detroit Dialect Study (Shuy, Wolfram, and Riley 1968, Wolfram 1969). All speech samples were taken from tapes of adult male, Detroit residents between the ages of 30 and 55. Three speakers represented each of the upper middle, lower middle, upper working, and lower working classes of the Detroit Negro population. Also included were three speakers in each of the upper middle, lower middle, and upper working classes of the Detroit whites.

The judges, or respondents to the tape stimulus, were 620 Detroit residents; 286 were sixth graders, 170 were eleventh graders, and 164 were adults. 256 were Negroes and 364 were whites. 305 were male and 315 female. In terms of social class, 167 were upper middle, 173 lower middle, 140 upper working, and 140 lower working class.

One of the judges' tasks was to listen to the tape, then respond to several seven-point semantic differential scales using polar adjectives:

awkward ___:___:___:___:___:___:___ graceful
relaxed ___:___:___:___:___:___:___ tense
formal ___:___:___:___:___:___:___ informal
thin ___:___:___:___:___:___:___ thick
correct ___:___:___:___:___:___:___ incorrect

The responses were then quantified, using slot one as 1, slot two as 2, and so on. Table 1 displays some of the response means to the correct-incorrect scale.

TABLE 1. Response means to semantic differential
Correct-Incorrect Scale

Male and female respondents	Negro stimuli				White stimuli		
	UM	LM	UW	LW	UM	LM	UW
Children	3.26	4.27	4.44	5.32	2.70	3.34	4.71
Teen-agers	3.13	4.46	4.87	5.97	2.52	3.44	5.35
Adults	3.13	4.01	4.93	5.95	2.29	3.55	5.53
Negroes	3.02	4.25	4.81	5.88	2.65	3.33	5.03
Whites	3.31	4.28	4.64	5.57	2.44	3.51	5.24
All subjects	3.18	4.27	4.72	5.71	2.53	3.43	5.15

One may recall that the objective data for Detroit as shown in Figure 3 demonstrate that there is very little difference between the speech of UM and LM whites. But there is a clear demarcation between the speech of LM Negroes and UM Negroes. Some of the subjective reactions as revealed in our research indicate that respondents similarly have a difficult time differentiating between UM and LM whites, but generally distinguish between LM and UW, reflecting the contour breaks of the objective data shown in Figure 3 (see Table 1).

For the Negro judges, the subjective reactions to the SES of the speaker on the correct-incorrect scale indicates that UM is regarded quite different from LM and UW, which are considered quite similar. UM is considered relatively neutral, but LM and UW are considered somewhat incorrect. In the actual taped speech samples, UM and LM are differentiated from each other by phonological features, and UM and LM are differentiated from UW and LW on the basis of both phonology and grammar. It is therefore interesting to note that in the subjective reactions UM are distinguished from LM and UW, which were seen as quite similar. Thus the grammatical differences between LM and UW were apparently overlooked in favor of the phonological features differentiating UM and LM. On this basis, one may suggest that a Negro speaker who retains certain phonological features indicating racial identity will be considered on the same level with the speaker having stigmatized grammatical and phonological features.

Although the similarities of the social stratification revealed by objective language data and subjective responses to these language data are limited here in quantity, let it be known that other examples may also be found. Our research gives clear indication that subjective language data can be used to great advantage in linguistic studies of this sort and that the researcher may get as much mileage out of a speaker's receptive behavior as from his sending functions.

The useful correlation of objective and subjective language data was by no means the only issue with implications for current sociolinguistic theory. From this recent research we may also gain insights into the current controversy over whether or not there is something called Negro Speech, the nature of social markedness, the ability of the general public to make judgments about social dialects and the tools for measuring these responses to taped stimuli.

The issue of Negro Speech

There has been considerable discussion among linguists as to whether or not it is possible to characterize a kind of speech as Negro Speech or, more recently, Black English. There are those who say that there is essentially no difference between the English used by Negroes and whites in certain parts of the South. Others say that there are clear differences in the South which contrast a creole origin of the speech of Negroes to the European origin of the whites. Still other linguists are less interested in the historical origins but point to synchronic differences between Negro and white speech. Our research deals with the synchronic situation without ruling out this possibility of diachronic influences on the synchronic description.

It is clear from our results that the speech of Negroes and whites is consistently distinguished in Detroit, since the judges correctly identified Negroes 80% of the time and white speakers 81.2% of the time from as little as 20 to 30 seconds of continuous speech. Furthermore, in nine short stimuli of from three to five seconds each, Negro speakers were identified correctly 70.1% of the time and whites 67.3% of the time.

What is particularly interesting about this information is that Negro judges did only slightly better than whites in identifying Negroes (3.8%), and whites did only slightly better than Negroes in judging whites (7.2%). Age does not particularly increase ability to determine the race of a speaker. Children, teenagers, and adults vary only 2.4% in their ability to identify Negro speakers. The socioeconomic status of the listener-judges also seemed relatively unimportant in identifying Negro speakers. Upper middle, lower middle, upper working, and lower working groups varied only 2.3% in identifying Negroes. Upper middle class judges are only slightly better than the other socioeconomic groups in identifying

white speakers, but the total range of variation is only 10.4% between
all four groups of judges in identifying whites.

From these data, it seems relatively clear that Detroiters of all
ages do extremely well in identifying the race of the speaker. Frequently it had been suggested that there is no such thing as Negro Speech
and that it is unfair to speak to the Negro nonstandard English. The evidence of this research makes it rather clear that in Detroit, regardless
of the age, race, sex, or socioeconomic status of the listener, Negro
identity of taped speakers can be made accurately from a minimum of
74.4% (adult white females) to a maximum of 86.2% (adult Negro females)
of the time. From this it appears that there is a clear polarization in
Detroit (and probably elsewhere) which enables residents there to think
accurately along the lines of race with respect to the speech of their city.
One might suggest that further research must now determine the extent
to which Southern whites and Negroes can identify the race of speakers.

The issue of social markedness

The most significant results of our research into the ability of a
listener to correctly identify the socioeconomic status of Detroiters is
that the lower the socioeconomic status the more accurate the identifi-
cations. All respondents identified upper middle class speakers accurately only 29.6% of the time, lower middle class speakers 31.8% of the
time, upper working class speakers 40.8% of the time, and lower working class speakers a whopping 60.8% of the time.

When the identification of both race and socioeconomic status of the
taped recorded speakers are examined, it is clear that the lower the
socioeconomic status, the more accurately Negroes are identified;
whereas for whites, the higher the socioeconomic status the more accurately they are identified. Of particular interest here is the fact that
Negro upper middle class speakers were identified accurately by Negroes 17.8% and by whites only 8.2%. If UM Negroes were excluded
from the tape stimulus, no doubt the overall accuracy of identification
would increase from 80% to 95% or so.

These data have several important things to say to students of language. It seems clear, for example, that the most outstanding fact in
the differentiation of social dialects in Detroit is the presence of 'stigmatized' grammatical and phonological features in the speech of lower
SES groups. The speech of the middle class is typified by the absence
of these features. This is not to say that there are no prestige features
in the speech of middle class informants. Indeed, objective research
(Fasold 1968) does indicate the presence of certain prestigious forms.
But since the current study reveals that it is easier to accurately identify a lower class than a middle class speaker, one can conclude that
prestige features of the middle class are not nearly as obtrusive as the

stigmatized features of the working class. One may say that the speech of the working class seems to be socially marked and the speech of the middle class socially unmarked.

It is of further interest to note the social markedness of speech clusters in different ways across race. Social markedness of Negro Speech is distributed so that N UM speakers are distinguished (subjectively and objectively) from N UM, UW, and LW; and N LM and UW speakers are similarly distinguished from LW. UM and LM white speakers, on the other hand, are clearly distinguished from UW.

The issue of popular judgments regarding dialects

In a search for a terminology by which language judgments can be made meaningfully by laymen, the semantic differential scale which was used for five speech concepts (Detroit Speech, Negro Speech, White Southern Speech, British Speech, and Standard Speech) proved interesting though not always useful. Detroiters of all types seem rather neutral about the speech of their city. Unlike some cities, such as New York, there appears to be no distinct entity conceived of as Detroit Speech by Detroiters. On the other hand, it is worth noting that the higher the SES of the judge, the higher he values British Speech. This concept, however, is neutral or less valuable to lower SES groups.

These data support previous research in which it was suggested that Negroes regarded white Southern Speech more negatively than did whites, and whites regarded Negro Speech more perjoratively than did Negroes (Lambert 1960). What is of more interest, however, is that whites saw less difference between Southern Speech and Negro Speech than did Negroes. Negroes view Negro Speech and Detroit Speech about the same; whereas whites see Negro Speech and Detroit Speech as rather distinct. Since both Negroes and whites assign about the same values to Detroit Speech, this suggests that Negroes consider their speech patterns as Detroit Speech even though whites distinguish Negro Speech from Detroit Speech.

This exploration into subjective reactions to speech concepts may be regarded as an interesting step toward understanding a broader spectrum of language in society than is provided by either the objective use of language or the judgmental reactions from a tape recorded stimulus. Further investigation into other speech concepts is in order, and cross-sectional studies of such concepts as Negro Speech may be quite revealing of a changing social climate.

Using the semantic differential scale

On the basis of this exploratory use of the semantic differential scale in response to speech samples and language concepts, it is clear

that this can be a useful tool to compensate for the general inarticulate-
ness of the public in evaluating speech. On the correct-incorrect scale
which accompanied the speech samples, for example, the judgments of
all subjects stratify quite neatly according to socioeconomic status of
the speaker: UM $\overline{M}$ = 2.86, LM $\overline{M}$ = 3.85, UW $\overline{M}$ = 4.93, LW $\overline{M}$ = 5.71.

It appears that semantic differential responses to speech samples
stratify in ways that would suggest value judgments being placed on
those linguistic features which are used to identify race and SES. This
reaction is also seen in response to other scales. Some scales are apparently more meaningful to judges concerning their subjective reaction
to language concepts. For example, it appears that generally the thick-
thin scale does not elicit this kind of stratification. It would appear that
further research might suggest scales that are more relevant to individuals' judgments concerning language.

Our pretesting indicated that the semantic differential response to
speech samples could not be used in this experiment with working class
respondents without interfering with their performance on the other
tasks presented. However, middle class sixth grade children use the
semantic differential scale as well as eleventh graders or adults. The
responses of sixth grade children were not essentially different from
other subjects on the correct-incorrect, graceful-awkward, tense-
relaxed or thick-thin scales. There is adequate evidence here to suggest that the semantic differential scale can be used with children as
early as the sixth grade in language judgment experiments.

When the semantic differential scale was used in connection with
speech concepts, sixth graders seemed to be as competent as teenagers
on the evaluative scales; but they responded differently on the presumed
potency scales. This suggests that the technique can be useful with sixth
grade children as long as evaluative scales are used.

In summary, this brief report has called attention to a type of research on language which holds considerable promise: (1) for supple-
menting information obtainable through objective speech samples (note
the supportive nature of objective language data and subjective responses to such data), (2) for enlarging our knowledge of public con-
ceptions of social speech communities (such as Negro Speech), (3) for
providing insights into the nature of how standard and nonstandard varieties of English may be discussed (social markedness), and (4) for
discovering a vocabulary, or technique, with which laymen's evaluations and attitudes toward language may be observed.

REFERENCES

Berlin, C. I., A. Dill, L. Eisenberg, and S. Frank. Class and Race
    Effects on the Intelligibility of Monosyllables. Baltimore, Maryland:
    The John Hopkins Medical Institutions.

Buck, Joyce F. 1968. The Effects of Negro and White Dialectal Variations upon Attitudes of College Students. Speech Monographs,
Volume XXXV, No. 2, June.

Harms, L. S. 1961. Listener Judgments of Status Cues in Speech.
Quarterly Journal of Speech, XLVII, 164-168, April.

Kurath, Hans. 1954. Handbook of the Linguistic Geography of New
England. American Council of Learned Societies. Menasha, Wisconsin: George Banta Publishing Company.

Labov, William. 1966. The Social Stratification of English in New
York City. Washington, D. C.: Center for Applied Linguistics.

Lambert, Wallace E., R. C. Hodgson, R. C. Gardner, and S. Fillen-
baum. 1960. Evaluational Reactions to Spoken Language. Journal
of Abnormal and Social Psychology.

Nader, Laura. 1962. A Note on Attitudes and the Use of Language.
Anthropological Linguistics, Florence M. Vogelin, Editor: Volume
IV.

Pickford, Glenna Ruth. 1956. American Linguistic Geography: A Sociological Appraisal. Word 12: 211-235.

Putnam, George N. and Edna M. O'Hern. 1955. The Status Significance of an Isolated Urban Dialect. Language 34, No. 4, Part 2.

Shuy, R. W., Joan C. Baratz, and Walter A. Wolfram. 1969. Sociolinguistic Factors in Speech Identification. Research Project No.
MH 15048-01. Center for Applied Linguistics.

_____, Walter Wolfram, and William K. Riley. 1967. Linguistic Cor-
relates of Social Stratification in Detroit Speech. Cooperative Research Project No. 6-1347. East Lansing, Michigan: Michigan
State University.

Wolfram, Walter A. 1969. A Sociolinguistic Description of Detroit
Negro Speech. Washington, D. C.: Center for Applied Linguistics.

DISCUSSION

Ralph Fasold, Center for Applied Linguistics: I think that the data
that Dr. Shuy has just presented will provide the sort of justification
which we have for using terms like Negro Nonstandard English, Black
English, or Negro Dialect; that is, that the Detroit respondents were
so much better at identifying the race of a person by his speech in the
case of the lower socioeconomic classes. The reason for this is that
the upper socioeconomic classes, of course, spoke English in much the
same way that the same class of white speakers spoke English. So what
this means is that, while not all Negroes speak Black English, practically everybody who speaks Black English is Negro. So, there is mu-

tually exclusive distribution which goes one way but not the other; and on this basis you can justify this sort of terminology.

William Labov, Columbia University: I think it is extraordinary how many rich conclusions Dr. Shuy was able to draw from this data. I think that it is also evident from his tables that Negroes and whites show an extraordinary agreement in their judgments, which runs across social classes too. This is an example of sharp stratification in behavior corresponding to unanimity in judgments about speech. But I wonder if you would comment on the other reverse aspect of the question: whether people are able to identify black speakers. While we want to be able to say that there is such a thing as Nonstandard Negro English, or Black English, the racial applications of the term are always in some people's minds. If anybody is under the impression that we are dealing with a genetic characteristic, you have clearly disproved that too. In our own 'Family Background' tests in Harlem, we used really tough cases: negroes raised in white communities, and the other way around. People showed very little ability to identify their original ethnic group. If you take the 67% success figure that you have, that shows that people were wrong 33% of the time.

Shuy: I would like to observe here that there are any number of things that might be done in addition to what was done here. Joan Baratz, Walter Wolfram, and I are not terribly happy with the fact that we have had to stop with this particular phase. It would be fascinating, as it has been pointed out to me before, and as I indicated in the paper, to get some white Southerners into the sample and see what happens to the judgments at this point. On the other hand, in the tape stimulus we could have included a little white girl who lives as a minority in a black community whose speech could have caused the results to go in a different direction. She is not a completely Black English speaker, as Ralph Fasold has indicated; but enough of the features would be interpreted, I think, as Black to cause her to be identified in that way. And concluding a report of this sort leaves you always with an unsatisfied empty feeling. There are many other things that need to be done at this point. We used only adult males, for example; and it would have been nice to find out how Detroiters view the speech of females, children, and many other variables.

Joan Baratz, Education Study Center: My one reaction relates also to what Professor DeCamp said before about borrowing concepts and methodologies from other disciplines and putting them into the linguistics discipline. One of the things that has been borrowed by sociolinguistics is a sophisticated terminology of social stratification, including labels which assign individuals to various social classes. However, in taking this framework for designating informant social-class status, they have neglected to take the necessary procedures for analyzing the numerical data which result from such classifications.

My one concern about much of the data from the New York, Detroit, and Washington studies is: What does such-and-such number mean? Indeed, what does a 'mean' mean—since these numbers presented here are 'means'? Linguists tend to presume that the numerical units 2.6 and 3.3 are statistically the same, since they look like they should be the same. But 5 next to 3.3 looks like it should be different. Yet, we really have no way of knowing that that is so from the manner in which this data is presented. Perhaps it is indeed so, though it may turn out that 3.3 is different from 5 statistically. It may also turn out that 2.6 is different from 3.3. So we really have to find out more about what these 'means' mean before we can make sure whether there is or is not a difference—especially so, when the examples are in terms of the percentages that were discussed Friday night, yesterday, and to-day. Where you can look at the numbers and say, 'Gee, it seems that this data must be significant; there appears to be a "sharp vs. weak" delineation that is ethnically matched. Although one set of figures varies only from 5.5%-15% and the other from 2%-33%, they may both be significant; and they may both delineate social class groups within and between ethnicity.'

David DeCamp, the University of Texas at Austin: I am delighted to hear that other people are working with the Osgood semantic differential in matters of this sort. It may be of interest that one of my graduate students at Texas, Mr. Scott Baird, just finished his dissertation which will be the first portion of a probable two-part treatment of listener reactions across racial lines and other social lines. Not all the answers are available as yet, because this is only a part of it. For instance, we only had one racial match; that is, so far we have only differential reactions of white listener subjects to Negro Speech. The other combinations are not in.

There is one point, however, which we have established. By 'we' I mean Baird, Dr. Walton Stolz, and myself. What we used as our variables were a series of features which are widely recognized; and the teachers all talk about them as being the shibboleths of Black English. That is, teachers of black children all pointed out these black features as the very ones which they are dealing with as usage matters. Like whether you have porch or poach for porch; this kind of thing, that is supposed to be the stereotype shibboleth differentiating different kinds of black speech. Listener subjects, when presented these as minimal pairs on tape and asked to distinguish which member of the pair was preferable, which was better English, consistently identified the standard forms and marked them higher.

When we presented the subjects with tapes, however, in which we had all possible combinations (ranging from all black features included down to a matter of not a single one of them included), which should have then given a whole range from relatively high evaluation to a low evaluation, we turned up with a surprising result. When faced with the Osgood semantic differential, virtually all of them—well, 92-93%—recognized the speakers as Negro. Among all of those who did so recognize the race of the speaker, the prejudicial reaction overrode all other responses. What came out from all these people was a differential scale which showed that the woman speaking was loyal but not terribly reliable, that she was intelligent and kind. In other words, the entire bit of the stereotype, the white stereotype of the American Negro, completely short-circuited, overloaded the semantic differential. Subjects could distinguish social level on the basis of just a single pair of sentences; yet when given the Osgood differential to work with, these stereotype attitudes just completely overrode it.

A SECOND DIALECT IS NOT A FOREIGN LANGUAGE

VIRGINIA F. ALLEN

Temple University

Abstract. When newspaper headlines proclaim 'English to be taught as Foreign Language to Negroes', it is time to slow down and try to explain what we mean. True, students whose home dialect is a nonstandard variety of English have problems in common with those for whom English is a foreign language. (Some of these common problems are spelled out.) But significant differences between second-language and second-dialect students must be noted. Procedures devised for speakers of Hawaiian pidgin and for inner city schools are described.

ENGLISH A FOREIGN LANGUAGE TO NEGROES, a recent newspaper headline declares. Below the headline there is a description of a second-dialect program which, according to the report, centers around the use of tape recorders in a laboratory. There the students hear and repeat material originally intended for foreigners because, says the article, English to Negroes is 'virtually a foreign language.'

News stories like this one are turning up all too frequently in the public press. It is disturbing to wonder how the students involved (and other members of their ethnic group) feel about such articles. Surely few can feel elated over finding themselves treated not even as second-class citizens, but as foreigners in their own native land.

Of course most writers of such reports mean no harm. They simply have done what journalists have done since time immemorial—failed to get all the facts quite right. It is up to us in the language teaching profession to try to set the record straight.

Misinterpretations of present trends in second-dialect teaching are of particular concern to me, because I am partly responsible for setting the trends, having initiated correspondence with the Office of Education which led to the funding, in 1961, of San-su Lin's Claflin Project in South Carolina. It was through working with Claflin students and their teachers that important differences between second-dialect teaching and foreign-language teaching began to be clarified for me. Since then, the distinctions and the parallels have become clearer, thanks to the work of many colleagues, and to my own experience with Harlem teachers, gang leaders in North Philadelphia, and speakers of Pidgin in Hawaii. There is still a great deal more to be learned than any of us will ever learn. But before misunderstandings become compounded, it would be well to review some of the observations we have made so far with regard to second-dialect learning vis-à-vis the learning of a foreign language.

What do people mean when they say that present-day approaches to the teaching of Standard English to speakers of other dialects have much in common with modern approaches to foreign language teaching, especially the teaching of English as a foreign language? Five points of similarity stand out:

(1) Both foreign-language programs and second-dialect programs are based on a contrastive analysis of the target language (or dialect) and the students' home language (or dialect). And the 'target' chosen for analysis is not the literary form of the language, nor the idealized language prescribed by the older grammar textbooks, but rather the 'language of educated ease'.

(2) Both foreign-language programs and second-dialect programs view the target language and the students' home language as equally valid systems of communication in their own respective orbits. The target language is not considered 'better'; the students' vernacular is not considered 'faulty'.

(3) Both programs tend to be structure-centered. That is, major attention is given to the grammatical structure of the target language or dialect, not to the vocabulary.

(4) In both second-dialect classes and foreign-language classes, the linguistic system of the target is presented to the student in a series of small steps, each step rising out of the one before.

(5) Both programs emphasize habit-formation. Success is measured in terms of the students' oral fluency in handling the language patterns that are habitual among native speakers of the target language or dialect. Achievement is not measured by the students' ability to recite rules or definitions, or to diagram sentences, or to label parts of speech.

In these five ways, among others, second-dialect programs have more in common with foreign-language programs than with 'English', as that subject is traditionally conceived. There are also similarities apart from general principles and policies—similarities in classroom techniques. In both second-dialect and foreign-language teaching, standard procedures include mimicry, repetition, and substitution. That is, the students first hear, then say, a number of utterances which repeatedly exemplify the linguistic point featured in the day's lesson. The students then construct similar sentences which 'fit the pattern', but they replace some or all of the words in the 'model' with words of their own choosing.

It can readily be seen, then, that current programs for teaching Standard English to speakers of other dialects do significantly resemble modern programs for teaching foreign languages, or for teaching English to speakers of other languages.

The fact remains, however, that a second dialect is not a foreign language. To the inner city American, to the Hawaiian child who speaks Pidgin English with his playmates, to the boy on a Navajo reservation who uses Boarding School English with his peers, to anyone who uses English of any sort for everyday communication, English is not a foreign language. Teachers in second-dialect programs had better remember that.

Because second-dialect learners are not foreign-language learners, procedures that have proved generally acceptable in teaching English as a foreign language cannot be carried over into a second-dialect situation without modification.

Take for example the mimicry-repetition-substitution sequence previously mentioned. Since English is not a foreign language for second-dialect students, and since most second-dialect students have already achieved passive dialectalism (they can respond appropriately to grammatical signals employed by standard dialect speakers, even though they do not consistently use those signals themselves), many members of a second-dialect class may need to be convinced of the need for mimicry-repetition-substitution exercises on a given grammatical feature. Until the student has recognized that he individually is not yet ready to control a specific linguistic feature on the level of oral production, many teachers find that mimicry, repetition, and substitution accomplish practically nothing. The student has to know that a problem exists, for him, before he can give due attention to an exercise designed to solve that problem.

There is value in an old pedagogical precept: never start a drill until the need for that drill has been demonstrated. As far as second-dialect teaching is concerned, it is not enough for the need to be perceived by the teacher: it must be perceived by the individual student himself.

Suppose the teacher has decided that most members of a class need practice on the preterit ending -ed, as in waited, wanted, needed, landed, etc., because those students seem to be saying things like We wait a long time yesterday and He need a doctor last night. Before

the class is asked to hear and repeat a string of sentences in which the
-ed inflection occurs, two or three minutes ought to be invested in
finding out just which students need that sort of drill, through an exercise that makes each of those students aware of his need. A simple
means is the following:

The teacher writes on the chalkboard: Every day we wait around.
Next the teacher announces: 'I'm going to keep changing Every day to
some other time expression, like Yesterday, or Last week, or Every
morning, or Three days ago. Depending on which time expression I
say, you'll finish the sentence by saying either wait around or waited
around. We're going to work fast. I'll call on you one by one, and I
want you to finish the sentence immediately. There won't be time to
stop and think. Are you ready? All right, Every morning we . . . ,
Last Wednesday we . . . , A week ago we . . . , Every Tuesday we . . . ,
The summer before last we . . . ' (etc., etc. until each student's control over the -ed inflection in such phonetic environments has been
gauged).

Quick oral quizzes of this sort, which Robert L. Allen had long used
in his own teaching, worked well with the Claflin second-dialect students, who dubbed them 'pop tests'. The essence of a 'pop test' is
speed. The teacher must keep one mental foot in the present while
the other is in the future; he must be thinking ahead to the next 'trigger'
while noting the student's response to the preceding one. The students
must be required to respond instantly: a faltering response should be
interpreted as a sign the student needs further practice along mim-
mem-substitution lines (known as 'fluency drills' in some programs).
Naturally the responses should be individual, though half a minute of
choral work may come first, to set the pace. And of course the students should be called on in random order, so that no one will know
whose turn will come next.

A device like the 'pop test' also has its uses in advanced classes in
English as a Foreign Language, where an individual student may require proof of the gap between his receptive and productive skills. But
it is even more useful in second-dialect teaching. It helps supply the
kind of short-range motivation that is essential there. Once a student
has been made to notice that he has yet to achieve oral control over a
linguistic feature he thought he had mastered, he feels challenged to
prove that he can produce sentences of that kind after all.

In EFL programs inspired by the Michigan prototype, everything
possible has been done to protect the student from the risk of making
wrong choices. At the beginning of each lesson, the class is given a
model to hear and imitate. The substitutions that are later called for
involve relatively 'safe' areas of the sentence. 'Teaching before testing' is the slogan; accuracy before fluency is the aim. But a second-

dialect student is already fluent in his own brand of English; and sometimes he has to be tested before he can really be taught.

Of course the 'pop test' device is only a small piece of a big puzzle, a small answer to this big question: how can we enlist the student's interest in the language-learning enterprise? Here is where one finds the most crucial difference between second-language and second-dialect learning.

Teaching Burmese to a platoon of American paratroopers during World War II was not child's play, but at least it had some advantages: the paratroopers knew their survival might depend on their mastery of Burmese, and the Burmese language had what Jespersen has called 'the charm of the unknown'. These two advantages have also characterized many classes in English as a Foreign Language, classes for adults in particular. Generally, however, neither of these advantages can be enjoyed by a teacher of Standard English as a Second Dialect. One can expect to find inertia and even hostility when Standard English is being offered to young Americans, each of whom is understandably attached to some other dialect.

Some resourceful teachers have taken this into account, and have done something about it. They have decided that practice materials for the second-dialect student need to do more than merely put him through certain linguistic paces. They have observed that many students get little out of repeating a series of sentences like Susan lives in Memphis, My aunt gives piano lessons, Our school needs a new gym. Being human, students expect language to communicate something either edifying or entertaining. When all the words in a sentence sound familiar, yet add up to nothing worth saying, the exercise seems pointless to many in a second-dialect class. Moral: add another dimension to the pattern practice, a dimension calculated to make the exercise seem worthwhile from the students' point of view.

If, for instance, the students need practice on -s endings, some teachers engineer the repetition of third-singular verb forms within the context of a song or a game (for younger students) or (for older students) as a series of answers to vocabulary questions. Sample: 'Who can say what each of the following does? An undertaker; a pawn broker; a blood donor; a night watchman.' After it has been decided what each of these functionaries does, some of the resulting sentences with -s are repeated aloud. Chances are, they will arouse more interest than the ones about piano lessons and the new school gym.

If no one in the class knows what an undertaker does, the class can learn. However, many second-dialect students know far more words than they are credited with knowing. Hence this sort of exercise is better adapted to second-dialect learning than to foreign-language learning, where one cannot count on nearly the same familiarity with lexical items.

Practice materials that do something more than exemplify a linguistic point are being improvised by teachers in many parts of the country. Several other varieties could be mentioned, but for present purposes the message has already been spelled out: since second-dialect speakers have grown to expect English to <u>say</u> something, they lack patience with sentences that merely illustrate a point—especially if nothing has been done to make the student realize he, personally, needs to work on that point.

A second dialect is not a foreign language. We have been reviewing a few of the many implications of that fact. Mainly they have been implications related to classroom techniques. But there is something more important than any instructional device. That is the attitude of the teacher toward the students, toward the total learning situation in which teacher and students interact.

Obviously the teacher of Standard English as a Second Dialect stands in a very delicate relationship to the students in the class. The students need acceptance and approval; yet there comes a time when the teacher must let them know their English usage is not acceptable under all circumstances, must help them face certain disagreeable facts—the fact that they have yet to master the kind of English required for success in school, the fact that there are new speech habits to be acquired, the fact that important decisions may go against them if they do not learn another way to talk.

The student of English as a Foreign Language has already faced these facts. Though he may not like them, at least they are not in much danger of undermining his self-respect. Somehow the second-dialect student has to be kept secure in his own identity and self-esteem while learning to talk like somebody else. How is this to be done? Evidently it <u>can</u> be done; good teachers have always found ways of making changes in students without damaging them. The following trivial anecdote may suggest how.

Not long ago, two young college students were overheard discussing their courses. 'How are you doing in Creative Writing?' one of them asked.

'Just great!' was the enthusiastic reply. 'Today I got back a paper, and guess what he had written across the top of it. "<u>This</u> story is worth revising."!'

More than the foreign-language student, more than the native speaker of Standard English, the second-dialect student needs to know his teacher considers him truly 'worth revising'.

REFERENCES

Allen, Virginia F. 1967. Teaching standard English as a second dialect. Teachers College Record. 68, No. 5, 355-370.

Dacanay, Fe R. 1963. Techniques and procedures in second language teaching. Dobbs Ferry, New York: Oceana.

Finocchiaro, Mary. 1969. Teaching English as a second language. New York: Harper.

Jespersen, Otto. 1904. How to teach a foreign language. London: Allen and Unwin.

Lin, San-su C. 1965. Pattern practice in the teaching of standard English to students with a nonstandard dialect. New York: Teachers College Press.

Marckwardt, Albert H. 1968. Teaching English as a foreign language. Language Development: Selected Papers from a Ford Foundation Conference on the State of the Art. 15-31. New York: Ford Foundation.

DISCUSSION

Irwin Feigenbaum, Center for Applied Linguistics: I agree with you that there are many similarities; however, one point where English as a second language and standard English as a second dialect would be different is in the use of contrastive analysis. In an EFL program, we don't usually contrast the two language systems in class activities. In teaching standard English, one of our problems is that the two dialects may appear to be very, very similar. I would suggest many activities in which there is contrasting of standard and nonstandard pronunciation and grammar.

Another point: in discussing mimicry, repetition, and substitution, you said that several or many of the students would have to be convinced of the need for going through these three steps. I, too, must be convinced of the need for mimicry and repetition, since many of the differences—and I would guess the important differences—between the two dialects involved are in grammar. Repetition and mimicry wouldn't serve the purpose as well as some type of grammatical manipulation. There is another problem: my work in the D.C. schools has shown that the students don't like mimicry and repetition. They are hard to do because the students won't put up with them. Substitution, other types of grammatical work, and response activities would be more to the point.

V. F. Allen: Thank you. You've raised a very interesting point. First of all, you mentioned the use of contrastive analysis. I work with teachers; I try to make the point that what linguists have for us is a body of knowledge, some of which we apply directly in the classroom and the rest of which is good to know because it guides us in what we do, even though we may not use the data directly. I would say that contrastive analyses are certainly useful to the teacher in showing where the areas of special difficulty will be, and in suggesting reasons why the students have the difficulties that teachers observe. As for the student consciously contrasting the two dialects, it seems to me that the age of the student is rather crucial here. For older students, it may be best simply to come right to the heart of the matter and say: 'Here are two dialects we are working with; let us notice when we are using one and when we are using the other, and let's decide which situation requires which dialect.' For the younger children, I suppose one can get at it through role-playing and through game-style activities. We can use narrative and dramatic material involving prestige persons in which the children act out the roles of the queen, the princess, the prince, and so on, using the standard dialect.

Now, about the mimicry, repetition, and substitutions. All of those are helpful, and so is code-learning. It seems to me that both are really necessary, especially with older students. They do need 'cognitive code-learning'. They need to notice the mechanics of the standard dialect. It is helpful for them to discuss it and for the teacher to identify the components of the system. However, I would not discount the need for repetition or mimicry in mastering grammar patterns, because there is so much muscular coordination required here. The youngsters can have an intellectual grasp of the fact that they are supposed to put /-s/ or /-z/ or /-ɨz/ at the end of a certain word; but unless they have plenty of chances to do it themselves, through repeated oral practice, they are not likely to use it in communication situations. So I'd say that in second-dialect learning there is a need for what could be called 'fluency practice', though it needs to be put in the right perspective, and it cannot monopolize the programs.

William A. Stewart, Education Study Center: In a way, I suppose I am at least partly responsible for the use of the term 'foreign language teaching techniques for second dialect speakers.' Yet, I would like to argue against the term from one point of view that wasn't made explicit today by Mrs. Allen, but was made the other day by Mr. Labov. This was that part of the difficulty with the foreign language analogy is that those who believe in linguistic deficit in the Negro child take our statements as an indication that the children have no language. It isn't a question, in their minds, of standard English as a foreign dialect for someone who speaks a different dialect of English, but rather it is interpreted as standard English as a foreign language for a child who has no language at all. Thus it is that statements about the teaching of standard English as a foreign language, as made by the linguist, have been used to support the views of the deficit theorists, currently so popular among educators and spread around. From that point of view, I would argue it. In response to this situation, one could overcompensate in the direction of Mrs. Allen's warm, motherly approach by throwing the linguistic baby out with the psychological bath

water. Yet, I would like to keep looking for similarities between foreign-language learning and foreign-dialect learning, since similarities
obviously exist. (It seems to me particularly far-fetched to sweep things
like Hawaiian Pidgin English and Gullah under the 'variety of English'
rug.) Indeed, I would like to reinforce the suggestion which has been
made as to actually using nonstandard dialects side-by-side with standard English in the classroom.

Finally, Mrs. Allen was lamenting the fact that, in teaching English
as a second dialect, we don't have the 'charm of the unknown' that we
have so often in foreign language teaching. Yet, one of the most exciting aspects of second-dialect teaching is the growing awareness in the
students, not so much of the new dialect being taught, but rather of the
structural viability and historical legitimacy of their own nonstandard
dialect. Here, there is also the 'charm of the unknown.' It just so happens that what is known least about is the learner's native dialect, not
the one being formally taught.

V. F. Allen: I agree! The more we can stimulate the students' interest in language as something worth observing and mastering, the
less need there will be for mechanical drills.

Mary Grigsby, Emmanuel College, Boston: I'd like to make an observation about the entire meeting: and the first one is that I am outraged and insulted by this meeting. First of all, because you have the
audacity to determine Black Speech as being nonstandard. And I would
like to know why white people can determine for black people what is
standard and what is nonstandard. Secondly, I would like to point out
that there are no black people on any of these panels, except at the end
of the program on the last page—the old 'back of the bus' bit—there is
the mention of the Howard professor; and I wonder when black people
are going to be able to speak for themselves?

David DeCamp, The University of Texas at Austin: I was trying, at
the time you rose here, to get recognition to say much the same thing.
I am awfully pleased that you brought up this question of motivation.
The fact is that the child isn't convinced somehow that this is as important to him as, say, learning Burmese is to the paratrooper. But so
many people read into this an assumption that of course it really is just
as important; but the child is just too limited in his scope and perspective, and so on, to be able to see it.

I think the time has long passed when the white man has any ability
or justification for trying to tell the black man what he ought to do.
This has been going on for a long time. It has been done by those with
malevolent motives. It has been done by those with benevolent motives,
and the kindness can kill as well as the hate can. At any time any group

of individuals, the black teacher or the black student or the black student's parents, want help and have made their decision of what they wish to do, we have a moral obligation to give assistance in it. But to establish (unilaterally) programs on the simple assumption that, of course, what everyone wants to do is to somehow join this establishment and adapt absolutely and completely to the white man's English: we have no right to do this.

William A. Stewart: I would like to make two comments on the complaint of the young lady who spoke from the floor. The first concerns her assumption that, when linguists use a term like 'nonstandard' in reference to a particular linguistic system, it necessarily means that they themselves consider that linguistic system to be functionally inferior. This assumption is commonly made by non-linguists, but it is quite wrong. As used by sociolinguists, the term 'nonstandard' is a technical one, and simply indicates the investigator has found that the linguistic system referred to has limited social prestige (not among linguists, mind you, but among those who frequently come into contact with it). In the case of Negro dialect, it is striking how much even monodialectal speakers of it will agree with white, middle class speakers of standard English that the former is less prestigious than the latter. Both Labov's study of language attitudes in Harlem and Shuy's study of language attitudes among Detroit Negroes make this quite clear, and of course Negro attitudes toward the two forms of English are embodied in their own sociolinguistic terminology, which labels what linguists call nonstandard dialect as 'talkin' bad' and what linguists call standard English as 'talkin' proper'.

Secondly, I would like to point out that it has been primarily whites who have fought the battle to get Negro Speech studied, described, and accepted as legitimate language. (One notable exception was, of course, Lorenzo Dow Turner. But his espousal of the generally unpopular thesis that Negro Speech showed African influences, and his use of linguistic techniques of mixed quality to prove that thesis, led to widespread rejection of possible implications of his work on Gullah for Negro dialect in general. The other exception has been Beryl Bailey, but it is probably no accident that she is a Jamaican and a creolist.) Recently, I had occasion to track down all the master's theses and doctoral dissertations which have been done on Negro dialect over the years. Surprisingly (if one accepts the young lady's implication that Negro dialect has been generally accepted as worthy by Negroes and downgraded by whites), they turned out to be a monopoly of predominantly white universities. And at such Negro universities as Fisk and Howard, one finds a striking silence on the subject. Now, I ask this: If Negroes have generally refused to study, describe, and defend Negro dialect, then who would have done it if whites hadn't?

Perhaps this white preponderance in Negro-dialect studies is merely the tail end of an older phase, in which the objective study of Negro dialect by Negroes was stultified by self-deprecation. Perhaps, now, negroes will begin to take up the study of Negro language and culture in greater numbers. The combination of their in-group insights with scientific objectivity could certainly produce some exciting results. But I warn the young lady that I for one will not stand silently by if militant nonlinguists try to distort the issue of Negro dialect (which has involved whites and Negroes against whites and Negroes) in order to use it as a phony ploy in political confrontations.

Subsequent written comment by William A. Stewart: After the session in which the foregoing comments were made, I was informed that the young lady who initiated the exchange, one Mary Grigsby of Emmanuel College in Boston, walked out of the auditorium immediately after speaking—thus sheltering herself effectively from the embarrassment of having to back up emotion and bombast with fact and reason. Apparently the complaintif did not count on responses being made—even in her absence—and the whole exchange being recorded and published. I mention this to show that little is to be gained by 'rapping' at linguistic conventions. It all gets noted down, and merely becomes additional data for the sociolinguist to analyze and use as evidence for his theories.

I didn't respond to the lady's comment about 'no black people on any of these panels' at the time because, frankly, I was confused by it. I happened to have been sitting next to Frederic Cassidy, a Jamaican (of Jamaican mother and English father) who gave a paper on Jamaican Creole on that very panel. Perhaps Miss Grigsby has a special way of classifying light-skinned Jamaicans as whites. Or perhaps she was unaware that Cassidy was in fact a Jamaican, as she was apparently unaware that Professor Applegate of Howard University appeared on the first, not last, panel of the series, and that the organizers of the Round Table had wanted black representation on Negro-dialect discussions, but had to settle for Professor Joseph Applegate of Howard University, a specialist in Berber languages, as the closest they could come! Now, although Professor Applegate has done no work on Negro dialect that I know of, the choice was not at all a bad one—since he happens to be an excellent all-around linguist. On the other hand, they could have invited (probably much more to Miss Grigsby's racial satisfaction) a self-styled militant like Charles G. Hurst, Jr., who waxes eloquent in public gatherings about white racism in linguistics, but who in his own publication, (Psychological Correlates in Dialectolalia, Howard University, Communication Sciences Research Center, 1965) has described the dialect-influenced speech of Negro freshmen as 'defective speech ... abnormal speech' containing 'oral aberrations' and 'phonetic distortions, defective syntax, misarticulations, mispronun-

ciations, limited or poor vocabulary, and faulty phonology' (pp. 1-2).
In discussions on racial problems, it has become fashionable for black
militants to tell white social scientists to go back and examine racial
attitudes in their own communities. Well, let me turn the tables by
telling Miss Grigsby to go back and examine sociolinguistic attitudes
in her own community before she tries to 'rap' on sociolinguists again.

Tsung Chin, Georgetown University: I rose to make a comment,
but since the situation has changed a little because of the previous discussion, I think I should make a wise statement; it is wise for me to do
this. I am a non-citizen of the United States; I am not a native speaker
of English; I am non-white; I am non-black; I am yellow. That means
I am neutral. If you read the title of Dr. Allen's paper (which I enjoyed
very much) which says that a second dialect is not a foreign language,
we might feel that, at first glance, there is a bit of tautology and confusion; because in a nation state once we define a certain variety as a
dialect, it will necessarily exclude the possibility of its being called a
foreign language. But I am not criticizing its title; I am praising its
title. It is well chosen, because it does point out the issue very clearly.
But I would add this: This teaching second dialect business is a universal phenomenon, a problem for all the countries in this world which
do have some sort of standard or whatever you call it, dialect, which
has to be learned by other dialects speakers. Now I can think of one
example in China. For instance, in Taiwan, we have to teach Mandarin, so-called, which is the superimposed social dialect, to people who
speak another dialect, Amoy. For that matter, in the whole of China
Mandarin has to be learned by speakers of all other dialects. Now we
don't have this problem in China or Taiwan, simply because of two
things. First, it is the tradition. We call this Mandarin dialect Kuv
Yu, which means the National Dialect or accent, whatever you call it.
It is national. Secondly, it has prestige, so people do want to learn it.
Because of these two factors there is no problem for other dialects
speakers to learn this language. We have never had this problem. In
the United States, I would say, now there is a bit of hesitancy to call a
certain variety a standard dialect. But once a certain norm is established, a certain label is fixed, and once this is realized, for some
reason, social or whatever you call it, as a dialect which has to be
learned, then there won't be any problem.
My second point is this: Now when we hear people say 'teaching
standard English as a foreign language, ' actually we shouldn't be over-
excited because simply we know what people mean by that. People want
to emphasize the point. When they talk about foreign languages, they
are talking about techniques. Dr. Allen has pointed this out clearly.
If we analyze her speech we know, actually, she has pointed out two
things. First, linguistically, teaching a dialect is the same as teach-

ing a foreign language: the techniques are the same. On the other hand, the psychology is different: we need to convince the learners this is the dialect that they should learn. We have to use the same techniques as in teaching foreign languages. We shouldn't be over-alarmed as linguists, as long as we know what they are talking about. Probably, if we want to be clear, we should say something like 'teaching a second dialect is not the same as teaching foreign languages.' Thank you very much.

Wesley Ponunzio, Southeastern Massachusetts Technological Institute: I am changing my topic in view of the comment by the young lady from Emmanuel College. I am going to be called upon once again, next fall, to teach a course in phonetics which will be oriented, principally, toward a group of students with predominantly French-Canadian background. I present this topic now because I think that there is a possibility of parallelism when we seek to determine what our attitudes should be toward other folk. In this particular instance, there is the attitude of the so-called 'continental' or otherwise labelled 'Parisian-French' speaker toward the Canadian. There is the attitude of the instructor, who himself is a foreigner, endeavoring to teach a continental or Parisian French to his speakers of English. And superimposed upon that, the situation of that same instructor endeavoring to modify, if it should be a question of modification, the inherited dialect or a variety of French of the local people who have spoken it in their family for 12 or 14 years.

The attitude that I will maintain in this course is analogous to that which Mrs. Allen has set forth, namely that of presenting two varieties. I will endeavor to present them without any value of prestige more for one than for the other; although I am not sure that this is fully realistic. I think it is true that the Continental French does have the prestige in view of its status as a national language, and that the other local dialect is, to be realistic about it, at a secondary level. And so, as far as the question of nonstandard English as it has been labelled for want, perhaps, of a better epithet, I think that the same attitude of good will must maintain. I feel that those such as Mrs. Allen who are endeavoring to bridge the gap between the two parts of our American culture should be commended, and that those who are black should find in her endeavors a cause of support, and should realize that this is a way of building a single nation where people of every color in some fond day, in the Utopian sense, will attain what is the right of all of us.

William Labov, Columbia University: I would like to compliment the young lady who was outraged at this meeting, for the way she posed her statement. I think that she demonstrated how well she could make an objection and how well she can express herself in perfectly standard grammar. And I think that she agrees perfectly well with Rap Brown, Stokely Carmichael, and almost every other nationalist leader on this point. They know that there is an appropriate dialect for platform work, and that dialect happens to be standard English. They want the kids in Harlem to learn to be able to use that too. There is no disagreement in practice in the Harlem community about that, as our work shows, or in the Detroit community, as Roger Shuy's work shows. There is no tendency for anybody here to impose a 'white' standard on the Negro community. On the contrary, as the young lady demonstrated to us by the grammar she used in making her objection, there is unanimous agreement on what dialect should be used in public speech.

TEACHING STANDARD ENGLISH TO SPEAKERS OF CREOLE IN JAMAICA, WEST INDIES

FREDERIC G. CASSIDY

The University of Wisconsin

Abstract. The home language of the mass of Jamaicans is basically a form of Creole English, though most also have some command
of Standard English. Even in the cities most children learn first a
speech which is officially banned from the schools. Teachers have
been 'required' to teach in Standard (British) English, though for
most in the public schools this is an ideal not often achieved; very
few of the teachers themselves are speakers of this kind of standard,
though they achieve what is sometimes called 'Jamaican Standard'
which has the local differences from British English. No formal
provision has been made to bridge the children over from Creole to
Standard; it has been sink-or-swim for them. Teachers are forced
on occasion to break the official rule and explain things in Creole in
order to get any comprehension. One university English Department
teacher has made a strong plea for teaching Standard English 'as a
foreign language', or actually teaching the first years of school in
Creole, but the idea has won very little acceptance. Some attempt is
being made, however, to help teachers to understand the problem, to
recognize that Creole is a real folk idiom rather than merely a
'broken' form of Standard. There is somewhat less disposition today
to denigrate and eradicate Creole. It is becoming slowly accepted
that the Creole speaker needs to acquire Standard as a second, prestige
dialect, without necessarily rejecting Creole.

My title may make you wonder whether English language teaching in
a Creole-speaking West Indian island can have any relevance to our

present problems in the United States. I believe that there are some
real parallels which you will see for yourselves—which I will not need
to point out. The situation in Jamaica is extreme by comparison with
ours, which brings common problems into sharper focus. Perhaps
you will be interested, at least, in how these problems strike the Jamaicans and what they are trying to do about them.

Jamaican Creole English, or JC for short, is, like other Creoles
of the New World, a language of local and recent growth, no more than
three hundred years old. It is definitely a language—not an auxiliary
or pidgin speech, but the chief or only speech of a million and a half
people. It has a structure which differs to a considerable degree from
that of any kind of standard English, British, Jamaican, or American,
in all of its parts: in phonology, morphology, syntax, and lexicon—to
the point where newcomers to the island cannot understand it. When
the first Peace Corps group was going to Jamaica in 1962 it was considered necessary to prepare a Language Guide to Jamaica (Bailey 1962)
for their use. This JC is the native speech of fully 80% of the population
—the entire working class, skilled or unskilled, agricultural laborers,
small tradesmen and shopkeepers, and necessarily, to some extent, of
those higher up the economic scale who have to deal with them, even
though these also know and can use something closer to Standard English (SE). More accurately, there is a sort of scale or continuum,
with the conservative or old-fashioned Creole at one end, SE at the
other, and varying infusions of Creole features between. The divid-
ing line, I think, is syntactic; Creole sounds and words may be found
all along the scale; but the use of Standard or Standard-like syntax
marks the decisive step toward the Standard end of the continuum. Almost any JC speaker can switch to the Standard spoken code on occasion and within limits; but in his daily life and with his own kind, the
ordinary man normally speaks Creole. Educated people at the top
speak Standard English of a British type. Jamaican Standard might
be described as British Standard with Creole effects, the most tenacious of which are prosodic.

As I have said, JC is a full language. All but technical matters can
be expressed in it with considerable accuracy and, on the lips of many
speakers, with wit, aptness, and even poetry—the last effect being in
part due to the archaism of the vocabulary. The Creole began as a
pidgin speech, probably developed in the first place along the coast of
West Africa; but when the slaves brought to Jamaica in the 17th and
18th centuries forgot their African languages, and when their children
(as is so often the case today with non-English-speaking immigrants to
the U.S.) refused to keep up the ancestral tongues, they developed the
pidgin into Creole as their first language. This was done partly on the
already existing resources of pidgin; African, English, and other elements were added; and certain grammatical features differing from

those of both English and African languages were developed. But because English was the language of the masters, of Government, of public life, of the professions, and of print, it had the prestige and was
the chief donor to the developing Creole.

At the time when this Creole speech was being developed, it should
be noted that the negroes outnumbered the whites 9 to 1, that the mass
of negroes had little opportunity to hear 'good English' spoken, that
many of the whites with whom they had contact were themselves dialect
speakers, hence that the acquisition of SE by the negroes was rendered
virtually impossible. Thus Creole became firmly established and
though the slaves were given their freedom 26 years before the United
States Civil War even began, this form of speech is still very much a
going concern today. The bulk of Jamaican children acquire it in their
homes; it is the only language they have when they start school. But
since the schools are required to teach in SE, the psychic shock to the
children may be imagined when they discover that the only way they
can speak is the wrong way. I am referring here to the public schools,
not the private schools to which the people who can afford it send their
children. These latter are on a par with American 'prep' schools,
though English in orientation. It is no surprise that public school
children speak Creole; but the fact is that some effects of Creole are
felt right up the economic scale. Even the private school boys and
girls often revert, at play, to modified forms of Creole.

Let me very quickly sketch the main features in which JC differs
from SE. First as to pronunciation. The 'th' phonemes /θ/ and /ð/
are missing: /t/ and /d/ take their place. Thus thin and then are tin
and den. Until this century /v/ was hardly used: /b/ took its place,
as in /beks/ for vexed and /neba/ for never. There is no schwa vowel: carrot and robin are /kyarat/ and /rabin/. There is a sort of
Cockney effect: [h] is frequent but not phonemic: it may be present
or absent unpredictably—thus one may equally often hear /eg/ and
/hat/ or /heg/ and /at/. The mid-front and mid-back diphthongs correspond in occurrence to those of SE, but instead of being upgliding
they are downgliding. Thus bay and row are /bie/ and /ruo/. The
SE contrast between /æ/ in hat and American /a/ in hot (or /ɔ/ in
British) is neutralized, making these words homonyms: /hat/ or /at/.
Anyone who has tried to help a Spanish-American speaker to distinguish
the vowels of heat and hit will appreciate what the JC speaker faces in
splitting /at/ three ways into SE at, hat, and hot. Parallel with substandard American speech, JC reduces final consonant clusters: post
to /puos/, hand to /han/, hold to /huol/, and so on. Initial clusters
that give trouble may be similarly simplified in JC, spoil, string,
scrape becoming /pwail/, /tring/, /kriep/. These are only the most
striking phonological differences. For a full historical phonology see
the Dictionary of Jamaican English (Cassidy-Le Page 1967).

Morphological differences are great in that there is virtually no inflection in JC. Nouns have only one form for singular, plural, and possessive; verbs have only one for present and past. Even the pronouns are severely reduced in conservative JC: number is formally marked but gender and case are not. Thus the statement /im brok im fut/ may mean he, she, or it breaks, or broke, his, her, or its foot, or feet. The precise distinction is made contextually. Inflection is used only for the -ing form of verbs: /komin/, /taakin/, and for comparison; but the latter system is multiple, so that better may come out as /muo beta/ and best may become /besis/. A number of these features are paralleled in the U.S. in old-fashioned lower-class speech. JC has developed some new markers—as for the plural, where dem (for them) is suffixed to the noun: /di fut-dem/ meaning the feet, /di tiit-dem/ meaning the teeth. New verb phrases have been formed, using as auxiliaries /a/, /da/, or /de/ to mark the durative aspect: /mi a kom, mi da kom, mi de kom/ mean I am coming. As in most pidgin and creole languages, the copula is omitted, hence the tea is hot is /di tii hat/. Again, one may see parallels to certain American usages.

As to syntax, word order is the chief relational device and corresponds to that of SE for simple declarative sentences. But there is no inversion for questions, nor use of introductory do or did: questions depend on a sharp rise of intonation. Thus for Have you seen it or Did he break it, JC has /yu^1 siit^3/ or /im^1 brok it^3/. The system is fairly complex, with introductory /a/ and floating /no/ having various functions of emphasis. /Jan siit/ is a simple statement John saw it; /a Jan siit/ identifies John firmly as the seer: John is the one who saw it; /no Jan siit ?/ is a rhetorical question equivalent to Isn't it evident, since John saw it? or Since John saw it, how can it be doubted? These are some of the most striking features; others may be found in Jamaica Talk (Cassidy 1961), a popular treatment, and in A Transformational Grammar of Jamaican Creole (Bailey 1966).

As to the lexicon, that includes hundreds of nonstandard words, most of them from archaic or dialectal English; also a considerable number of African loans such as poto-poto 'mud', ninyam 'food', kakanabú 'nonsense'; sprinklings also of Portuguese, Spanish, French, and Indian words. While the SE word for almost any simple, daily matter will be known, these other Creole words may be preferred and come more readily to a speaker's lips. But in addition to nonstandard words there are many nonstandard meanings for ordinary words. Ignorant is used for indignant, tall for long, grudge for envy, and so on. In short, JC has a system of its own; though it coincides at many points with SE, it is different at probably as many points. With so many differences between JC and SE, no teacher could possibly impose any Standard all at once. What may be the best strategy of teaching, under

the circumstances, is doubtful. Meantime, the pupil's submission to
school methods makes its mark on him.

In the public schools as recently as eighteen years ago, when Prof.
Madeline Kerr of the University of Liverpool published her excellent
study Personality and Conflict in Jamaica (Kerr 1950), the textbooks
in use were printed in England, made for English children, and dealt
with many things which the Jamaican child would probably never experience, while ignoring the world he actually knew. For example,
there was a lesson on the botany of the primrose, which does not grow
in Jamaica, but nothing about the hibiscus or bougainvillea. School-
teaching was of the traditional type, hardly getting beyond the three
R's and relying on memory work and set questions and answers—con-
ceiving of the teacher as a container from which the established materials were to be poured into passive receptacles, the pupils. Question-
ing and discussion were practically impossible anyway under prevailing conditions. I have seen a one-room country school with over a hundred children—far more than it could hold—so that they carried their
benches out under the trees, sorting themselves out by size to left and
right of the building. When a tropical downpour began they all squeezed
under the one roof. The teacher, unable to do anything else, made
them sing—which they did with enthusiasm and fine harmony. The
moment the rain was over they burst into the open air again and re-
sumed the interrupted lessons.

Though Jamaica became an independent nation in 1962 and has been
making heroic efforts to improve the educational system, it is, in fact,
slowly losing ground. Poverty, overpopulation, the reluctance of Government pundits to listen to professional educators, and the enormous
weight of tradition make for little real change. There are some new
textbooks in history and geography of Jamaica. But only about half of
the teachers get professional training (Figueroa 1966 : 14-16) and since
most of them start life as speakers of Creole their version of Standard
language is in many cases far from perfect. Thus not even the teachers are adequate models for the children. When released from classroom pressure, Jamaican children immediately relapse into Creole
speech. This the teacher cannot officially countenance, yet even in
the classroom she is often forced to resort to the only language which,
for the children, carries the sanction of immediate comprehension.
So the Creole speech goes merrily on. Prof. Kerr tested Jamaican
school children in a number of ways; but to me her most interesting
test was that in which they were asked to draw a house and the people
who lived in it. The preschool children or beginners drew pictures
full of freedom and vitality (Kerr 1950: opposite 176, 177); but the older
ones, after several years of schooling, drew pictures on the same subject that were flat, conventional, depersonalized (Kerr 1950: opposite

192). The personality of the child was seen to be deteriorating as a
result of the school experience.

Educators in Jamaica, under the leadership especially of the University of the West Indies, have long been aware of the language problem as lying close to the core of their troubles. The traditional method
of simply 'expecting' the child, under the influence of books and the
teacher, to acquire SE has obviously not worked. Of course the bright
and well motivated children come through all right—you can't keep a
good mind down—but the less bright merely go through a baffling and
even stunting experience. The prestigious key to all advancement and
self-realization is beyond their grasp; they can only accept their inability to achieve it, hence admit to a lower personality status. Professor Kerr (1950: chapter 15) finds this an important contributory
factor to a widespread reluctance among Jamaicans to take charge of
their own lives—to feel, instead, a need to be directed. Her conclusion is that their personalities have not matured, hence they easily fall
victim to degrading forces.

To try to cope with this situation at least one language teacher at
the University (Dr. R. B. LePage) proposed as early as 1955 or 1956
to consider teaching the first year or two of school in Creole, as in
Sierra Leone, Africa, where the Krio speech, related to that of Jamaica, has some official sanction. During this period the children would
be taught SE 'as a foreign language'. This proposal was either not taken
seriously or was considered shocking. Since it never became official I
can refer only to the reaction expressed in the newspapers. One colum-
nist in particular, Vere Johns in the Kingston Star, damned it as a per-
nicious and insulting idea. In Jamaica, though most of the populace
speak Creole, those higher up consider it utterly degraded and associate it with poverty and ignorance. The notion of giving it any degree of
school sanction was intolerable; but it was also deeply insulting, as if
'good English' were a foreign language to Jamaicans. This unfavorable
public reaction, plus what it would have cost to institute any such program, killed the idea at least for that time.

There may be something for us here: even if we can afford to put in
programs to bring our disadvantaged children to a par with those better
off than they, it must be done without the element of insult. Linguists
know and must continue to insist that one language or dialect is not in-
trinsically better or worse than others, and further, that a child may
command two dialects, the one he brings from home and the one he
uses in school, without derogating the one in order to recommend the
other. To know both gives him a double strength: he can better adapt
his speech to varying environments or needs and not be shut off from a
whole range of experience by being merely monodialectal.

The Creole language, even for the most cultivated speaker of SE, if
he has known it at home or at school, has a force of intimacy that the

upper language can never offer. In Sierra Leone, in Haiti, In Curaçao, the native intellectual knows this—some things can be said or suggested in Creole more effectively than in Standard. In Jamaica, now, the same feeling is slowly growing. Since independence (1962) British English is recognized to be exotic: Jamaican is fi wi ting—that is, 'something all our own'. So, at least, among the younger generation of writers, artists, and teachers. A home language becomes profoundly implanted in us; any attempt to eradicate it is made at our peril. Now we know that the school language can be acquired 'in addition to', not 'rather than' the home language. Teacher training in Jamaica today is attempting to instill this idea—to reduce thereby the sense of guilt in the Creole speaker.

As I said, the University of the West Indies is leading in the attempt to bring the educational system up to date. New textbooks have been and are being developed; programs of teacher retraining are beginning —and more basically—experiments which may guide the directions of change. In April, 1964, a conference was held at the University on Language Teaching, Linguistics, and the Teaching of English in a Multilingual Society (UWI Faculty of Education 1965). The Report has been published and contains accounts of several of the experiments being made. One big question seems to have been what kind of Standard the schools were to aim at—SE as in the past, or some new Jamaican Standard (SJ), and if the latter, what was to be its nature. Some of the linguists present took a rather hands-off position, arguing that language development takes its own course anyway and one cannot interfere with it. The educators, on the other hand, faced with immediate problems and needs, called for some sort of codification. No practical compromise was reached but perhaps the teachers took away a clearer idea of the distinction between formal and informal language requirements, the understanding that if anything is to be codified at present this can be only for formal or written language, and they agreed in the need for specific experiments with new methods such as the discussion method in teaching writing (UWI Faculty of Education 1965: paper 4).

Notably, there was a return to the idea of teaching the Standard (which some preferred to call 'Educated Jamaican') as if it were a completely different language from the Creole, seeing Standard as even more difficult for a Creole speaker to learn than another European language would be for a speaker of SE. I quote (UWI Faculty of Education 1965: 25-26):

> The conclusion to which one is driven is that the Creole speaker must learn by rote the forms and patterns of SE syntax. His own syntax, unlike that of French, for example, is too unlike SE syntax to be much help in learning SE from within. He is unquestionably without.

Tentatively the compromise was considered of recognizing: (I quote again, 27):

> a West Indian Standard English which would allow certain
> well-established features of WI speech the prestige of SE
> equivalents, and remove something of the vast differences
> which separate the Creole dialects from SE. (UWI Faculty
> of Education 1965 : 27).

But this too was dismissed on the ground that the reduction of this distance would be so slight as not to solve the problem. The basic problem is the truly bilingual situation in which the popular speech has no prestige and can hardly ever attain it, being in competition with a world language, English. If the child's life is not to be automatically restricted to the world of Creole speakers, he must learn some kind of Standard English too. The question reduces itself to how early, how widely, and by what method.

May I say that if I were in a position to do anything about it I would first recognize the unideal 'fact' that poverty is the chief foe of social 'upward mobility'; that in a country where poverty may be palliated but not removed, the mass of the population simply have to learn to live with it; that only those individuals with natural ability, strong motivation, and some luck, can rise above or escape such a situation. I consider it inexorable and unquestionable that unless great economic improvement can be achieved, the mass of Jamaicans will continue as speakers of some form of Creole.

Nevertheless, the educator must set himself the goal of providing and improving 'opportunity'—opportunity for the abler individual, regardless of how poor his background may be, to get the fruits of his ability, for his own good and for the ultimate good of society. For the sake of the few who will grasp it, opportunity should be held open to all. It should not require generations for native ability to force its way up the social scale. In Jamaican schools, then, the goal of learning SE (or SJ) should be held to firmly, and if starting it at once, from the moment the child enters school, seems to be the most effective, that is when it should be started. If teaching SE or SJ 'as a foreign language' offends public sensibilities, some less unflattering phrase could be found—such as 'Early Intensive Language Training'—without abandoning the effective method. I would begin with those features in which Creole differs most from SE —in other words, with the syntax, especially verb syntax, and drill this in by pattern practice and other such devices. This is the deep structure, here the overlap with SE structure is at a minimum. I would let lexical differences wait, or take their chances along the way; they are surface features and cannot be treated as systematically anyway.

Such a program would require, first of all, a set of new textbooks made by linguists who knew the Creole thoroughly, which made no attack on the Creole but simply presented SE in the order of its differences from Creole, descending from greatest to least. These texts would have to be practically self-teaching; even so, teachers would have to be retrained to use them and encouraged not to relapse into the old ways. Certainly a pilot project should be run before the books were printed in official form; a monitoring program should be provided in expectation of revision after a few years' experience with the books and the method. Some kind of incentives should be provided for the teachers, financial and otherwise. While the expectation would be to switch as soon as possible to SE for all classroom activities, it would have to be understood that sympathetic communication with the children was the first necessity, and the teacher would have to be permitted to use Creole when that was the most effective means. Use of Creole should even be encouraged within bounds: for songs, games, stories. But the emphasis would go increasingly on SE, and good grasp of it should of course be a qualification for higher schooling.

Finally, I would be wary of the temptations to delay, always very powerful in a poor and traditional country. A general looks at a war as an opportunity to test his tactical theories and new weaponry; he is less eager than the man in the front line to 'win' the war. In this analogy the generals are the linguists and professional educators; the front-line fighters are the teachers. In my opinion, enough is known already about JC so that linguists could make the necessary texts and educationists set up the necessary programs immediately. Yet it is tempting to postpone action, excusing it on the ground that more experimentation is necessary. More experimentation is always necessary, but the need to reform the system is greater, and reform should not wait.

Perhaps you have seen for yourselves some parallels to the situation we face in poor communities in the U.S., both isolated rural ones and undigested urban ones. Our concern, as educators, should be to keep opportunity open, to remove accidental environmental barriers, to provide more aid to students who need it, and thus to prevent the loss of human potential from which everyone in our society suffers.

REFERENCES

Bailey, Beryl L. 1962. A Language Guide to Jamaica. U.C.W.I. (for Peace Corps).
_____. 1966. A Transformational Grammar of Jamaican Creole. Cambridge: University Press.
Cassidy, F. G. 1961. Jamaica Talk. London: Macmillan.
_____, and R. B. LePage. 1967. Dictionary of Jamaican English. Cambridge: University Press.

Craig, Dennis. 1966. Teaching English to Jamaican Creole Speakers. Language Learning 16: 1, 2.

Evans, P. C. C. and R. B. LePage. 1967. The Education of West Indian Immigrant Children. London: National Committee for Commonwealth Immigrants.

Faculty of Education, University of the West Indies. 1965. Language Teaching, Linguistics, and the Teaching of English in a Multilingual Society. Old Woking: Gresham Press.

Figueroa, John J. M. 1966. Notes on the Teaching of English in the West Indies. Kingston, Jamaica: New World. Cropover.

Kerr, Madeline. 1950. Personality and Conflict in Jamaica. Liverpool: University Press.

DISCUSSION

Diane Gottesfeld, Winthrop High School, Brooklyn: I would like to know, faced with the reality of the New York City School System, would you put a Jamaican child who is not reading, in a corrective reading class with slow learners, or in a non-English class?

Cassidy: Would I put a Jamaican child in New York City who is having a difficult time in school with language into a non-English class or into a slow learners' class? I wish I knew enough to answer that question; I am afraid I don't. But you might get some help out of a little book that has been published in England quite recently (I have it here and I would be glad to show it to you) on what happens to West Indian children in English cities. They face a very similar problem in England. They have an undigested West Indian group. The children learn their Creole from their parents at home, but they have to be on a par with the English school child, and they face this problem head on. The English school teachers and the education system in the places where this happens most, which is the big cities—London, Liverpool, Manchester, and so on—are facing the problem and they are working through Dr. LePage, the man I mentioned before. He it is who first suggested this system in Jamaica, and is one of those concerned with it. And they are at least linguistically equipped to do something about it. I don't know quite what their solution will turn out to be; they have to test things.

William A. Stewart, Education Study Center: Fred, as one who was at that conference that you referred to and, incidentally, had a hand in the formulation of the statements on both standard Jamaican and on the Creole, I would question your symbolic comparison of the general with the linguist, and the teacher with the soldier on the front line. You said that the linguist was the general who was engaging in delaying tactics by his saying that more experimentation was always necessary—the implication being that linguists are the ones who are holding back the acceptance of Creole in the Jamaican Public Schools. As a linguist interested in Jamaican Creole, and as one who has been directly involved in this off and on, I don't really think this is so. The times that I have been in conferences on education in Jamaica, it has been quite clear that the many cretins in the Ministry of Education were responsible for the delaying tactics, rather than linguists, either at the University of the West Indies or those of us from outside. Although the Jamaican teacher may have some attitudes which would conceivably get in the way of the use of Creole in the public school curriculum, this can be overcome. I think the biggest barrier is the Ministry of Education itself, and not the teacher or the linguists.

Cassidy: Dr. Stewart has the advantage of me; he was at that meeting and I wasn't, and he is quite right, of course. I should not put the linguists and the professional educators in the same basket. They are, however, not faced with the same problem as the teacher who is in the front line and has to fight the battle directly, and has to get hit when something starts flying. That was one thing.

I should say that I tried to qualify that statement by saying that the tendency was to delay—the temptation, that was my word, the temptation was to delay. I am speaking now quite specifically of two people who I think are adequately equipped to do this job, but are not getting to it. Maybe that is because they can't get support—I am not quite certain; but at any rate what they are saying is: If we knew more about it, we could get on with the job. So they are applying for fellowships and a year abroad and things like that, so that they could learn more. I have a feeling that they know enough already, and that the job should be got on with; that's the thing I had in mind.

David DeCamp, The University of Texas at Austin: One thing I can report: that although the primrose is no longer in Jamaica the required flower for botany—so I guess there is progress—countering this is the fact that in the zoology lab in high school they still require the fish to dissect to be the dogfish, which has to be imported from Scotland.

I think there is some chance of hope, and I think none of it rests in what Bill described here. I think there is some chance of enlightenment coming out of, not the top level at the Ministry, or other official sources, but out of the minority of the rank-and-file teachers (despite the God-awful, appalling conditions under which they have to work, in spite of the fact that they are deficient in training and so on); a minority of these people are seeing for themselves and are awakening to many of these problems.

I conducted a two-day seminar workshop for teachers down there, and was trying to get them to talk about these things. After about three hours, a young man spoke up. He said, 'You know, I've always simply corrected the students whenever they speak in Creole and called it an error; but one of the boys in the class said—pointed outside and said—"The road is <u>poto-poto</u>." Of course, I corrected him and said, "You must say the road is <u>all muddy</u>." Very respectfully, the boy said, "That isn't what I mean. It isn't just <u>muddy</u>, it is <u>poto-poto</u>. It is like <u>ploto-ploto</u> and it certainly isn't <u>mek-mek</u>." ' The teacher asked, 'Do you think this has any relationship with this business that we had to read in the readings for this course about the Eskimo having a whole lot of words for snow, simply because that is something that is very important to him to have distinctions about? And if so, who is right?'

I think that the fact that you can get people spontaneously coming up with questions of this sort indicates there is some hope there.

SOCIOPOLITICAL ISSUES IN THE LINGUISTIC TREATMENT OF NEGRO DIALECT

WILLIAM A. STEWART

Education Study Center

Abstract. The rapid growth of the linguistic discipline has had its impact on pedagogical theory and practice. First influential in shaping thinking on foreign language teaching methods, the linguistic view has more recently been extended to the area traditionally known as 'remedial English'—i.e. the teaching of standard English to speakers of nonstandard dialects. Since most such speakers are lower-class Negroes, the nature of nonstandard Negro English, and its relationship to both standard English and the nonstandard English of whites has received increased attention by linguists. Yet, the objectivity which linguists have traditionally shown in dealing with unstandardized languages or dialects in the past has not been the rule in the linguistic treatment of Negro dialect. The problem seems to be that, since the subject is the speech of lower-class Negroes, there is a great deal of interference from current sociopolitical views on the Negro's place in American society which shapes and distorts theoretical descriptions of Negro dialect's place in the range of dialect differences which make up 'English' in its most comprehensive sense.

In this talk, I will address myself to certain problems which seem to have arisen along with the development of both theoretical and applied treatments of nonstandard Negro dialect. In particular, I would like to deal with the blatant intrusion of sociopolitical issues into the scientific study of Negro speech.

Language teaching in schools has become quite contingent upon applied linguistics for its general perspective as well as for methodological details. This has been true for some time now with respect to the teaching of foreign languages, and seems likely to become so for the teaching of standard English to speakers of problematically non-standard varieties of the language as well. If this is true, then many English teachers will become dependent upon linguistic theory and research to an even greater extent than the foreign language teacher is, since the linguistic and social variables are so much more subtle. But, the fact that so many speakers of nonstandard dialects of American English are Negroes introduces a whole host of attitudinal complications in both the theoretical and applied sides of what is already a technically complicated area, and thereby renders the chances for successful linguistic and successful English teaching much more remote in this area than American linguistics and American education can afford. Since these attitudinal complications are many and diverse, it is very difficult for the linguist or the language teacher to avoid them all. Yet, they are chronic because they are woven right into the fabric of our society and our history. The total effect has been to warp linguistic objectivity in Negro-dialect research and to stultify the application of what research has been forthcoming to educational methodology.

To clear the air somewhat, I would like to violate some of the topical taboos which currently hold in polite Negro-white dialogue, by bringing into the open some of the most tenacious and prevailing social and political issues which I find interfering with the linguistic and pedagogical treatment of Negro dialect. In doing so, I will undoubtedly question some of the social beliefs and offend the social sensibilities of many who are present. Yet I do this because I am convinced that leaving these issues undiscussed is precisely what has allowed them to endure too long. The issues are: (1) racism, particularly as it involves the American Negro, and (2) Americanism, and particularly the way we perceive American society and the Negro's place in it. For, as I will attempt to demonstrate, these all affect linguistic and pedagogical views of Negro dialect. Now, if there are any white liberals or black militants who feel a glow of satisfaction at my assertion that I am going to deal with racism, I must warn them that my treatment of the subject may not be what they expect. For I have come to the conclusion that a particular kind of anti-racism is more troublesome at the moment than the older racism that we all know and abhor. For I intend to show that the reaction to anti-scientific racism has merely been anti-racistic scientism and that, while the two are philosophically opposed, neither is the more objective or useful for it. And if I open myself to the charge that I am not dealing with linguistic phenomena at a linguistics conference, I would point out that what is needed to resolve the attitudinal dilemma of which I speak is not more linguistic data; it is a much-needed historical perspective. For, it is one of the main tasks of the historian to assess the development of scientific thought in terms of the general social context and attitudes of the times. In the role of historian, then, I will examine the effect of American racism and the American concept of a national society on the linguistic treatment of Negro dialect.

In dealing with racism, it is important to understand exactly how the term is used. In its most technical sense, it refers to the belief in a genetic basis for differences in the behavior of different human populations, although another, and more political, use refers to any unfair treatment of one caste by another.

As genetic racism affected the white colonial view of the African slave in what became the United States, it was manifest in a widespread tendency to regard Africans and their descendants as innately inferior to Europeans and their descendants. Of course, a supportive theory of genetics had not yet been developed at that time, but it was nevertheless thought that there was something in the 'blood' of the Negro which made him inferior to whites in ways that affected intellectual capacity and many kinds of behavior—including language behavior. With the development of the Darwinian theory of evolution, there was a perhaps inevitable extension of the evolutionary concept to the social level, so that many came to feel that, even if individual Negroes were capable of acculturation to European life-ways, Negro society was itself retarded and inferior. Called 'social Darwinism', this theory held that societies formed by Negroes were further behind in the scale of social development or evolution than societies formed by Europeans. Since the social Darwinists were all products of European culture, it is probably natural that they would see European behavior as more advanced than non-European behavior—particularly in an intellectual climate as yet unchallenged by anthropological relativism. (Incidentally, if the position of social Darwinism seems similar in many ways to the hierarchical ordering of middle-class culture as more advanced than lower-class culture by such modern educational psychologists as Deutsch, Engelmann, and Bereiter, it is because both schools of thought share many basic premises with respect to the relationship of Negro behavioral norms to white behavioral norms.)

Of course, the supposed innate inferiority of the Negro, and the supposed retardation of African culture, was a handy justification for slavery from the very beginning. When they came into contact with Africans who worked on New World plantations, many slave-owners undoubtedly noticed behavioral differences between those Africans and themselves. And, of course, the African behaviors were invariably taken as ipso facto evidence of Negro inferiority. As far as the language of the early slaves was concerned, African tribal languages were often regarded as consisting of random grunts and clicks—just as American Indian languages often were. When African slaves acquired unique forms of English (probably influenced in many ways by African patterns), these were also considered to be inferior and unstructured.

That, in general, American Negroes continued to behave in ways which were distinct from the ways in which white men behaved, generation after generation, was taken by many whites as evidence that Negroes were incapable of ever behaving as whites. And those patterns of behavior which were unique to Negroes became embodied in generalized stereotypes of the Negro. Now, it has often been charged that such stereotypes were totally inaccurate, that there was a deliberate distortion on the part of whites in describing Negro behavior as different, and that this distortion was due to racism. But even if the racism was there, it is important to realize that the distortion or invention of 'typically Negro' behavior was not necessary, because behavioral differences between whites and Negroes did exist, and those associated with Negroes were interpreted as ipso facto evidence of Negro inferiority. That there might also have been some distorting of the descriptions is certainly possible (and obviously occurred in the minstrelsy tradition—created by Northerners and not Southerners, incidentally). The interesting point is that when one compares the serious descriptions of Negro behavior by white racists, one finds indications of behavioral patterns which can be found today through scientific research in American Negro communities. (This is perhaps one reason why Negro-image-oriented militants and community spokesmen have often opposed social-science research in the inner city.) And this is no less true for Negro speech than for other kinds of Negro behavior.

These racist interpretations of Negro-white behavioral differences either caused or coincided with similar ones within the Negro population itself. Indeed, with some historical validity, Negroes often called their own distinctive behaviors 'Af'ican' in the plantation jargon, as opposed to 'proper' for European-type behavior. There was a tendency on the part of antebellum Negroes to be ashamed of, to try to explain away, or to try to hide from public view, any distinctively Negro behavior, and this practice has survived right down to modern times. In her study of the folklore of the South Carolina Sea Islands, for example, Parsons reported the following incident, which illustrates that even young children had learned such attitudes:

> One day I arrived at Edding's Point school during recess.
> About a dozen girls, large and small, were crowded together
> in a compact circular group. Their knees were bent, their
> buttocks protruding; they shuffled from one foot to the other
> as they clapped their hands. Only one word was clearly ar-
> ticulated—jibber; and the game or dance was, I suspect (an
> old ring-game of slavery times called 'You Kyan't Dance
> Juba') ... Not long after the girls noticed me watching them,

they broke up their game, drew nearer, and re-formed to play
'The Farmer in the Dell'.[1]

It is significant that the first and, ultimately, the most successful
reaction against racism was an abolitionist attack on the institution of
slavery, which left the underlying racism intact. Indeed, many aboli-
tionists were themselves convinced of the innate inferiority of Negroes.
Their point was that it was morally wrong for whites to enslave Negroes, just as it would be morally wrong to coop children up, keep
them prisoner, and force them to work. This is why the early aboli-
tionists often advocated African colonization (that is, the shipping of
freed slaves 'back to Africa'). And as a matter of fact, the growth and
development of Liberia was connected with one successful stage of the
colonization movement.

One characteristic of the early stages of 19th-20th century social
science was that, although it believed in the innate equality of people,
it still did not really believe in the innate equality of cultures; that was
to come later, with the relativism of cultural anthropology. To show
that Negroes were equal to whites, it was felt necessary to show that
they were identical to whites in their behavior and social traditions.
Thus there was the development of a tradition which tried to explain
away distinctively Negro behaviors as mere relics of European behaviors. So, for example, Negro folk songs were claimed to be trans-
planted British folk songs that happened to survive among the Negroes,
but not among the whites. And Negro dialect was presented as a composite of British dialect features from here, there, and everywhere in
the British Isles, which had come into the speech of Negroes in the colonial period. Of course, if one compares American Negro dialects
with English dialects in the British Isles, they do not look alike at all.
But there was a tendency to make this kind of a connection on the basis
of superficial word forms because it was part of what I would call the
Anglocentric tradition—the tendency to regard Negroes in the United
States as part and parcel of Anglo-Saxon culture. It should be obvious
that Anglocentrism was merely one way of accommodating the view that
non-European behaviors were inferior to the view that non-European
peoples were not inferior; the Negro could be seen as equal to the white
only if his behavior would be claimed to be identical to that of the white.

The obvious result of this was that people tended to deny any Negro-
white differences they could deny. Liberal whites denied them, as did
upwardly-mobile Negroes. And the social sciences, dominated by the
liberals whose feelings of race-guilt made them overly responsive to
Negro sensitivity, were affected. Since racist stereotypes of the Negro
had focused on distinctively Negro behavior, all evidence of distinctively-
Negro behavior was subsequently dismissed as racist stereotypes. Thus,
when confronted with literary attestations of early American Negro slave

speech which showed it to be quite different from that of the colonial
whites, many philologists and dialectologists dismissed them as racist
inventions—even though many of the structural details of these attestations reflected present-day American Negro and West Indian usage, and
even suggested very plausible kinds of interference from African languages.

With the rise of cultural anthropology, anti-racism was extended to
the cultural domain. It was shown that behavioral differences can and
do exist between peoples, but that these have no implication of inferiority or superiority at all. In the moral and behavioral relativism of
cultural anthropology, the American Indian and the white became equal
while different. As a matter of fact, the whole early history of American anthropology involved coming to understand and appreciate how different, yet how inherently equal as alternative designs for living, different cultures could be. And since the early stages of American linguistics involved the study of American Indian languages (an offshoot of
cultural anthropology), the principle of relativism was applied to language.

But while the Navajo could now be accepted as different from, yet
equal to, the white, the principle of relativism was somehow never applied to the American Negro. Where Negroes turned out to be different
from whites, the difference couldn't be attributed to innate physical
differences (since this would be racism), so it had to be attributed to
a poor environment, to ignorance, to general causes in the environment which set the basis for the cultural-deprivation theory. The false
assumption responsible for this was, of course, that the acculturation
of Africans to the New World Anglo-Saxon culture was both rapid and
complete. In short, the application of the anthropological view of cultural differences to the American Negro was stultified by the melting-
pot myth. Unfortunately, this situation was reinforced by the upwardly-
mobile Negro's reaction to racism, which was a full commitment to
Anglo-Saxon culture and, with it, an excessively normativistic view.
Many observers have remarked on how absolutist Negro teachers of
English often are in school, and how carefully middle-class Negroes
adhere to general mainstream norms. But this excessive normativism
was much more general than just within English teaching; it involved
all areas of conscious behavior. Surprisingly, from today's standards,
it even extended to the preservation of Negro spirituals. As the folk
song collector Lydia Parrish observed a quarter of a century ago:

> But genuine Negro music is confronted by a real menace in
> the scornful attitude of those Negro schoolteachers who do
> their utmost to discredit and uproot every trace of it. (At
> Hampton Institute, when I protested at the way the old tunes
> were altered, a music instructor loftily informed me: 'When

they are wrong, of course they must be changed.') Instead
of being inordinately proud of their race's contribution to the
music of the world, as they have every right to be, too many
of them treat it like a family skeleton. In the schoolroom,
even in sections where spirituals may be said to be indigen-
ous, they are suppressed, and the supposedly 'more artistic'
Europeanized book versions are laboriously learned. This
misplaced zeal even follows the pupils into the schoolyard.
Such musically commonplace English game songs as 'The
Farmer Takes a Wife'—although I admit the action is pic-
turesque—are substituted for such joyous Afro-American
melodies as 'Go roun' the Border, Susie'—for all the world
like carrying synthetic coals to Newcastle![2]

The recent Negro revolution started out as essentially sociopolitical
in its orientation, being largely committed to the goal of integration—
a thoroughly middle-class Negro aspiration. Since it sought socioeconomic opportunity for Negroes in white-dominated society, it tended to
accept and reinforce the normativism of the earlier period. Militant
Negroes tended to say, for example, 'We want our children to have the
opportunity to learn effective standard English. We know that Negro
dialect is bad, so we want to get rid of it.' More recently there has
been a happier trend (let us call it 'black awareness') which seeks to
understand the differences between Negroes and whites. But so far,
the black-awareness movement has tended to emphasize world-wide
Negro identity—what Negroes in Africa and America and other parts
of the world have in common. It has not yet focused on distinctive
North-American-Negro cultural reality, except in certain areas like
music—ones which can easily be transvalued within a newly-developed
concept of black 'soul' culture. This is why there is still focus on
Swahili, rather than on American Negro speech. Swahili is considered
a legitimate language by people who belong to this movement, while
Negro dialect is still considered by many as the product of a 'lazy
tongue' and of ignorance. Thus, the older Anglocentric tradition of
studying the American Negro is strangely reinforced by much of the
present Negro Revolution, which is as yet dominated by Negroes who
are politically militant and separatist, but socially conservative and
assimilationist. Because such quasi-militants feel that Negro dialect
is inherently 'bad' (as did conservative Negroes before them), they regard it as a product of white racism. Thus, they see any attempt to
describe and scientifically record Negro dialect as nothing more than
a white-racist exploitation of Negroes.

The effect of these views on scientific research and on the teaching
of English is profound. It produces a scientific environment, for example, in which the proof level for scientific generalizations about the

nature and distribution of Negro dialect are quite different from what
they would be for other dialects or languages. If one needs, say, fifteen examples of unique forms to show that a particular white dialect
exists, one needs 100 to show that a particular Negro dialect exists.
When one does historical reconstruction, one is automatically expected
to derive Negro dialect directly from Britain, and to avoid postulating
such plausible additional factors as pidginization and structural interference from African languages. And, above all, in attempting to implement the concept of Negro dialect as a unique form of language into
the schools, one encounters resistance and hostility from middle-class
Negro teachers who want nothing distinctively Negro, and over-cautious,
politically-oriented white school administrators who want nothing con-
troversial. In spite of the fact that community control is now being advocated as a panacea for Negro education, I suspect that one will find
inner city Negro mothers who are no more tolerant of a school curriculum oriented to the reality of Negro culture than suburban white mothers
often are. Although they are at first often embarrassed to talk about it
in public, Negro school children will probably turn out to be the strongest advocates of the recognition of Negro dialect in the school curriculum. But then we know that the interests of children tend to be shunted
aside, when they conflict with the insecurities of adults.

On the optimistic side, there is a growing number of anthropologi-
cally-oriented Negroes and whites who see that the melting-pot view of
American society is as mythical for the Negro as it is for the Navajo,
and that the African, in coming to the New World, became more a con-
tributor than a copier. That large numbers of distinctively-American
cultural patterns originated with the Negro (and have, in fact, been subsequently borrowed by whites) means that we have at least two full-
fledged historical sources for our national cultural heritage. There is
exciting history here, something totally missed in all the early Negro-
History talk about heroes (the best boxer, the best bicycle-rider in the
world, etc.), a history which involves, among other things, development and survival of a new kind of English in a largely hostile sociolinguistic environment. It seems to me that this is going to involve
more research, rather than less research. With our eye on linguistics, rather than on the issue of racism, we can argue objectively
whether or not Negro dialect is the same as white speech, without feeling any social or moral pressure to say it is when it is not. I think we
will then have a more objective social-science treatment of the Negro,
and a more valid linguistic treatment of Negro dialect. And if that does
not directly improve the educational opportunities for lower-class Negro children, then my intuitive feelings about the central importance
of language in school achievement will have been wrong.

NOTES

[1]Elsie Clews Parsons. 1923. Folklore of the Sea Islands, South Carolina. Cambridge, Massachusetts: American Folklore Society, pp. 199-200.
[2]Lydia Parrish. 1942. Slave Songs of the Georgia Sea Islands. New York: Creative Age Press, Inc., p. 10.

'WHAT A THING IT IS!'

ALBERT H. MARCKWARDT

Princeton University

Abstract. The limitations of educational research, particularly
with respect to language learning, are generally recognized. The difficulty of establishing controlled conditions but for a single variable,
the gap between linguistic theory and its application, the ever-present
possibility of the Hawthorne effect, the undeniable fact that different
methods and approaches suit different teachers all contribute to the
establishment of a credibility gap, or if not that, at least to a reluctance
to accept any one set of results as definitive. This raises the question
of a source of guidance for the individual teacher: if the answers to
fundamental questions lie only in part in educational research, where
else are they to be found?
    One valuable and often neglected source of information is simply
the first and second language-learning experience of the teacher himself. Every teacher has learned at least one language and has expanded
considerably his capacity to use it. He may, in the course of his
education, have shifted dialects. Foreign-language teachers have
either learned English as a second language or the language they are
teaching. In fact, each one of us is constantly altering, day by day,
his command of at least one language.
    Much is to be learned from sophisticated individual introspection
relative to such matters as the acquisition of new vocabulary, the
adoption of new syntactic patterns and the expansion of old ones, the
operation of linguistic taboos, not merely verbal but structural as
well, and the way in which written material is composed. Properly
carried out, this inventory of personal experience can lead to a re-
examination of language attitudes, an appraisal of grammatical
theory, a tough realistic base for the judgment of pedagogical prac-

tice. Above all, it focuses attention where it should, upon the student
and the learning process. 'O this learning, what a thing it is!' exclaims Gremio in The Taming of the Shrew. Our principal task is to
find out just what sort of thing it is, and without question one important source of information lies in individual experience.

I must confess to a somewhat inordinate fondness for cryptic titles,
a weakness in which I indulge myself from time to time. It stems, I
fear, from the apprehension I occasionally feel when I look at my own
bibliography, wondering if I have spent my entire academic life writing
different versions of the same article.

Nevertheless, the relevance of the quotation from Shakespeare I
have taken as a title becomes a little more apparent when Gremio's
speech in the second scene of the first act of the Taming of the Shrew
is given in its entirety. 'O this learning, ' he exclaims, 'what a thing
it is!' All of us have, of course, just spent the past two days in hot
pursuit of this elusive problem—not only what it is, but just how one
finds out anything about it. And even the most optimistic of us must
confess that as far as the learning of language is concerned, we know
precious little, and some of that rests upon a fairly shaky foundation.

The initial sentence of a recent article by John B. Carroll reads,
'The process by which children learn their native language is in many
respects a mystery.' (Kosinski 135) The first three sentences of another article in the same collection of essays, this one by Robert B.
Ruddell, suggests a reason for our uncertainty about many of these
matters. 'Within the last four decades, the language development of
preschool and elementary school children has been carefully examined
under the austere lens of the psychologist and the language specialist.
These researchers have attempted to identify specific variables directly
related to children's language development. Only partial success has
been attained in this endeavor. ' (Kosinski 153)

For an indication of just how partial this success has been and the
extent to which the austere lens to which Mr. Ruddell refers has been
either cracked or clouded over, I turn to an as yet unpublished paper
by Ralph Robinett in which he sums up the present state of knowledge
with respect to one particular aspect of language learning, namely that
of the bilingual child. 'What does research tell us ?' he asks. The reply: 'Almost anything we want to hear: that bilingualism is good; that
it's bad; that a statistically significant number of bilinguals stutter;
that native speakers of English have just as hard a time learning "big"
words as do non-native speakers; that non-English speakers don't do
very well on English I. Q. tests; that bilinguals do better on both verbal
and nonverbal tests. For those of us in the business, there is a marked
tendency to quote—shall I say "selectively" ?' (Robinett 3)

My purpose is not to ridicule, not even to suggest that the so-called austere lens cannot do better than the eye behind it, but rather to call attention to the difficulties that are posed by the conventional pattern of educational research when it attempts to deal with language-learning problems, particularly in relationship to what is done in the classroom.

As we all know, language acquisition is by no means confined to the classroom or the school, as is the case with many other learning activities. The student brings a considerable command of the language with him when he enters kindergarten, although probably not as much as some linguists have optimistically declared. Moreover, his experiences with the English language are by no means confined to his language-arts instructional program, or even to his total school environment. The English language, or generally some form of it, surrounds him from his first to his last waking hour during the course of every day. Under circumstances such as these, how is exposure to be controlled in any sense?

Nor do the difficulties inherent in the situation stop at this point. Obviously any research in language learning must depend on one description of the language or another in order to identify the units or segments which the student is supposed to learn. This means a commitment to, or a preference for, one grammatical approach over another. But what may seem to be progress or increased mastery in terms of one grammar, and even transference to a productive or receptive command of the language, may turn out somewhat differently in terms of another.

It is evident, too, that progress in language performance must be measured. This leads to the problem of constructing tests, developing measuring instruments which are not only valid but 'culture free', if one accepts some of the current strictures on the evaluation process. There is in addition the necessity of separating levels and functional varieties of the language, at least to the extent of knowing what we are dealing with. Finally, there is the ever-present question of the Hawthorne effect on any experimental procedure.

Eight years ago the National Council of Teachers of English set one of its committees the task of reviewing all the research on the teaching and learning of composition, that is to say, learning how to use the written language effectively, in order to determine which of the studies were the most soundly based and worthy of publication in summary form. The committee, under the chairmanship of Professor Richard Braddock of the University of Iowa, examined more than five hundred studies and found only five which they were willing to classify as 'distinctly superior', defining this term not as 'perfect in all respects', but far more conservatively as 'the most soundly based of all those studies available'. The report goes on to say, 'There are many variables to control in research on written composition. There are so many that it is an unusual study which does not leave several important variables uncontrolled or undescribed. Consequently the writers of this report were tempted more than once not to select any "most soundly based studies" to summarize at length.' (Braddock 55)

As they found it with composition, so it is with other aspects of language learning. After all, dealing with learning in any intellectual field is difficult. The human mind is complex; it operates in a variety of ways. Language, as a form of human behavior, is equally complex and equally variable. Clearly, there is more than one way of learning and one way of teaching. As a consequence, one can scarcely escape the feeling that the classically structured pedagogical experiment is not likely to lead to conclusions about language learning in which we can place even a fair degree of confidence. I have always disliked the arrogant introductory clause, 'Research tells us', which my colleagues in education are likely to use as a preface to the statement of their beliefs of the moment. Research, or at least the kind to which they refer, has told us very little, as Mr. Robinett so trenchantly pointed out, and under the circumstances, it is not likely to tell us much more.

What, then, are we going to do about it? Do we give up the entire enterprise of trying to find out how language is learned and how it may best be taught? Certainly not, I would say. But I must confess that I see very little hope in stopping up the holes in the leaking vessel. We must try to tap some new, or at least hitherto unused, sources of information.

One such source is the individual experience of the teachers of English, of a foreign language, or of English as a foreign language. Every one of us in the profession has learned at least one language—his own—and is likely to have acquired some degree of competence in at least a second, if not a third or a fourth. And if what he has acquired is perceptibly less than competence, possibly there is something to be learned from his failure. Moreover, it is well known that for most teachers in this country, their current position represents a rise in social status, a fact which in itself is laden with implications for language learning, or at least dialect transference. This adds up to a considerable amount of learning experience for any one of us to fall back on, and I have in mind here the teacher in the classroom, not just the specialist in linguistics or pedagogy or psychology. Much of the experience may seem rather vague when attention is first directed to it, but it is surprising how much comes back, how many vague memories move into sharper focus when one begins to examine his past language experiences in detail, for the purpose of recalling specific instances of the way in which his own command of his native and of foreign languages developed.

Vocabulary is always a convenient starting point in exercises of this kind, since every one of us has multiplied his word stock many times since the beginning of his school experiences. We may best begin by trying to think of ten or a dozen fairly recent acquisitions. What was their source: reading or hearing them spoken? Was their meaning immediately clear, either totally or in part? To what extent did contextual clues furnish some concept of the meaning? How long was the term merely a passive element in the lexicon, and what were the circumstances which gave rise to its active use?

Vague or general answers to these questions will not be of much help. They must be asked in connection with specific words. Which words continue to give trouble because of some uncertainty about their sphere of use? I must confess, personally, to constant uneasiness with <u>heuristic</u> and <u>parameter</u>, and I have at least a suspicion as to the reason, namely that I encounter them so frequently in contexts that scarcely seem to justify their use, and I become over-cautious as a result. To become very specific, what is the history of your use of <u>atavism</u>, <u>adumbrate</u>, and <u>anaphoric</u>, to select a noun, verb, and adjective respectively, all beginning with the first letter of the alphabet?

Word composition is another important aspect of the learning of vocabulary. Again, in terms of specific experiences, let me ask to what extent is your facility here the result of a firm knowledge of certain word-forming prefixes and suffixes, and to what extent is it a catch-as-catch-can process. And if it is a firm knowledge, was it acquired by conscious effort or is it the result of a kind of osmosis, stemming from a familiarity with Latin, Greek, and French? On the very day that these remarks were written, I found myself on the horns of a dilemma, faltering between <u>judicious</u> and <u>judicial</u> as the most precise term in a particular context—this in connection with something else that I was writing. I blush to say that I finally gave up and used <u>temperate</u> instead.

As I have already suggested, we must not overlook our experiences in attempting to master the vocabulary of a foreign language. Here we run much more directly into the problem of trying to acquire a large number of words in a relatively short space of time. I still remember with distaste the self-teaching grammar of Italian that I used, with about sixty new vocabulary items in every lesson and virtually no planned repetition or re-entry for any of them. By careful experiment I determined a kind of average capacity for new items per lesson and let the rest go hang. I also remember, with a sense of triumph, my discovery of a series of correspondences between initial clusters in Italian and Spanish, a language with which I had some familiarity, and the help in word recognition that this gave me.

There is also the matter of social adjustment and of coping with current fads and the consequences of these for language development. How many in this audience have given up <u>tux</u> or <u>tuxedo</u> in favor of <u>dinner jacket</u>? When did the change begin, and under what circumstances?

How many will use <u>black tie</u> in a situation where <u>dinner jacket</u> seems a bit stilted? Did the impetus to change, if there has been one, come from reading, and if so what kind, or from observing the talk of others? This is just one example of operative social taboo, but the same phenomenon may be observed in connection with our terms for noon and evening meals, and for the household room which serves as the principal gathering place, to mention only two others.

Carefully recollected answers to questions such as these will serve two purposes. They should provide a number of useful clues to the way in which students acquire and employ the lexicon of the language, whether native or foreign. Certainly, unless we can answer such questions for ourselves, we can scarcely hope to answer them for anyone else, or to assist someone wisely in the growth and development of his stock of words. Moreover, the answers will be useful in calling into question some of the dubious and hoary superstitions relative to vocabulary and to vocabulary acquisition. 'Use a word five times and it is yours.' 'Consult the dictionary for every word you don't know.' What a ghastly prospect! It might even dispel the tired myth about the five-hundred word peasant vocabulary, no matter what language is being referred to and irrespective of how words are counted in it, and currently being applied to the lexicon of the culturally deprived.

Admittedly vocabulary acquisition is no more than a starting point. I began with it because it is tangible and because some of our lexical <u>faux pas</u> stand out in our memories so very sharply, and the scenes of triumph as well, I hasten to say. But we must go on to other matters. Phonologically, I suppose the most valuable experiences will be those connected with foreign-language learning, although I find it fascinating to watch my own linguistic behavior whenever I get to England. But again, to fix upon some specific questions, how successfully have you acquired the front round vowels of French and German, the lenis stops of French and Spanish, the uvular $\underline{r}$, the back unround vowels of Russian? For myself, I realize that I have just unconsciously listed these in an order of increasing difficulty and decreasing competence in their production. If you have acquired something like a native pronunciation for any of these, did the mastery come quickly or slowly, and were there recognizable stages? If only partially successful, what are the trouble spots, and why? A former professor of mine once discovered that the way in which he could most easily produce uvular $\underline{r}$ was to lie flat on his back, but this entailed certain difficulties in its practical use. Nevertheless, a thoughtful inventory of personal experience and difficulty here is not without its value in teaching a new dialect as well as a new language, and an equally comprehensive analysis of hearing difficulties will be relevant as well.

Next there is the grammatical apparatus to be considered. Much

of the morphology of the native language is internalized before we begin to go to school, so here again we must lean rather heavily upon
our experience in foreign-language acquisition. Fortunately the German and French that so many of us have been exposed to, taken together
pose a number of significant problems. What is your success with gender in these two? Arbitrary as it is, it is no more so than strong verbs
in English. If you have a firm grasp of the mixed declension of German
adjectives, or the forms of the subjunctive in French, when and how did
you acquire it? What were your adventures with the noun-adjective order in French, the transposed word order in German dependent clauses?
Are there clues here for the mastery of some of the morphological
trouble spots in Standard English?

When it comes to syntax, however, we can learn a great deal from
our fairly recent experiences in the native language and even from our
current practices. How do we manipulate language structure when we
communicate, both orally and in writing? What kinds of false starts
and construction shifts are you most given to in conversation or in
speaking extemporaneously? The soul-shattering experience of listening to a tape of yourself will go far in furnishing an answer to this last
question. What kinds of restructuring are typical when you convert a
first draft to a finished piece? Do you find it necessary to shift modifying elements in the interest of clarity and tightness, or are they happily placed in the initial version? Does the same hold true for the
avoidance of repetition, both structural and lexical? Which structures
do you overwork in a first draft, and at what point do you alter them?
How often does embedding occur when you first set down your ideas,
and to what extent does it reflect later manipulation?

How much do you remember about the way in which you acquired
whatever facility you may have in prose composition? At what point
did you develop the trait of beginning sentences with adverbial phrases?
Before or after you had developed the use of the initial adverbial
clause? When did you begin to use appositives, both restrictive and
nonrestrictive? Do you use them more frequently in speech or in writing? Does your writing show a tendency toward overuse of the passive?
Toward an excess of initial there and it? Do you vary sentence length
consciously? Use fragmentary sentences consciously—as I have done
just now?

These are but a few of the questions pertinent to anyone's awareness
of how he employs the language today and how he came to use it as he
does. Each one of us is constantly altering, day by day, his command
of at least one language, and for most of us the alteration is still in the
direction of greater expertise in its use. It is difficult to believe that
our own experiences toward this end are without significance for those
to whom we are trying to impart a heightened facility and competence.

I am not foolhardy enough to assert that the kind of sophisticated individual introspection I have been describing will answer all of our questions about language learning or language teaching. Nevertheless, given the difficulties attendant upon some of the pedagogical research which I mentioned at the outset, I believe that an inventory of personal experience is a valuable but hitherto almost totally neglected source of useful information which can scarcely be acquired in any other way. Properly conducted, it can lead to a re-examination of language attitudes, an appraisal of grammatical theory, and most important of all, a tough realistic base for the judgment of learning materials and pedagogical practice. It has the prime virtue of focusing attention where it should, upon the student and the learning process. It has the further virtue of developing the critical faculty and self-reliance of the person on the firing line, the classroom teacher, of protecting him from the three greatest threats to educational advance: the so-called expert, the zealot, and the hidebound. Let me, in concluding, repeat the quotation which furnished the title for what I hope has been at least a provocative suggestion: 'O this learning, what a thing it is!' Our principal task is to pursue precisely this point; and without question, one place to discover it lies in the experience of the individual with the languages he speaks and writes.

REFERENCES

Braddock, Richard, et al. 1963. Research in Written Composition. Champaign, Illinois: National Council of Teachers of English.
Kosinski, Leonard V., ed. 1968. Readings on Creative and Imagination in Literature and Language. Champaign, Illinois: National Council of Teachers of English.
Robinett, Ralph F. 1969. Bilingualism, the Education of Bilinguals, and Bilingual Education. Unpublished. Delivered at the National Advisory Council on the Teaching of English as a Foreign Language, February 27, 1969.

DISTINCTIVE LINGUISTIC CHARACTERISTICS OF BLACK ENGLISH

RALPH W. FASOLD

Center for Applied Linguistics

The question of whether or not there are distinctive differences between the nonstandard speech of poor black people (which we can call Black English) and the speech of whites has been much discussed in recent years. Almost any conceivable position on the subject can find its advocates. The view of those who are unfamiliar with the systematic nature of Black English is usually that Black English is simply English pronounced sloppily and with many grammatical errors. In other words, there are no differences between the two kinds of English which are not the result of carelessness in speaking. In this view, the differences would disappear completely if only black people would use more care. Unfortunately, this view can be found even in the work of some who have achieved some recognition in the field of English for the disadvantaged. Thus, we find Dr. Ruth Golden treating a set of standard English and Black English sentences as if they were on an ascending scale of correctness. [1]

> Individuals use different levels of language for different situations. These levels vary from the illiterate to the formal and literary. For instance, starting with the illiterate, He don't be here, we might progress to the colloquial, He ain't here, to the general and informal He isn't here up to the formal and literary, He is not present.

From Dr. Golden's perspective, we find a sentence like He don't be here, which appears to be very different from anything which would appear in the English of whites, treated as if it were not different at all, except that it represents an extreme of deterioration from standard English.

Apparently in reaction to this view, a number of linguists began to take the opposite position; namely that features used by Black English speakers which are apparently the same as those in standard English are actually very different. A few citations from the literature will illustrate this. In an article in the Florida FL Reporter, J. L. Dillard indicated that sentences with the 'zero copula', while they sound much like standard English sentences, are really quite different. [2]

> The 'zero copula' as in He there ... can pass (almost in the racial disguise sense) for He's there with a 'lightly articulated' -s.

In an article in a later issue of the same journal, William A. Stewart argues that the wide differences between Black English and the dialects of whites, while profound, are likely to remain undiscovered by dialect geographers and non-linguists. [3]

> One further reason why both language teachers and dialectologists have failed to appreciate the extent to which nonstandard Negro dialects may differ from nonstandard white dialects (even in the Deep South) may simply be that such differences now remain mostly in syntax (i.e. grammatical patterns and categories) rather than in vocabulary or lexicophonology (i.e. word forms), and are thus not normally uncovered by the word-comparison techniques which dialectologists and non-linguists rely on so heavily.

Stewart goes on to give four illustrative sentences, one in standard English, one in a white nonstandard dialect, one in Negro nonstandard basilect, and one in Gullah and to argue that the Negro nonstandard sentence, while superficially very similar to the sentences in the two white dialects, is really more similar to the Gullah sentence, in spite of the fact that the Gullah sentence looks very different from the other three.

Perhaps the most extreme example of this movement in the study of Black English is the work of Marvin D. Loflin. In an article published in The English Journal, Loflin makes the statement that: [4]

> ... efforts to construct a grammar for Nonstandard Negro English suggest that the similarities between it and Standard English are superficial. There is every reason, at this stage of research, to believe that a fuller description of Nonstandard Negro English will show a grammatical system which must be treated as a foreign language.

Elsewhere, Loflin has constructed a grammar of the Black English verb structure which is radically different from the corresponding structure of the standard English verb system.

It will perhaps surprise no one that careful research has supported a view of the status of Black English which is somewhere between these two. But before going any further, it is necessary for us to distinguish two subvarieties of Black English. One of these spoken by almost all adults and most older children can be called Mainstream Black English. Mainstream Black English has many rules of grammar and pronunciation in common with standard English, other rules which are not in standard English but are shared with other nonstandard dialects, and a few which belong exclusively to Black English. There are also speech features not found in the mainstream dialect which are used by very young children. These features have been cited by Stewart and others as examples of the 'basilect' Negro dialect. [5] However, beyond a few citations and some speculations about possible origins in creole languages, little has been published about the basilect. In any event, its speakers are so few in number, at least in the northern urban setting, and they so quickly outgrow the use of basilect features, that it will be safe to ignore the basilect in the remarks that follow.

When the use of a feature like invariant be is examined with rigor, it turns out that it is certainly not a form on the illiterate level from which one might progress to the literary and formal is. The invariant form of be is distinct from all inflected forms of be and is the marker of a distinction which standard English can only make paraphrastically. The use of the present tense forms of to be in Black English can be used to indicate either a momentary or a completely uninterrupted action or state. In I'm a man, the constant state is intended. In I'm here, the momentary aspect may be the appropriate interpretation. But to express an action or state which is recurrent, the form be is used. Thus I be here means that the speaker is not here just for the moment, nor is he here perpetually, but he returns here periodically.

To demonstrate this, we can examine some data on the adverb co-occurrence with invariant be and with the present tense forms. In the speech of 56 speakers of Black English from Detroit and D. C., invariant be occurred 357 times. Of these 357 examples 111 co-occurred with a time adverb. Of these 111 time adverbs 92 were of a type which specify repeated occurrence, such as sometimes, usually, every day, or mostly. [6] This means that the form be co-occurred with an adverb of repeated occurrence in 25.8% of all its occurrences. Furthermore, an analysis of the remaining 19 time adverbs with which be co-occurred but which do not indicate repeated occurrence showed that none of the 19 contradicted the notion of repeated occurrence.

These figures are more impressive when we compare them with the occurrences of time adverbs with present tense forms of to be in the speech of some of the same Black English speakers. Of 538 instances of present tense be, adverbs of repeated occurrence appeared with only two. While invariant be co-occurred with such an adverb over 25% of the time, the present tense forms occurred with these adverbs in less than 1% of all their occurrences. It hardly seems likely that this situation is accidental.

It is interesting to note that the time adverbs now and right now were the most frequent adverbs with the present tense concord forms but never occur at all with invariant be.

In other cases, alleged gross differences between Black English and standard English have been shown to be relatively superficial. Labov has shown conclusively that the absence of forms of to be in Black English results from a rule which allows for the deletion of the remnants of contraction of the present tense forms of to be.[7] His analysis revealed that to be is absent only when it is in the present tense. With modal auxiliaries, when the form is infinitive, or when the past tense forms are used, the expected forms of to be are always present. Labov further showed that even when to be occurs in the present tense, it is only absent under conditions in which contraction is possible in standard English. Furthermore, the form am is virtually never absent. It seems clear that the most compact analysis would allow for the removal of the remnants of the contraction of the present tense form of to be, provided that what is left is not the 'm of am. These considerations are only a small part of the evidence that this is the correct analysis.[8]

Even when a Black English sentence contains an instance of invariant be, this is not sufficient to prove that it is a sentence which is completely different from what occurs in standard English.

The use of invariant be is potentially ambiguous in three ways in Black English. Consider these three sentences, each illustrating one of the three meanings.

Lou be home next week.
Last year, he told him he be writing to him.
Usually I just be by myself.

In Lou be home next week, the auxiliary will is understood. The rules of Black English pronunciation provide for the deletion of will in two steps, as in the case of is and are. First, will can be contracted to 'll, as in standard English. Black English has a further rule by which 'll can be eliminated. Similarly, the second sentence, Last year he said he be writing to him is understood to contain would. Just as will can be contracted and its remnants removed, so would can be contracted to 'd and the 'd removed by a similar process. The third sentence, Usually I just be by myself, on the other hand, has no understood auxiliary and no parallel in standard English.

Consider the following sentence, which is ambiguous in all three ways:

If somebody hit him, Darryl be mad.

Under the first interpretation (understood will), it is a prediction as to how Darryl will react if he is hit. If it is interpreted as containing the auxiliary would, it expresses a hypothesis as to how Darryl might react. If the be in the sentence is taken as distributive be, it is a statement of Darryl's regular reaction to being hit. The sentence is only ambiguous because it is a positive statement. In negative sentences, contraction of will to 'll and would to 'd is not possible. The three interpretations of the above sentence would each be denied in a different way, namely:

If somebody hit him, Darryl won't be mad.
If somebody hit him, Darryl wouldn't be mad.
If somebody hit him, Darryl don't be mad.

On balance, it seems that rigorous research will reveal that although there may be some features of Black English which are surprisingly and extensively different from anything in any English dialect spoken by whites, most of the differences between the speech of whites and Black English will be relatively superficial. This conclusion hardly means that there is no problem. Far from it. The differences which exist, both profound and superficial, are socially stigmatized and can contribute to the limitation of opportunity for those who speak Black English. What may be worse, attempts by formal education to eradicate these features by condemning them as sloppy or bad speech can seriously undermine the child's sense of dignity and self-esteem. It is important to realize that the differences between standard English and Black English are in no sense careless deteriorations from standard English. Rather these speech forms conform to grammar and pronunciation rules which are just as rigorous as any rule in a grammar text.

NOTES

[1]Ruth I. Golden. 1963. Effectiveness of Instructional Tapes for Changing Regional Speech. Unpublished Ed. D. dissertation. Wayne State University, p. 171.

[2]J. L. Dillard. 1967. Negro Children's Dialect in the Inner City. The Florida FL Reporter, Vol. 5, No. 3, pp. 7, 8.

[3]William A. Stewart. 1968. Continuity and Change in American Negro English. The Florida FL Reporter, Vol. 6, No. 1, p. 16.

[4]Marvin D. Loflin. 1967. A Teaching Problem in Nonstandard Negro English. English Journal, Vol. 56, p. 1312.

[5]See for example, William A. Stewart. 1965. Urban Negro Speech: Sociolinguistic Factors Affecting English Teaching, in Social Dialects and Language Learning, Roger W. Shuy, ed. Champaign, Illinois: National Council of Teachers of English, p. 15. Also J. L. Dillard, op. cit., p. 7-10.

[6]Mostly is a time adverb of this type in Black English, although it is not in most standard dialects.

[7]William Labov. 1968. Contraction, Deletion and Inherent Variability of the English Copula. Unpublished manuscript. New York.

[8]The fact that this rule also applies to the 've contraction of have has lead Marvin Loflin to the erroneous conclusion that have + -ed does not exist in Black English (Marvin D. Loflin. On the Structure of the Verb in a Dialect of American Negro English. To appear in Linguistics). Current research by Walter Wolfram and myself has shown that have + -ed indeed does function in Black English. Since Loflin's contention that the verb structure of the black dialect is radically different from the verb structure of standard English depends crucially on the alleged absence of have + -ed in Black English, we must conclude that the verb structure he constructs is invalid.

HISTORICAL AND STRUCTURAL BASES FOR THE RECOGNITION OF NEGRO DIALECT

WILLIAM A. STEWART

Education Study Center

1. The issue. Because of the current focus on the nonstandard speech of lower-class Negro school children by current educational problems and curriculum needs, the issue of whether or not there exists a distinctive Negro dialect has come to underlie pedagogical as well as scientific efforts to help such children, and has flared up openly in academic circles. In itself, the issue is not new; the existence of Negro dialect, while traditionally accepted by the general public and most literati, came under question by philologists and dialectologists in the early decades of the present century. Using the philological technique of word-form comparison, they showed that the lexicon and lexico-phonology of uneducated American Negroes contained little or nothing which could not be found in the speech of southern American whites, or rural Englishmen. Thus, they argued, it was unreasonable (and, by implication, probably racistic) to treat uneducated Negro speech as an entity distinct from uneducated white speech. It should be kept in mind that the issue was debated at a time when linguistic descriptions and linguistic comparisons were made primarily (and almost exclusively) on the bases of phonology and lexicon; sophisticated techniques for describing the grammatical features of languages and dialects were not yet due for several decades. Because of this, grammatical similarities between Negro and white nonstandard dialect were assumed, rather than determined. Furthermore, it was probably no accident that the view of Negro-white linguistic unity was advanced—and quickly accepted in educated circles—at a time when there was an upsurge of motivation within the Negro population for incorporation into the white world (and increased willingness on the part of at least the

white scholars to accept Negroes), and at a time when it was becoming understood that physical differences between Negroes and whites did not necessarily imply the physical inferiority of the Negro. It was not yet understood, however, that behavioral differences between Negroes and whites did not necessarily imply the cultural inferiority of the Negro. Thus, to demonstrate that Negro speech was identical to white speech was, at the time, the only way to assert the linguistic equality of Negroes to whites. Once this view became established among philologists and dialectologists, it was largely self-perpetuating. Since the linguistic forms used by Negroes were considered to have all come originally from white sources, then any occurrence of a linguistic form in the speech of a Negro, even if absent in the speech of local whites, was assumed to be or have been present in the speech of some white, sometime, somewhere. Any recorded examples of Negro speech which deviated extremely from known white dialect patterns were accordingly dismissed as racist inventions (e.g. literary dialect texts), or, where 'scientific' recordings by dialectologists had been made (as in the case of Gullah), explained away as a historical anomaly.[1]

As long as the issue of Negro dialect remained a purely scholarly matter, there was little chance of the theory of Negro-white linguistic unity being questioned. Since the theory predicated the questions and interpretations embodied in formal dialect research, it was self-fulfilling in the field. The only possible challenge was from outside the philology and dialectology establishments. But Negroes, who might have challenged the theory on ideological grounds, were not ready to do so. Usually happy to be considered white in any way possible, they were hardly anxious to question the beliefs of the one branch of social science which did that most successfully. (The first Negro to eventually do so, Lorenzo Dow Turner, came—significantly—out of the Negro History field. But his studies concerned African survivals in Gullah, which allowed philologists and dialectologists who considered Gullah anomalous to deny the relevance of his conclusions for other kinds of American Negro speech.) Therefore, any serious challenge to the unity view of Negro and white speech in America would have to be scientific, not ideological, and it would have to originate with a group of professionals who were interested in the Negro as a possibly unique entity culturally and linguistically, not in the Negro as a parrot of European language and culture. So, when the challenge did come, it was natural that it came from Caribbeanists and Africanists. Their challenge was made on three bases: historical, comparative, and synchronic.[2]

2. The historical-comparative basis for Negro-dialect autonomy. The historical arguments which Caribbeanists and Africanists have advanced in favor of Negro dialect being something more than just a conglomeration of British linguistic features are based primarily on the

existence of early literary attestations of North American Negro speech which show it to have differed markedly from any known kind of British or white-colonial dialect. Precisely because of this, most dialectologists and language historians have been inclined to dismiss these attestations as racist inventions having no real basis in the reality of early American Negro usage. (It is interesting to note that one of the most prominent historians of the English language in America, George Philip Krapp, did indeed see that many of these early attestations might be fairly accurate.[3] But, working before the advent of the serious study of pidgin and creole languages, he tended to dismiss the clearly pidginized examples as real enough speech, but not well-formed language. Thus, the possibility of treating these pidgin-creole varieties of early American English as a legitimate historical alternative to British dialects as a source for more recent American Negro speech was not seriously considered by him.) A comparative study of these attestations certainly suggests that most of them were as realistic as literary-dialect norms of the day permitted. Some showed African phonological interference in English with surprising accuracy, while most exhibited such real and widespread creolisms as zero copula, zero possessive, object pronominal forms (from the British point of view) with subject function, uninflected verbs, etc. The obvious structural relationship between the kind of early North American Negro English suggested by these attestations and varieties of creole English which were (and still are) used in the West Indies on the one hand, and many nonstandard varieties of Negro speech (especially—but not exclusively—of the Gullah type) on the other, make it difficult if not impossible to maintain that African slaves coming to North America acquired British or colonial English the way it was spoken by whites, and passed it on in that form to their descendants. Instead, it seems clear that the English of New World Negroes has been different from the speech of New World whites (and Old World whites as well) from the very beginning—and, in fact, gets more different the further back one goes. Thus, in spite of the fact that they are made much of by white dialect geographers and middle-class Negro image-makers, cases of Negroes who speak exactly like whites must be recent and exceptional rather than traditional and typical. This means that any distinctive characteristics of Negro speech have their origin in linguistic history rather than in oppression, and represent normal language differences rather than the direct effects of poverty, ignorance, or genetic inferiority.

3. The structural basis for Negro-dialect autonomy. If it is the case that the speech of American Negroes never was identical to that of American whites, and that, in fact, the two diverge more and more as one goes back through time, then it stands to reason that the Chomskian assumption that different dialects which derive from a single source will differ primarily in trivial surface features, while possibly

valid for white dialects of American English, may not necessarily apply to the differences between Negro dialects and white dialects. This means that the attempts of many linguists to derive Negro-dialect forms from underlying representations which are identical to those which seem to exist for white dialects, while comforting to the social conscience of white liberals and the social insecurity of middle-class Negroes, may nevertheless obstruct accurate analysis. Furthermore, the assumption that superficially similar linguistic phenomena in Negro and white speech are caused by the same factors may lead to conclusions about Negro behavior which are far more unfair than assumptions about linguistic and cultural differences, whether real or imagined, could ever be. In a recent work on nonstandard Negro speech, for example, as cautious a linguist as William Labov, while rightly taking Carl Bereiter and his associates to task for assuming that a sentence like Me got juice (heard from a Negro child) represents unstructured language, attempts to explain away the use of me in subject position as a developmental phenomenon—the incomplete mastery of the I/me alternation of adult speech, simply because that is what such a sentence would be in the mouth of a white child.[4] But the fact is that the use of such pronominal forms as me, him, her, dem in subject position and with subject function can be heard from adult as well as infant Negroes, which, if one were to accept Labov's explanation, would mean that a teenage or adult Negro's use of Me got juice would have to be regarded as evidence of retarded language development! Once one rejects the idea that similar Negro and white speech forms need be the result of the same process, however, and comes to understand that such forms as me, him and dem were normal subject pronouns in older American Negro speech, then present-day occurrences of them (even their use by octogenarians) will lose all suggestion of pathology.

In the same work, Labov's attempt to treat Negro-dialect zero copula as a low-level phonological deletion of a word-final sibilant resulting from contraction à la standard English (e.g. an underlying form something like He is big becomes He's big, and then a deletion rule for the /z/ of the contracted form He's big produces He big) gets him into more trouble. At one point, Labov is forced to consider a sentence of the form I'm onna say why what they say you have to have a high school diploma as, in his words, an 'unsolved puzzle' insofar as its grammatical structure is concerned.[5] Now, it could be that this sentence has an intrusive what put in it through some sort of surface confusion, and ought to be I'm onna say why they say you have to have a high school diploma. To anyone who knows Negro dialect well, however, it will be apparent that the sentence is perfectly well-formed as originally recorded. With a zero copula before the last noun phrase, the sentence means, in a more standard type of English: I'm going to say why what they say you have to have is a high school diploma. Apparently, Labov was prohibited from considering this possibility by his theory of the standard-English-like nature of Negro-dialect zero copula, since standard English would not contract _is_ in this position in the sentence under consideration. That is, standard English would not have _I'm going to say why what they say you have to have's a high school diploma_. In addition, Labov's theory that Negro-dialect zero copula is merely an extension of standard-English contraction fails to deal with the fact that a Negro-dialect sentence like _He workin'_ is not really an exact grammatical equivalent of standard English _He (i)s working_, since the Negro-dialect construction indicates immediate action in contrast to _He be workin'_ for repetitive or extended action. This Negro-dialect distinction, which obviously goes deeper than mere surface phonology, is difficult to relate to standard English in any credible way. Moreover, the fact that Negro-dialect _be_, used in this way, has the tag _do_ (e. g. _Do he be workin'_?) precludes the possibility of its being derived directly from the _will be_ construction of standard English by, say, a phonological deletion of the contracted form /l/ of the auxiliary _will_. [6]

Now, this criticism of certain details of Labov's analysis of Negro dialect should not be taken as a general condemnation of that analysis. On the contrary, it is precisely because Labov's research on Negro speech has generally been so thorough and insightful that I regard his explanation of the use by Negroes of _me_, etc., in subject position and his analysis of Negro-dialect copula as inconsistent with his usually healthy views. Labov makes a strong case for the structural and logical integrity of Negro dialect, but then would agree with Bereiter in principle if not in degree that a sentence like _Me got juice_ would represent language pathology if heard from an adult. Labov demonstrates that Negro dialect has its own system of grammatical and phonological rules, but would explain the Negro-dialect use of the copula as essentially standard-English-like. And the worst part of it is that he ignores counter evidence which is available in his own data and conclusions. Part of his dilemma is etiological; if one assumes that the use of _me_ as a subject is natural only at a certain early stage of language development in children, then any instance of _me_ as a subject is, ipso facto, an example of retarded language development. But in the case of Labov's analysis of the Negro-dialect zero copula as merely the result of phonological deletion of copula contraction, the deletion rules he proposes do not seem to account very satisfactorily for another characteristic of Negro-dialect predication which Labov's research turned up—that the frequency of copula deletion was not the same for different grammatical functions. Most notably, zero copula occurred less before noun phrases than before verb phrases. [7] In keeping with his attempt to make Negro-dialect copula deletion standard-English-like, Labov tries to explain this difference as the result of a variable constraint which has moved to a 'higher level', producing a semi-categorical pat-

tern. Yet, it is precisely here that a willingness to consider other relationships than just with standard English become important in the analysis of Negro dialect. For, if many Negro-dialect forms and patterns could have resulted from earlier creole ones—in spite of superficial similarities between present-day Negro dialect and standard English or white nonstandard dialect—then a more plausible explanation
for the statistical difference in Negro-dialect copula deletion before
noun phrases and verb phrases could actually be the converse of that
given by Labov. That is, it might well be that the statistical discrepancy reflects an earlier categorical difference which, because of a
subsequent merger of the grammatical markers, has now come to look
like variability. In an earlier recorded form of Gullah, for example,
equation (i. e. predication with a noun-phrase complement) was marked,
apparently categorically, by means of a morpheme which we might
write /da/. Verb phrases roughly equivalent to English V + ing were
/da/ followed by the unmarked verb. Thus we had both <u>Dem da fish</u>
'They are fish', and <u>Dem da fish</u> 'They are fishing'. That these were
only superficially similar is made clear from a later change to V + <u>ing</u>
for the verb phrase, while retaining /da/ for equation, e. g. <u>Dem da
fish</u> 'They are fish', but <u>Dem fishin</u> 'They are fishing'. Later still,
the /da/ equative morpheme was relexified to /iz/, so that one said
<u>Dem iz fish</u> 'They are fish' but <u>Dem fishin</u> 'They are fishing'. Finally,
with the introduction of an optional dummy /iz/ in V-<u>ing</u> phrases, and
a partial collapse of verbal /iz/=∅ with equative /iz/≠∅, one can see
the historical process—entirely documentable—which could easily have
given rise to the statistical difference in copula deletion discovered by
Labov.

An even less defensible claim that Negro dialect differs only super-
ficially from standard English involves another aspect of verb phrases.
A number of linguists, including Ralph W. Fasold of the Center for Applied Linguistics, have questioned the view that the verbal system of
Negro dialect differs in the treatment of preterites and perfectives.
The debate has been motivated by Marvin Loflin's analysis of the Negro-
dialect verbal system as having no preterite vs. perfective distinction. [8]
Now, one of my long-standing disagreements with Loflin has been precisely on this issue, since all American Negro dialects and even creole
varieties of English seem to have some such distinction as is marked
by a <u>Dey/dem finish yesterday</u> vs. <u>Dey/dem done finish now</u>. Furthermore, even most American Negro basilects have a contrast, which is
most explicit in the negative, between <u>ain't</u> followed by an unmarked
verb (indicating the preterite) and <u>ain't</u> followed by a past-marked verb
(indicating the perfective), e. g. <u>He ain't go</u> meaning 'He didn't go' and
<u>He ain't gone</u> or <u>He ain't went</u> meaning 'He hasn't gone'. [9] To compli-
cate matters, there is the remote past marker <u>been</u> which is used in
many varieties of American Negro dialects. [10] But the arguments ad-

vanced by such linguists as Fasold against Loflin's analysis and in favor of a basic similarity in this aspect of the verbal system between
Negro dialect and standard English are simply that a sequence like He
gone is actually He have gone (and therefore perfective) with the auxiliary deleted through a contraction stage—presumably He's gone or
He've gone. But the point is that, even if this is so, it does not make
the Negro-dialect verbal system similar to that of standard English.
For, if He done it can be explained as He (have) done it, then contrasting forms like He done done it and He been done it should be explained
as He (have) done done it and He (have) been done it, which, if maximally standardized, would be He has done done it and He has been done
it—hardly standard English in form or meaning!

It would seem that the synchronic study of Negro speech as it exists
today, as well as the study of Negro-dialect history, would benefit from
an increased willingness on the part of linguists to look outside the
'melting pot' tradition of Negro-speech-qua-white-speech to non-
European sources for those features of Negro speech which seem strange
by white norms. In particular, a re-evaluation of early literary records of American Negro speech should prove helpful in settling disputed
or unclear points about the processes by which Negro dialect forms are
produced or have come about. Until synchronic studies of American
Negro speech face up to and explain the many striking similarities between it and attested forms of creole English used by colonial Negroes,
present-day Caribbean creole English, and West African forms of English, the results may be more appropriate as white-assimilationist
propaganda than as the scientific study of the American Negro.

NOTES

[1] In his review of Turner's work on Gullah (see n. 2, below) in Language 26 (1950), Raven I. McDavid, Jr. assumes that Gullah represents 'the unique example of a creolized language developing in the
United States' (p. 323). Since he does not admit the creole French of
Louisiana as another case, it must be that McDavid sees that the close
structural correspondences between it and the various creole French
dialects spoken in the West Indies are evidence that the history of creole French involves far more than local linguistic anomalies. But, although the structural correspondences between Gullah and such West
Indian varieties of creole English as Jamaican Creole are equally close,
McDavid seems to be content with the conclusion that these are merely
the result of a common African substratum and, therefore, that they
have no implications for a direct relationship between the creole varieties of English themselves. Incidentally, in the same review, McDavid takes Turner to task for not having presented 'a descriptive grammar' of Gullah in his study. This criticism rings especially false,

coming as it does from a prominent representative of a dialect-studies tradition which had never to that time (and has never since) produced a descriptive grammar of any American dialect.

[2]In order of appearance, the Africanist-creolist contentions that Negro speech has been shaped by African substrate influence and pidgination are: Melville J. Herskovits, The Myth of the Negro Past (New York: Harper & Brothers, 1941), particularly Chapter VIII; Lorenzo Dow Turner, Africanisms in the Gullah Dialect (Chicago: University of Chicago Press, 1949); Robert A. Hall, Jr., 'The African Substratum in Negro English' American Speech 25 (1950); J. L. Dillard, 'The Writings of Herskovits and the Study of the Language of the Negro in the New World' Caribbean Studies 4 (1964); Beryl Loftman Bailey, 'Toward a New Perspective in Negro English Dialectology' American Speech 40 (1965); William A. Stewart, 'Sociolinguistic Factors in the History of American Negro Dialects' The Florida FL Reporter 5 (1967) and 'Continuity and Change in American Negro Dialects' The Florida FL Reporter 6 (1968); J. L. Dillard, 'Non-Standard Negro Dialects—Convergence or Divergence?' The Florida FL Reporter 6 (1968); David Dalby, 'Black Through White: Patterns of Communication' (Hans Wolff Memorial Lecture, delivered at Indiana University, March 24, 1969, in press).

[3]George Philip Krapp. 1925. The English Language in America. 2 vols. New York: The Century Co. See particularly Vol. I, pp. 246-265.

[4]William Labov. 1969. The Study of Non-Standard English. Washington, D.C.: Center for Applied Linguistics. p. 48.

[5]William Labov. op. cit., p. 54.

[6]This practically universal occurrence of be to indicate an extended or repeated state or action in the nonstandard speech of American Negroes may or may not be the result of an earlier creole stage or an African substratum. The use of be in a similar way seems to occur in at least some varieties of nonstandard Irish English; see Jiro Taniguchi, A Grammatical Analysis of Artistic Representation of Irish English (Tokyo: Shinozaki Shorin, 1956), pp. 79-80. But if that is the origin of the Negro-dialect use of be (i.e. borrowed by Negroes, let us say, from Irish immigrants to North America), then why is it now so widespread among Negroes but so absent from the still somewhat Irish-sounding speech of many direct descendants of the Irish immigrants? J. L. Dillard has pointed out to me some early literary suggestions of uninflected be + verb in certain varieties of West Indian English, although this does not seem to be common in the Caribbean today. David Dalby has expressed to me the opinion that the form be may have been borrowed from some kind of European English to serve a grammatical function which occurs in many West African languages—one which is marked by blan in both Krio and an older variety of Gullah. This certainly seems possible. In the one West African language I am most

familiar with, Wolof, there is a particle, di, which functions almost exactly like Negro-basilect be; see William A. Stewart, Cheikh Babou, Dorothy Pedtke, et al, Introductory Course in Dakar Wolof (Washington, D. C.: Center for Applied Linguistics, 1966), section II, pp. 32-33.

[7] This characteristic of zero copula in Negro dialect has been noted by William Labov in 'Contraction, Deletion, and Inherent Variability of the English Copula' (a paper originally given at the December 1967 meeting of the Linguistic Society of America and, in expanded form, at the Conference on Pidginization and Creolization in Languages held in Jamaica in August 1968). It will undoubtedly be elaborated on in some of Labov's forthcoming publications.

[8] The analysis of Negro dialect without a preterite-perfective distinction is presented in Marvin D. Loflin, 'On the Structure of the Verb in a Dialect of American Negro English', to appear in a forthcoming issue of Linguistics.

[9] In forms which attempt to approximate standard English more closely, ain't becomes didn't in the preterite and haven't in the perfective, e.g. He didn't go vs. He haven't gone or He haven't went.

[10] As far as I know, this remote-past function of been was first pointed out (pp. 15-16) in my article 'Urban Negro Speech: Sociolinguistic Factors Affecting English Teaching' which appeared in Roger W. Shuy, ed., Social Dialects and Language Learning (Champaign, Illinois: National Council of Teachers of English, 1964).

LINGUISTIC CORRELATES OF SOCIAL DIFFERENCES IN THE NEGRO COMMUNITY

WALTER A. WOLFRAM

Center for Applied Linguistics

Within the last several years the speech patterns of lower socio-economic class Negroes have become increasingly important to a number of different disciplines, including linguistics, sociology, psychology, and education. Whereas one can certainly understand why scholars might focus on that variety of English spoken by Negroes which shows the most structural and functional contrast with standard English, it has become increasingly apparent that there is a need to study the speech of a wider representation of the black population. To understand the significance of speech as an indicator of social status in the black community it is insufficient to consider only one subset of the community. Also, in order to study the role of linguistic behavior in social mobility it is necessary to determine how different linguistic features correlate with specific social levels. Furthermore, as a practical basis for the teaching of standard English it is essential to have some understanding of what particular features characterize specific socioeconomic groups and at what age levels.

As a case study of the sociolinguistic parameters of the black community, Detroit was chosen as an example of a large Northern urban area. From over 700 original interviews conducted by the Detroit Dialect Study, 60 informants were chosen to evenly represent four social classes (conventionally labeled upper-middle, lower-middle, upper-working, and lower-working class), three age levels (10-12 year old preadolescents, 14-17 year old teenagers, and 30-55 year old adults), and sex differences (see Shuy, Wolfram, and Riley 1968, for a description of the field procedures).

This measurement of sociolinguistic behavior requires the formulation of a unit which can take into account continuous ordered variation within and across discrete linguistic types (e.g. within or across systematic phoneme boundaries). The unit that permits this characterization has been termed the 'linguistic variable' (Labov 1964: 15). The linguistic variable, itself an abstraction, is realized in actual speech behavior by 'variants'; that is, individual items which are members of a class of variants constituting the variable. For example, we may choose to consider what we will call the 'theta' variable in word-medial or word-final position. For this variable, generally represented orthographically as th in such words as mouth, nothing, and tooth, at least four significant variants are actually realized phonetically. These include an interdental voiceless fricative θ (e.g. [nəθɨŋ]), a labiodental voiceless fricative f (e.g. [nəfɨn]), an alveolar stop t (e.g. [nət n]), or no consonantal realization at all (e.g. [nəɨn]).

The formulation of the linguistic variable has important dividends for sociolinguistics in that it is the unit which serves as the basis for correlating linguistic with extra-linguistic or independent linguistic factors. The particular value of a given linguistic variable (x) may be viewed as a function (f) of its correlation with extra-linguistic or independent linguistic variables. For example, in the current study extra-linguistic factors such as socioeconomic class, sex, age, contextual style, and racial isolation are considered; independent linguistic factors taken into account are linear environment and construction type. This may be represented as:

$x = f(a, b, c, d, e, f. g)$
where a = socio-economic class
    b = sex
    c = age
    d = contextual style
    e = racial isolation
    f = linear environment
    g = construction type

The regularity with which much variation between forms, formerly dismissed as 'free variation', can be accounted for on the basis of extra-linguistic and independent linguistic factors has made the concept of the linguistic variable an invaluable construct in the description of patterned speech variation.

The study of linguistic variables rather than categorical constants adds a new dimension to the examination of speech differences, namely, the quantitative measurement of the variants of a variable. As quantitative methods are used, correlations between linguistic and social patterns emerge. The utilization of quantitative methods is, of course, somewhat of a paradox in linguistics since structural linguistics has been based on the classification of elements into discrete qualitative units, conceived as absolutely different from one another. That a qualitative model is adequate for a description of language as 'code' (i.e. its cognitive function) is not disputed here; however, the functions of language when viewed as 'behavior' (i.e. its social function) suggest that a qualitative model is inadequate in accounting for the patterned variation between forms.

The quantitative measurement of linguistic variables necessarily involves counting variants. Although at first glance this may seem like a fairly simple procedure, hardly requiring linguistic sophistication, Labov (1968: 14) has correctly pointed out that:

> ... even the simplest type of counting raises a number of subtle and difficult problems. The final decision as to what to count is actually the final solution to the problem at hand. The decision is approached only through a long series of exploratory maneuvers.

In the first place, it is necessary to delimit the number of variants which can reliably be identified and to select relevant categories of variants for tabulation. Take, for example, the case of syllable-final d in such words as good, bad, and stupid. At least six phonetically different realizations for syllable-final d can be transcribed, including a voiced stop [d], a partially voiced stop [d̥], a voiced flap [ɖ], a glottal stop [ʔ], an unreleased stop [t], and no consonantal realization at all [∅]. Although six different phonetic realizations can be noted, there are only three relevant categories for tabulation: (1) a stop with partial or full voicing, (2) a voiceless glottal or unreleased alveolar stop, and (3) no consonantal realization at all.

It is also important to identify the total population of utterances in which an item may 'potentially' vary (Labov 1968: 14). For example, in the consideration of copula absence for the Negro population (e.g. he nice) there are certain types of syntactic constructions (e.g. clause final, emphasis, past tense, first person singular, etc.) in which the presence of the copula is obligatory for all speakers regardless of socioeconomic class; in other types of syntactic constructions, however, the copula may or may not be present. To include both types of constructions in a quantitative measurement of variation is to skew the actual figures of variation.

Further, it is necessary to identify relevant linguistic environments (phonological, grammatical, and semological) which may affect the variation of items. In identifying and classifying different types of environments affecting variation, it is also necessary to exclude environments in which distinctions between variants are neutralized for phonetic reasons. Thus, in word-final consonant clusters in such

words as test, desk, and ground, it is necessary to exclude clusters
which are immediately followed by a homorganic consonant (e. g. test
day) from the tabulation since it is sometimes impossible to perceive
whether the final consonant of the cluster is present or absent. The
importance of identifying relevant linguistic environments is no less
for quantitative studies than it is for qualitative description.

With our previous discussion on the nature of the linguistic variable
in mind, let us now turn to the actual variables which were delimited in
our case study of Detroit. Four phonological and four grammatical variables were chosen for this study. The four phonological variables
were: (1) word-final consonant + stop clusters (e. g. desk, ground,
cold) whose variants are simply the presence or the absence of the final
stop, (2) medial and final th (e. g. tooth, with, nothing), whose variants
were given earlier, (3) syllable final d (e. g. shed, good, stupid) whose
variants are a voiced stop, a voiceless unreleased stop or glottal, and
no phonetic realization, and (4) postvocalic r (beard, fire, sister) whose
variants are simply retroflection and lack of retroflection. The grammatical variables were: (1) suffixal -Z, including third person singular
concord (e. g. he goes), possessive marker (John's hat), and certain
plural constructions (e. g. five cents)—the variants are simply the
presence or absence of -Z, (2) multiple negation (or commonly referred
to as 'double negative', e. g. He didn't do nothing), whose variants are
simply 'realized' and 'unrealized' multiple negation, (3) copula, whose
variants are a full form of the copula (e. g. he is here), a contracted
form (e. g. he's here), and the absence of a copula (e. g. he here), and
(4) the use of 'invariant be' forms where SE uses the conjugated forms
of the verb (e. g. he be busy). It is certainly beyond the limitation of
this paper to present a detailed analysis of each of the individual variables although this is, in fact, what was done in the actual sociolinguistic research (see Wolfram 1969). What can be summarized here
in this brief account is several basic research questions concerning the
function of the linguistic variable as a marker of social status in the
black community: (1) the intersection of various social factors in accounting for patterned speech variation, (2) the extent to which social
differentiation is quantitative or qualitative, (3) the relation between
socially diagnostic (i. e. features which mark off social groups from
one another) phonological and grammatical variables, and (4) the effect
of independent linguistic constraints on variability. First, let us examine the intersecting social factors which correlate with speech differences. The investigation of various social parameters indicates that
social status is the single most important variable correlating with linguistic differences. Of the four social classes delimited in this study,
the most clear-cut linguistic boundary is found between the lower-middle
and upper-working social classes and the least clear-cut difference between upper-working and lower-working classes. According to Lan-

decker (1960: 874), it is most difficult to determine sharp social boundaries at the lower end of the social scale. We thus observe that the least clear-cut linguistic boundary parallels the least clear-cut social boundary.

Although social class is the single most important social factor correlating with speech differences, there are other social variables which intersect with class in an important way. For example, within each social class it is observed that females generally approximate the standard English norm more than males do. Hannerz (1967: 2) has observed that the Negro male departs more from the mainstream norm of middle class behavior than the female. The sex differentiation of speech behavior in this study parallels Hannerz's general observation.

Age also correlates with differences in speech behavior. Adults generally use socially stigmatized variants less than teenagers and preadolescents. A comparison of the individual informants with each other indicates that there is more individual variation among middle class preadolescents and teenagers than among middle class adults. Middle class adults are relatively constant in their use of standard English, whereas some preadolescents and teenagers show considerable divergence from the standard English norm. On the other hand, there is more individual variation among working class adults than preadolescents and teenagers. Some of these adults approximate the standard English norm more than others, whereas the working class preadolescents and teenagers are relatively constant in their use of nonstandard Negro English. A comparison of age differences in the black community with age differences in the white community suggests that age differentiation plays a more important role in the black community.

An investigation of the parameter of style shows that there is considerable variation based on the differentiation of interview and reading style, the latter style consistently showing a closer approximation of the standard English norm. This stylistic variation indicates that the informants recognize (whether consciously or unconsciously) that particular variables are markers of social status. The more stylistic variation there is, the more socially 'marked' the linguistic variable. Both working class and lower-middle class informants have more stylistic variation than the upper-middle class informants.

Finally, the factor of racial isolation (as a function of peer group, educational and residential segregation patterns) is seen to be useful in comparing the speech of a number of upper-middle class informants who have integrated or predominantly white contacts with upper-middle class informants having predominantly Negro contacts. Racial isolation is observed to have some effect on the speech of preadolescents and teenagers, but there is very little effect on adults.

The second question, the extent to which social differentiation is qualitative or quantitative, reveals that differences between social groups vary slightly according to the individual variable being analyzed. However, despite the slight individual differences, we can make some general observations. For one, we observe that three of the four phonological variables investigated suggest that the differences between the four social classes of Negroes in Detroit are quantitative rather than qualitative. The one exception is the 'theta' variable—this variable tends to reveal the categorical absence of f among the middle class informants. But even among Detroit middle class residents (and particularly preadolescents and teenagers) one will find some incidence of cluster final stop absence, postvocalic r reduction (and this is despite the fact that the Negro community is surrounded by an r dialect area), and glottal or unreleased stop variants for syllable-final d. On the other hand, the grammatical variables most typically reveal the categorical absence of certain variants among the middle class population. If the variables chosen here are in any way typical of the actual social stratification of speech, we may conclude that phonological variables will more often reveal quantitative differences between different social classes of Negroes and grammatical variables will more often reveal qualitative differences.

A corollary of the above observation concerning qualitative and quantitative differences between social groups is the conclusion relating to the relative social diagnosticity of phonological variables as they compare with grammatical variables. In order to understand the relation most clearly we can suggest the use of two terms, namely what may be called 'gradient' stratification and 'sharp' stratification. Gradient stratification refers to a progressive increase in the frequency of occurrence of a variant between social groups without a clearly defined difference between contiguous social groups. The incidence of postvocalic r in the black community is an example of gradient stratification. Figure 1 illustrates the differences in r absence (i.e. lack of constriction) for four social classes of Negroes in Detroit, upper-middle (UMN), lower-middle (LMN), upper-working (UWN), and lower-working (LWN) class Negroes.

One observes that there is a progressive increase in the absence of postvocalic r between the four social groups; none of the groups are discretely differentiated on the basis of r. But there are other variables which indicate a sharp demarcation between contiguous social classes (i.e. sharp stratification) such as the absence of third-person singular, present-tense-Z. Note the incidence of -Z third person singular absence in Figure 2.

In contrast to the absence of postvocalic r, we observe that the middle class groups are sharply differentiated from the working class groups by the incidence of -Z. Contiguous social groups (in this case, lower-middle and upper-working classes) reveal significant differences in the incidence of -Z third-person singular. In the case of the grammatical variables we often find sharp stratification. But for the phonological variables we most generally find gradient stratification. In

FIGURE 1. Postvocalic r absence: an example of 'gradient' stratification

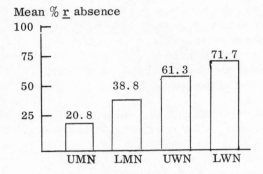

the sense that grammatical variables more discretely divide the population than phonological variables, we may conclude that they are typically more socially diagnostic.

FIGURE 2. Third person singular -Z absence: an example of 'sharp' stratification

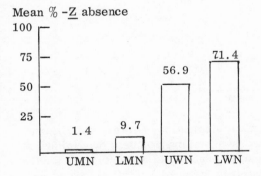

The fourth question, that of independent linguistic constraints on variability, is one which has received conspicuously little attention in sociolinguistic research. Whereas the last decade has witnessed an increasing awareness of systematic variation in speech as it correlates to social factors such as class, age, sex, and contextual style, the relative influence of independent linguistic constraints on variability has been overlooked. But this research reveals that there are linguistic effects on variation which have essential implications about the relative social stigmatization of particular features. Linguistic factors such as construction type and linear environment may greatly affect the social diagnosticity of a particular feature. Take the well known case of multiple negation. The tabulations of multiple negation reveal that one type of multiple negative involving a negativized auxiliary and a negative adverb (e.g. hardly never) is observed among the middle class population while multiple negatives involving a negativized auxiliary and an indefinite pronoun or determiner (e.g. don't do nothing) are categorically absent in the speech of most middle class informants. Similarly, copula absence involving is (e.g. he nice) is confined to the working class informants, although the absence of are, particularly with gonna (e.g. They gonna) is sometimes found in the speech of both the middle class and working class.

We also see that linear environment may have an important effect on the social diagnosticity of variables. Consider the case of consonant clusters given in Figure 3.

FIGURE 3. Effect of following consonantal and nonconsonantal environment on final member of word-final consonant cluster

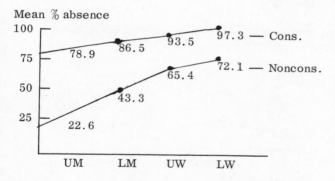

One will notice that the statistical discrepancy between the classes is much greater following a nonconsonantal environment than following a consonantal environment. Cluster reduction is quite common for the Negro middle class population (as it is for most English speakers when a potential cluster is followed by a consonant). But when followed by a nonconsonantal environment, the discrepancy between the social classes is much more apparent. We thus conclude that the absence of the final member of the cluster is considerably more stigmatized for the working class population in the nonconsonantal environment. It is quite inconspicuous, and therefore less stigmatized in the consonantal environment.

In sum, we have tried to show that in order to account for systematic variation between the variants of a variable a consideration of extralinguistic and independent linguistic constraints is imperative. Only a consideration of these two facets will reveal the fully systematic nature of variation and the various constraints on the relative social significance of certain variants.

REFERENCES

Hannerz, U. I. F. 1967. Another Look at Lower-Class Sex Roles. Washington, D. C. Unpublished paper delivered at the 66th Annual Meeting of The American Anthropological Association.

Labov, William. 1966. The Linguistic Variable as a Structural Unit. Washington Linguistic Review 3: 4-22.

_____. 1968. Contraction, Deletion and Inherent Variability of the English Copula. Unpublished paper given at Linguistic Society of America annual meeting.

Landecker, Werner S. 1960. Class Boundaries. American Sociological Review 25: 868-77.

Shuy, Roger W., Walter A. Wolfram, and William K. Riley. 1968. Field Techniques in an Urban Language Study. Washington, D. C.: Center for Applied Linguistics.

Wolfram, Walter A. 1969. A Sociolinguistic Description of Detroit Negro Speech. Washington, D. C.: Center for Applied Linguistics.

URBAN SPEECH ANALYSIS

JOSEPH R. APPLEGATE

Howard University

The importance of sociolinguistic studies cannot be denied; and when one considers the results that have already been obtained in this field of study, one can only look forward to many new possibilities that will be even more rewarding. Better understanding of the role of social dialects in defining the structure of societies is important and necessary in dealing with the problems of contemporary social systems. Many interesting investigations have already been completed, and more will undoubtedly be made. There are, however, some questions that may be raised at this stage—not as challenges or as criticisms—but as requests for information about the structure of the investigations and the theoretical frameworks within which they are being conducted.

One of the fields that currently occupies the attention of many investigators in the field of sociolinguistics is that of urban speech patterns. There is no doubt that the investigations in this area are of high priority because of the importance of urbanization in contemporary society and because the results may be useful in determining educational policies and, hence, the future evolution of society. Because the term is often loosely used, however, one must ask for a formal definition of 'urban speech'. In the discussions that have been presented at this meeting the term has started out with one meaning, i.e. the speech of people in an urban community. Attention has shifted, however, from the entire community to one segment of it, and the speech patterns of the people in that segment have been labelled 'deviant'. Because the speakers in that segment have been labeled members of a race, socially not physically defined, there are questions that arise. The basic question is this: At what point has the speech of these people been defined as deviant? The significance of this question can be seen when we consider the talks that have been given this evening. Much has been made of the use of statistical measurements as useful instruments for the analysis of differences between the lower and middle-class groups in the black community. At no point, however, has there been a satisfactory description of the use of statistical measurements in the definition of 'standard American English', a dialect which is assumed to exist in a specific form, a form from which the speech of black members of the urban community is said to deviate. As a matter of fact, there does not seem to be a definition of 'urban speech' itself. In other words, there seems to be a methodological fallacy in many of the investigations. Can the dialect which is being studied, whether it be standard American English or urban speech be described without including the speech patterns of one segment of the speakers? If these speech patterns are included, what will be the effect on the description of the standard dialect? If the studies are to be valid, satisfactory answers to these questions must be provided, and at no point have they been given.

Another point of methodology may be questioned. This is the accuracy of the descriptions. The language of an individual is based on a number of rules some of which vary from one social situation to another. Description of the language of an individual or a group of individuals cannot be considered accurate or complete unless all of the social situations have been considered. Data collected in many urban speech studies are representative of a single social situation so that the descriptions based on such data must be considered incomplete or inaccurate. Can such descriptions then be used for making generalizations about the language of the speakers in one segment of the urban community? It is quite possible that when the social situations are clearly defined and when data are collected carefully within those situations, the major areas of difference will be not phonological or syntactic as suggested here, but lexical and semantic.

In short, what I am suggesting is this: If a serious study of the speech of people in the black urban community is to be conducted, the methods that have been established for collecting data for sound linguistic descriptions must be used. First, let us have an accurate definition and description of the language called 'standard American English' as it is currently spoken. This should include consideration of the language used by all speakers in the American English speech community; no segment of the community should be arbitrarily excluded. Then, the descriptions should be as accurate and as complete as possible both for standard American English, for urban English, and for the speech of the black community. Only when these things have been done can we assume that we have established a firm base for discussions of urban speech patterns of the kind that we have heard this evening. Anything less implies that we are disregarding our responsibility as linguists and as scholars, perhaps succumbing to previously conceived ideas about the speech of certain ethnic groups.

LIST OF REGISTRANTS

Nancy M. Aaron
Rafael A. Abasolo
Maria Isabel Abreu
Luis Acevez
Rowena L. Adamson
Thomas K. Adeyanju
D. Adnani
Frances Aid
Audrey J. Ailer
Nobuo Akiyama
Riyadh Al-Any
James E. Alatis
Penelope M. Alatis
John Gage Allee
Charles L. Allen
Harold B. Allen
Susan K. Allen
Virginia French Allen
Richard Allsopp
A. Altmann
Barbara R. Alvarez
Harold Ames, Jr.
Angeline E. Anderson
Paul Angelis
Madlynn Anglin
Julia April
Louis A. Arena
Edwina Arnold
Matsuko Asakura
Hilda I. Ascunce
Luisa M. Atkinson
Janet E. Ayers
Yvonne Baker
Margarette Ballantine
Ruth Barnes
W. Barnes
Lillian J. Barret
Florence Baskoff
Evelyn Bauer
Sylvia Behar
John L. Behling, Jr.
Sandra A. Benedetti
Carol Berman

Joy Bernat
Lillian Bethel
Taddese Beyene
Josefina Bonangelino
Dusia Bondarew
Victor L. Bondi
Fred Bosco
Mary Boswell
Gertrude Bramkamp
Arthur W. Brewington
Eugene J. Briere
Lucy T. Briggs
E. W. Brockman
John P. Broderick
Peggy Ann Brown
Mary N. Bruder
Ruth Miles Bruns
Hugh W. Buckingham, Jr.
Edward I. Burkart
Brigid Burkert
Dolores M. Burton
Clifton H. Butcher
Jennifer Butler
Lois E. Bythewood
June R. Cannell
Debbie Carr
Gerald F. Carr
William S. Carroll
Fred G. Cassidy
Jorge Casteleiro
Jimmie E. Cato
Eileen Marie Celedon
Edward Cervenka
Joseph Chachulski
Raymond E. Chambers
Julia I. H. Chen
Cynthia Cherry
Arleen Cheston
Liliana Chiappinelli
Tsung Chin
Bernard Choseed
Neil Clancy
Martha K. Cobb

Elizabeth G. Cohen
Kip Colegrove
P. C. Collier
Rosemary K. Conley
Marilyn J. Conwell
Walter A. Cook, S. J.
Melvin E. A. Coomber
Ronald D. Coon
Paul V. Cooper
Alicia Coro
Edward T. Cortner
Karen Cossaro
Angelo A. Corretto
Ruth Cox
Mary-Howard Critchell
Robert Cromack
Diana Crone
Donald E. Crook
Daisy Crystal
Eva Garcia Currie
Daniel P. Dato
Walter Davison
Roberta Dawson
David DeCamp
Edith de Hamilton
Randy J. Dicks
Rose Marie DiGregorio
Dolores W. Dill
Ekaterina Dimova
F. P. Dinneen, S. J.
Robert DiPietro
Vincenzina DiPietro
Philip Doherty
Michael B. Duffin
Roy E. Eblen
Thomas J. Egan
K. B. Emmons
Wallace Erwin
Margaret Therese Evans
Frank L. Fadner, S. J.
Ralph W. Fasold
Crawford Feagin
Jamila Feldman
Carol Flamm
Jo-Ann Flora

Tatiana Fotitch
Nearlene J. Francis
Gloria O. Frank
William W. Gage
Aidan F. Gara
Arlene Geis
Nancy Gilmore
Adrian S. Gimate-Welsh
Doris E. Ginn
Walter B. Gleason
John Godfrey
Doris Gold
Barbara Gordon
Douglass W. Gordon
Diane L. Gottesfeld
Harry L. Gradman
Elsa R. Graser
Ann S. Gray
Stephen J. Greenberg
Mary Grigsby
Carol A. Guagliardo
Johanna Guccione
Doris V. Gunderson
Robert E. L. Hacke
Lawrence Hall
Aluizio Elia Hamilton
John H. Hammer
David P. Harris
Clarette Hart
H. A. Hatzfeld
Jane Hawkanson
Raymond Hebert
Michael J. Herrington
Fernando A. Hervias
Jurgen Heye
Cesar A. Hidalgo
Louis B. Hillman
Bill Hoffman
Reinhold Hoffman
John Hogan
Maurice Hohlfeld
Dao Thi Hoi
Catherine Buttery Hollan
Coletta H. Holloway
Mary Ann G. Hood

C. S. Hoover
Martha Horne
Rafael Hoyos
Herman Hudson
Carl S. Hundley
Joseph C. Hutchinson
Mary Iams
Maurice Imhoof
Maridale Jackson
Rodolfo Jacobson
Vicky Jamail
Winifred E. Jones
John F. Jordan
Eleanor H. Jorden
Grace J. Joseph
John Kane
Theodore B. Karp
Masako Kato
Anita Kaufman
David Kaufman
George Kelly
Carolyn Kessler
Buu Khai
Hae Chung Kim
James C. King
Timothy King
Aileen T. Kitchin
Donald Knapp
Mathilda S. Knecht
Kathleen Knodel
Christopher Kocher
Eric Kocher
Augustus A. Koski
Edna T. Kraft
Keith R. Krause
Carol Kreidler
Charles W. Kreidler
Yutaka Kusanagi
William Labov
Robert Lado
James E. LaFollette
David Lajmanovich
Maurice M. Lamarche, S. J.
Margaret Landis
Kichoon Lee

Marie Pius Lee
Marianne Lehr
Cheryl Lesmeister
Norman Balfour Levin
Mary M. Levy
Kathleen Lewis
Richard L. Light
Lucia Lobo
George R. Long
Jean B. Longmire
John Lotz
Ilana Luft
Robert C. Lugton
Gawaina D. Luster
R. Ross Macdonald
Fidelis MacEinri
Lucille Mack
Sam Maggio
James P. Mahoney
Anna Maria Malkoc
Grace S. Mancill
Gail C. Marble
Albert H. Marckwardt
Inge Marelli
Leonard R. Marelli
Joan Markessinis
George Mason
Egon Richardo Massing
Joseph A. Matesi
Paula L. Maurice
Edna D. Mayronne
Thomas C. McBride
Raven I. McDavid, Jr.
Emmett McKowen
Ginger McRae
Judith Meissner
Martha Millen
Mary Rita Miller
Barbara C. Mims
Edna K. Monsees
Ruth Montalvan
Jacquelyn R. Moore
Michael S. Moreno
Alice A. Morrison
Stephen T. Moskey

Lucille Muntz
Andrew F. Murphy
R. Paul Murphy
Harvey Nadler
Joy Newkerk
Linda E. Newman
Joan Noonan
Leopoldina Nowak
Maria V. de Nunez
Mrs. Loren Nussbaum
Virginia Simmons Nyabongo
Richard J. O'Brien, S. J.
Ostreicher
Milos Pacak
Leslie A. Palmer
Wesley C. Panunzio
Barbara Paramore
Gino Parisi
J. F. Pattiasina
Dorothy A. Pedtke
Harry Winfield Peter, S. J.
Kent Ponder
Wendy Powell
Jane Proctor
Robert Rainsbury
Clea Rameh
Lusn Ranta
Irmengard Rauch
David W. Reed
Frances Reid
Ilo Remer
Theresa Richardson
Eleanora M. Ridgley
Mary Rimblas
Diana Risen
A. Hood Roberts
Betty W. Robinett
Paulette M. Robinson
Maria Vicente Rodriguez
Petrona Rodriguez-Pasques
David S. Rood
Peter S. Rosenbaum
Marilyn Rosenthal
Jane Ross
H. L. Rosser

Joseph A. Roy
Rose Marie Ruffle
Marjorie Russell
Carolyn Rycyna
Amelia A. Sandique
Madeline Sapienza
Solomon Sara, S. J.
James F. Schaefer, Jr.
Kathleen Todd Schaefer
Richard A. Schuchert
John H. Schumann
Arletha T. Scott
Charles T. Scott
Eleanor L. Sebeok
Angela Sebis
Deborah A. Senbron
Hannah Shapiro
Joseph H. Sheehan
Marie-Antoine Shiels
Eugene L. Shiro
S. Shukla
Roger W. Shuy
Ann Gerard Siebert
Mahmoud E. Sieny
Sigrid Simlik
Kanchana Sindhvananda
Sadanand Singh
Myer Site
Linda Slagle
Margaret Slocum
Thelma Smackey
Victor E. Smilgin
Shirley H. Sneed
Dennis K. Snyder
William Solzbacher
Michael Sotiriou
Warren W. Spencer
Bernard Spolsky
Esperanza M. Spyropoulos
Norman C. Stageberg
Opal Y. Sterrett
Nic Stevens
William A. Stewart
Marie E. Stiller
William Stokoe

Edith Stone
James W. Stone
Albert Storm
Ignatius Suharno
Paula M. Sullivan
Rokeya Sultana
Muljanto Sumardi
Nguyen Hoang Tam
Robert H. Tarr
Grant Taylor
Joann B. Tench
Richard E. Tenney
Joan A. Thomas
Charles Thompson
Richard T. Thompson
Gail Thomson
M. J. Toconita
Zoe Tokatlian
Aurelie H. M. Tran
George Treadwell
Rudolph C. Troike
Virginia C. Tsien
Walter V. Tuman
Charmaine H. Turner
N. J. Twombly, S.J.
John Underwood
Howard M. Van Roy
Michael F. Vargo
Milton Velder
Patricia Venditto
Merle P. Venture
Amy Van Voorhis
Paul Voorhis
Daniel Ward
Ronald Wardhaugh
Lucia Washburn
Mark Hanna Watkins
Mary C. Wayne
William T. Weir
Regis Welch
Jean Francis Whalen
Adelia C. Wheeler
Gerald W. White
Della S. Whittaker
Maria Wilhelm

Cdr. R. T. Williams
Marilynne N. Williams
Robert M. Willis
Ethna B. Winston
Louise Winfield
Erma Withers
Wolfgang Wolck
Walter A. Wolfram
David R. Woods
Frances S. Woods
Elizabeth Wright
William H. Wright
Warren G. Yates
Sayo Yotsukura
John Young
Laura M. Zamarin
Michael Zarechnak
Charles Zisa
Joyce G. Zuck
Louis Zuck
Joseph Zuschmidt